Y0-DDO-861

Once again I offer a collection of stories based on real events – the real events of my life. Since my professional career has included several unique twists and my personal life has had the fortune of many memorable experiences, sometimes very little daylight exists between the fact and fiction of my stories. But I believe that every life has at least some cause for celebration; everyone has their own unique tale to tell, and every family has its treasured memories. What do you do when you get together with friends and relations? You share these stories, of course! Perhaps you do so with a bit of extra zeal, an extra punch of enthusiasm to add just the right tinge of unique magic to your experience. And why not? Your friends love it. Your family loves it. And the entire evening has an added wonder to it because you have offered your life story. This is certainly the case in my family and I thank God for it. The stories of our life, however, are far more than amusing anecdotes to share with those we love, of course. And in this I see an interesting, mysterious dilemma. Do the events of our life mold us into the man or woman we are to become – or does each experience simply bring us closer to the man or woman that we are from the moment of birth? Whatever the answer, life is an inevitable journey of transition and transformation.

John M. Regan
Graham, WA
12 May 2018

1

CONTENTS

THE POUGHKEEPSIE WITCH

I was fourteen years old and ready to pounce upon a remarkable period of freedom that summer. The fact that I had achieved this incredible slack in parental reins was notable in itself. Not that my parents were particularly strict; quite the opposite. But they both frowned on the friend I wanted to visit. Jim "Harry" Harrison had a fairly notorious reputation. Honestly earned, I'll admit. His gamut of notoriety included running away, school suspension, smoking, and extremely long hair – glaring indicators of an adolescent on the high speed highway to perdition by any parameter in 1967. But that was part of Harry's charm. He always knew the latest, coolest stuff to do. Stuff like getting high by smoking green pepper seeds. It wasn't true, of course, but Harry promoted the concept with such authority that we immediately scuttled into the basement of my house and cut off the tops of three big green peppers I'd snuck out of the refrigerator. Under Harry's experienced supervision we dropped lighted matches into the things, inhaled the damp smoke and waited for the monumental rush. We got runny noses instead. Undismayed, Harry corrected his theory by remembering that the proper ingredients were the dried scrapings of banana peels. No psychedelic experience there either but it smelled better. If only we had more bananas, Harry opined. But I knew if I asked for more fruit my mother would get suspicious. She was already giving me the raised eyebrow about the peppers.

Consciousness raising experiments aside Harry was a hit with my parents. Yea, they had misgivings over the divorce in his family, long hair, and a flagrant propensity for self promotion but he was intelligent and funny - and respectful to my parents. They took him in as though he was my wayward misguided brother. Harry was always welcome at our dinner table, and most nights he was there, too. There was a caveat to this admiration, however. Unsupervised companionship with him was frowned on. And when you consider that Harry and his divorced dad now inhabited a mobile home in a trailer park an hour and half away from Albany you have a near miracle of parental leniency in allowing my visit. But we'd been best friends for several years and remained that way even after his parent's separation and subsequent move to an oddly named city in the Catskill Mountains of New York.

Of course, it took a substantial amount of teenage moaning to secure the green light to board a Greyhound bus from Albany and ride it solo all the way to Poughkeepsie. But it worked. So there I was, clutching tickets and pacing around the bus station staring at the oddest assortment of humanity I'd ever seen. I had begun to question the wisdom of my journey when a garbled voice over a loudspeaker blurted out something that sounded like "Poughkeepsie." I jumped and ran outside. A huge bus with the word "Poughkeepsie" over the driver side squeaked to a stop. I took a breath, climbed aboard and selected an empty seat near a window. Now I don't know what Greyhound travel is like today but in 1967 it was not the preferred mode of travel for the upper class, middle class, or anybody else with class for that matter. That, of course, did not concern the human oddities in the station that followed me aboard and now swirled about in close proximity. These folks with their unusual morphology – and odor - were not prototypes of Fred Astaire movie characters. Thankfully, though, the seat next to me remained empty.

The driver put the bus in gear and we hit the road. Seemingly safe from the strange array of fellow travelers I relaxed. Less than thirty minutes later we made a stop to take on more passengers. My senses came back on alert as my adolescent mind conjured a vision of the beautiful girl destined to climb aboard, sit alongside me, and turn this into the most memorable trip of my life. To my delight several flower bearing young ladies had indeed decided to visit

Poughkeepsie. Back then long hair had a profound impact; it made a distinct statement about the bearer. Unfortunately, I did not have the hair, clothes, or appropriate maturity for consideration to be included in this group. The girls took up a seat two rows in front of me. The rest of my fantasy was cruelly destroyed when an old geyser who resembled a rotted tree stump slumped down next to me. He slammed his head against the back of the seat and passed out snoring and smelling like a troll. For the next ninety minutes, in between the troll's snoring, I listened to the beautiful giggling flower children several unreachable feet away.

We hit Poughkeepsie at two o'clock in the afternoon on Saturday. The tree stump troll remained thoroughly comatose as the passengers disembarked. I stepped over him taking care not to touch any part of his anatomy. There was no telling what kind of unpleasantness could result from contact with this unknown species. My luck held and I got off the bus unscathed.

The Poughkeepsie bus station had the standard seedy look that all Greyhound depots strived for back then, a kind of gray grime laden with body odor and just the right trace of urine. My fellow travelers clambered down the bus steps and melted away as did the hippie flower girls of my dreams. The stump troll somehow managed to exit the vehicle as well. He looked a little confused as he stepped down and I wondered if he even knew where he was. Well, he wasn't my problem. I looked around for Harry. A half an hour later I was still looking. I walked out onto the street a bit peeved and more than a bit worried. I'd just started to wander around when I heard a familiar voice holler out my name.

"Rick! Rick! Hey, slob, how you doing?"

There he was. A bit shorter than me, but possessed of a solid, wide shouldered physique. His red blond hair had attained shoulder length by now and it hung over a tie dyed tee shirt and bright blue eyes gleaming with his usual mischievous expression as he ran up to greet me.

"Man, I was getting worried," I said.

"Yea, sorry, Rick. It took me a while to hitch a ride down here. How's the bus trip?"

I describe the sorry state of my travelling companion and expounded at length about the hippie girls. To my credit I did not embellish on fictional exploits with them even though Harry begged for details. If he'd had been on that bus I know he'd have struck up a conversation somehow and he'd probably be walking them home, too. As if to reinforce my opinion Harry began lecturing me about the various techniques I should have employed. He was an authority in these matters but I thought the idea of pulling the bus emergency alarm in order to confuse the seating arrangement was too much.

We wandered out into the city, catching up and not at all concerned about where we were going. We found a little diner with the appropriate pinball machines and stopped in for lunch. Two hamburgers later we hit the machine. Of course, I was no match for Harry on the thing. He was a pinball wizard. But when school and normal restrictions aren't part of your life you get good at things like that. By five o'clock the main drag was crowded as we continued wandering, looking for the standard mischief that attracts teenage boys. Most of the girls we saw were young and afraid of us or older and disdainful despite our skillful manipulation of cigarettes. Shop owners kept a wary eye on our every move and I suspected more than one of them knew Harry by sight. That made me guilty by association, of course, so their fish eye tracked my movements as well. I took pride in this shared notoriety.

We were ogling some switchblades in a pawn shop window when something in the street distracted me. I turned and confronted an extraordinary sight. The woman was well over six feet tall. She towered over everyone on the street. Covered from head to toe in what looked like a black drape the lady looked ominous. I grabbed Harry by the shoulder and pointed wildly. "Look, man! Look!"

Absorbed in the pawn shop display window, my friend ignored me. I had to physically spin him around and by then she was directly in front of us. Long, white gray hair cascaded to her shoulders from under – I swear it – a pointed black hat. She was lean as a heron and had the same raptor intent eyes; sharp black orbs that glanced in my direction. I nearly ducked. But the strange woman ignored me and strolled on by. Her posture was rigidly upright, completely dignified, and oblivious to the stares she attracted. I noticed that people in front of her parted as though in awe. She strode silently down the street like a queen disdainful of her subjects. I could not believe what I was seeing.

Harry nodded knowingly. "That's the Poughkeepsie Witch," he said.

"What?"

"The Poughkeepsie Witch," he repeated, the nonchalance in his voice obvious. "She walks through town every now and then."

I was incredulous. "But what's her thing, Harry? Does she believe she's a real witch or what?"

"I don't know, man. All I know is everyone kind of stays away from her; they get out of her way when she walks."

"Yea, I noticed."

I continued to gawk as the woman walked away. Her tall black figure remained starkly obvious all the way down the street. Not a soul got in her way and she never stopped for cars at the intersection either – they stopped for her. Harry and I gabbed about her for a while until the conversation disintegrated into adolescent jokes. By the time we'd made our way down the street I'd written her off in my mind as just another Poughkeepsie kook. And that was not really hard to do. This little town in the Catskill mountains of New York was famous for the big "nuthouse" located just outside of the city limits. It was actually a major institution, and still is for all I know, but you can just imagine the images that kind of thing fired up in Harry and me. Like any city, Poughkeepsie was not without its share of odd characters but the presence of the huge psychiatric center magnified its reputation.

By the end of the day we'd had our share of exploring the city and decided to head to Harry's trailer. First, though, Harry informed me that we had a party to check out at a local park. It was the usual gathering of high school mischief makers replete with illegally purchased beer and the newly popular "weed" we kept hearing about so in vogue with all the hippies of the era. That this weed stuff had a technical name of marijuana I knew, but as for trying it I was still clueless. Harry, of course, could give line and verse about the plant, and state it with his usual authority. "It's great; really great," he'd say. Everything was "great" back in '67. "Better than booze but no hangover." I had no experiences with hangovers either, but I nodded sagely at this important information.

We arrived at the park toward evening. Respectable, normal, people were leaving and the crowd of fun lovers we'd come to engage were arriving. I remember it as a pleasant, lushly green place, built like a huge bowl with an enormous pond in the middle. The park fronted one side of the pond and had all the usual accoutrements: picnic tables, park benches, kid's playground; a couple of buildings here and there. You get the idea. None of which did we care about. Harry and I were looking for the alcoholic contraband and this weed stuff.

We were not disappointed. Getting our share of these marvels, however, proved more of a challenge. The main group of partiers were high school seniors who had just graduated. Mixed in with this bunch were some that looked as though they'd left high school long before the previous year. And for some mysterious reason none of these people was at all anxious or even willing to share. And despite all of Harry's considerable powers of persuasion two hours later we hadn't even scored a sip of beer. The weed we craved was absolutely unassailable. Harry and I thought this incredibly unjust. So much for the milk of human kindness. After careful commiserations about the gross unfairness of the situation we decided there was just one reasonable course of action – steal the stuff.

Harry immediately hatched a fool proof plan. I was to create a distraction and Harry would swipe the goods in the confusion. "What kind of a distraction?" I asked.

"Oh, you know, Rick; the usual stuff. Start a fire or something."

I was mulling over how to execute this feat in an open grassy park with nothing but a sporadic tree or building to light on fire when Harry had what he estimated to be a much better idea.

"This is even better!" he said with great enthusiasm. "You streak through the party! That's bound to get attention. I'll hold your clothes and snatch the goods. Then we'll link up on the other side of the park."

I received this idea with less enthusiasm than the arsonist angle. "Oh yea, right. And what happens if I get caught or we can't link up someplace?"

"Don't worry, Mike. If they get too close just dive into the pond and swim for it. They'll never go after you in there."

"Right, Harry. They'll just wait for me on the other side and pelt me with rocks when I climb out of the water. Great idea." For some reason my friend found this scenario extremely humorous. He burst out laughing and pretty soon I was bent over laughing at the idea, too.

We were in the midst of concocting further outlandish schemes when a solution materialized right in front of us; ironically it had an element of Harry's idea in it, too. Splashing and giggling wildly several of the older kids decided that the pond was an excellent venue for skinny dipping. Three of the girls, much to the pleasure of our astonished eyes, started stripping down. They dared the rest of the crowd to join them and raced off into the pond shrieking with laughter. We stared goggle eyed as one naked body after the other slipped into the dark water accompanied by a chorus of screams and giggles. Pretty soon about half of them had taken the plunge with the other half standing by the pond as an enthusiastic audience. Behind them a bounty of deserted six packs lay exposed on an old picnic table.

I slapped Harry on the arm. "This is it, man! Let's grab a couple and go!"

But at that point Harry had completely forgotten the illegal beverages. Mesmerized at the unexpected sight of feminine unclothed loveliness so suddenly near and freely splashing about Harry wanted nothing more now than to join the fun. Before I could say anything further he prepared to join the naked assembly in the water.

"C'mon, Mike!" he yelled. "We can't miss this!" His shirt flew into the air as he ran.

I stood rooted to the spot; stifled by indecision. On one hand Harry was indisputably correct. This was an opportunity extremely unlikely to be repeated in my lifetime. Just the idea of being in that wonderfully warm water with wonderfully real girls was an enormous incentive. On the other hand, though, it meant I'd have to do the same thing as everyone else. That was part of the bargain I was not quite ready to take up. There was another consideration, too. Why on earth was there any reason to expect that the guys who begrudged us a sip of Budweiser going to let us near their girlfriends under these exceptional circumstances? The more I thought about it the more I considered the possibility that we could get killed. Judging from what I'd seen it might be worth it, but we still be dead at the end of the experience and what good was that? And then I had an idea even better than Harry's. From the spot where I stood I now had a perfectly good view of more than just the thrashing and splashing antics of the pond crew – I had a great view of the unguarded stack of beer. I'd never been one to explode into action without some analysis; that was Harry's forte. But his spontaneous action in joining the skinny dipping crowd added just the right tipping point and it soon appeared that I was now one of the only clothed and dry humans left. I exploded into action. With a six pack in each hand I sprinted for the tree line.

Once safely hidden behind a line of great oak trees I stopped and looked back. With unbridled joy possible only in youth they roared their pleasure, frolicked, splashed, and romped in the pond. It was almost dark by now but a full moon was just clearing the tree tops. Wet bodies in the pond glistened silver but I was effectively invisible in the tree line. Now, how to get Harry's attention. Simply strolling down to the beach and yelling, "Hey Harry, I got the beer!" did not seem like a good plan. There was one other option, of course – go down there and join in the fun. This idea was gaining momentum when I heard a voice.

"You should not have done that."

The low, growling voice sounding as though it was right in my ear. Violently frightened, I spun about. The speaker unnerved me even more. Less than an arm's length away from me stood the Poughkeepsie Witch. Still draped in her gothic black cloak and monstrous hat the woman's body was ghostly invisible against the dark forest background; the towering visage of her white face seemed to hover in the air above me. I could not stop staring at the strange sight and I could not move either. A sudden burst of yelling from the direction of the pond broke the spell. The face disappeared.

I recovered somewhat and looked back toward the pond. The entire crowd was emerging from the water. Suddenly chilled by the evening air they were laughing and running for towels and clothes. My chance to escape! Suspecting that she might have a weapon of something I looked back at the witch before I bolted for safety. She was gone. Somehow that was more unnerving than if she had still been standing there. For the second time that day I exploded into action.

Harry had recovered most of his clothes by the time I ran to the beach. He was still laughing with exhilaration over the experience but he knew something was amiss by the look on my face. Struggling to drag dry clothes over his wet body he gasped out, "What's the deal, Mike? You look messed up, man."

"You can't believe this, Harry! You can't believe this!" was all I could manage.

"What the hell are you talking about?"

I started to tell him about my haunting experience but there were too many older guys around. It was going to be bad enough explaining this to Harry; with a bunch of the older guys around it'd be nearly impossible.

"Forget it," I said. "Just get your clothes on."

As Harry dressed several of the guys and girls called him by name and even seemed friendly. I should have known. Harry could make friends in an empty room. Give him a pond full of skinny dipping kids and he was bound to be a hit. This was not going to make things any easier. The witch business was bad enough but new found friends who discover that you had ripped them off could be a dangerous prospect. Trying to be as nonchalant as possible as I walked with Harry and the others away from the beach. I soon had a fear almost as real as the spooky woman I'd just encountered. We were walking directly back to the picnic table where the beer had been stored. Since there were only four six packs to begin with, and I had swiped two of them, the missing beverages were going to be impossible to miss. Once again I exploded into action.

"Harry," I said while grabbing his arm, "c'mon over here a minute; I've got something I have to show you."

Harry, a big fellow, and a brunette girl walking with us slowed their pace and gave me the *what are you weird or something* look. I laughed it off. "I'll explain later, guys. This is just one of those things that has to be discussed in private. You know what I mean, right?" That last bit about assuming their intelligence worked. The group nodded as though they understood completely. Harry rolled his eyes but finished putting on his shirt and followed me as I led him away from the gang.

"Okay, Rick," he said, "what is it?"

We were still too close in my estimation; I kept leading Harry away at a right angle from the crowd and toward the tree line. I stopped about ten feet way from the big oak tree where I'd left the beer. The cans were invisible from where we stood and there was no way the original purchasers could see it. I whispered just the same.

"I took a couple of six packs, Harry. They're over there behind that tree." I nodded my head in the direction of the tree line and admonished Harry not to look over there.

Harry gave me an appreciative nod and risked a discreet glance in the direction of the tree. "Good work, Mike! Now we gotta figure a way to get out of here."

I could tell he was ready to make a break for the trees and the beer so I stopped him. "That's not the thing, Harry!" I rasped out the words. "While I was standing over there I saw the witch!"

"What?"

"I saw her I tell you! The Poughkeepsie Witch. I put the beer down and I was watching you guys in the pond. All of a sudden I hear the voice behind me say, 'You shouldn't have done that.'" I did my best to imitate the awful voice.

All Harry could to was to stare at me and repeat, "What!?"

"I'm serious, man! I heard the voice and I turned around – there she was standing right behind me. She looked like some kind of black ghost I'm telling you; scared the shit out of me!"

Harry was considering this incredible possibility when a huge commotion broke out among the gang at the other side of the park. I had an immediate suspicion about what had caused the uproar; a suspicion confirmed when I heard amidst a cascade of swearing words to the affect

"Those SOBs stole our beer!" We looked at them. They looked at us. We ran.

They should have caught us. Harry and I were about half their size and our pursuers were not old men, they were all in their late teens or early twenties. But whenever I think back to that day I am reminded of an old bit of Indian wisdom about betting on the fox or the rabbit. Most of the time the rabbit wins. The fox is running for his dinner but the rabbit is running for his life – which certainly described our situation that night. Those guys may not have wanted to actually have us for a meal but they surely wanted to kill us. Harry and I had no illusions about why we were running away.

We darted into the woods at the side of the park and here we had a stroke of good luck. Harry had managed to put his sneakers on, and since I had never taken mine off, we were well shod as we tore into the forest. The beer deprived group coming for our scalp, however, were still mostly clad in skinny dipping apparel. Outraged curses quickly gave way to whoops and howls of pain, immediately followed by a return to outraged curses. Harry and I were not about to return and confer sympathy. Running like the rabbits we were we continued our headlong dash into the safety of the forest and disappeared into the night.

Twenty minutes of this frantic sprinting and we stopped to catch our breath. We bent over panting with our hands on our knees, struggling with laughter and oxygen deprivation. These physiological requirements finally equalized but the exhilaration at having escaped with our lives was soon tempered by the realization that we'd lost the very thing we risked our hides for – we had no beer. Well, you can't have everything.

"Where the hell are we?" I asked.

Harry looked around with a knowing nod. "In the woods," he announced.

"Brilliant," I said. "Does this forest have an end or do we just walk on to oblivion?"

"Where's that? Sounds cool."

Well, hanging around with Harry was always an adventure. What could I say? I signed up for this after all. We decided on a strategy to head back in the direction of the park but stop short enough of the place to scope out the situation. The gang chasing us might stay there all night but at some point they'd pass out or go to sleep, right? Then we'd sneak past them. Flawless plan.

We'd podded on for what seemed like an hour before we stopped. In the dim, almost non-existent light Harry and I looked at each other. At the same time we both said, "Where the hell are we?"

"Oblivion," I answered. Harry agreed.

"Might as well keep going this way, Rick. Sooner or later we'll run into a road or something."

"Probably later, but it beats standing here with the mosquitoes."

We hoofed on. A rising terrain combined with the moonless night and overhanging oak trees made for a stumbling hike that quickly fell into a rhythm: four steps forward - fall down - swear - get back up. A hike like that would put me in hospital now, but when you're fourteen years old not only are you immortal you are injury immune as well.

The hill we had been assaulting finally leveled off and we stopped for another breather. At the summit we looked around trying to get our bearings. Harry pointed at something. "Look, see that?"

I peered around the tree that separated us. A yellow light glimmered in the distance. It seemed to be about a football field length away from us but it was hard to tell. The slightest wind rustled leafy branches and caused to the light to wink in and out of sight. We stared at this for a while and at last convinced ourselves that we had actually seen a light and not some mirage.

"At least it's some kind of human inhabitance," I said. "Let's head for it, Harry."

We headed off repeating the step, fall, and swear rhythm this time in a downhill direction. Aided by gravity, however, the falls outdistanced the steps so we made good time. When the ground leveled and the trees thinned progress came a bit easier and before long we made out the dim outlines of a house. The single yellow light we had seen hung from the back of the house over a door that opened onto a concrete patio. No lawn furniture or anything else, just a large square patch of concrete. We stopped for another strategy session. What was a house doing out here in the middle of nowhere? Outside of its location the place didn't look especially sinister but there were no other signs of humanity. Something was not right. After much commiseration, about five minutes worth, we settled upon a plan of action that we considered especially clever. It held the least amount of risk and the greatest potential of return. Our plan had three phases. Phase 1 – creep up to the house. Phase 2 – peak inside a window. Phase 3 had two contingencies dependent on what we discovered in Phase 2:

1. Run like hell

2. Ask for help.

We commenced Phase 1 in classic manner; we'd seen plenty of movies and knew exactly what to do. Head down and arched over we approached in a crouched run, stopping every ten feet or so to pause and ensure that we had not been discovered. A massive oak tree stood off to one corner of the house. We hid behind it and prepared for the final assault. Even our teenaged minds knew enough to stay out of the single porch light while peaking in the window. We opted for an indirect approach at the side of the house, bolted from the tree, and dashed to our objective.

I have three very distinct memories of that assault: Harry tripping and falling, a loud "OOOMPH" as I stomped and tripped on his back, and a very loud WHACK as my skull collided with the side of the house.

I came to with Harry pulling at my shirt and frantically whispering. "Man, man! We gotta get outta here! We gotta get out!"

Still somewhat delirious from my encounter with the side of the house I vaguely agreed with this proposal but was powerless to act upon it. I mumbled something that Harry seemed to find unsatisfactory because his repeated instructions to "get outta here" became more hoarsely frantic.

With his hands gripping my tee shirt Harry began pulling me to my feet.

"WHAT ARE YOU TWO IDIOTS DOING?"

The voice was loud, imperious, and very angry. Standing behind Harry I caught a terrifyingly familiar sight glimpse of the Poughkeepsie Witch. Harry let go of my shirt and the back of my head collided with the house again.

"Idiot number two is waking up, ma'am."

"Give him this."

I stared at a cup of vaporous broth, the steam from it curled and swirled in the air. It did not smell particularly good. I turned my head away.

"DRINK IT!"

The witch was standing over me and glaring. To the right of the recliner I sat in a familiar figure knelt and pushed the cup at me. "Drink it," he said. "Good stuff."

"Go ahead, Mike. It's alright, I had some." I recognized Harry's voice. He was kneeling on the other side of the chair. "It'll make you feel better."

I was all up for that. The back of my head and top of my head throbbed, and my neck sparked in pain whenever I moved. I took the cup in both hands and sipped. It did not taste any better than it smelled; sort of like minty fish soup, old minty fish soup. But I was desperate. As I took another sip my eyes peered over the top of the cup. I dropped the thing and spilled fish soup over myself and the recliner. The liquid exploded from my mouth in a powerful spray into the face of the man who'd handed me the drink. It was the tree stump troll from the bus!

The guy grimaced, shook his head, and fell backward swatting at his face with his hands. He lay there for moment then struggled to his feet growling curses at me. The guy was frightening enough to look at but with his face dripping fish soup he looked even worse. His yellowed beard glistened in gray droplets of the stuff that he tried to wipe off. In the frenzy to clear his face he must have rubbed some soup into his eyes. He was not happy.

"Ahhh – it burns!" he screamed and rolled backwards onto the floor.

The witch turned her attention to the troll. "Oh stop that nonsense, Rollie. The only thing burning you is the dirt you rubbed in your eyes," she commanded. The Rollie troll did not argue and immediately ceased squealing.

The witch turned away from him. "Ashay, Ashay," she said. "Take Rollie to the bathroom and wash him out."

An unseen voice answered. "Yes, ma'am." An enormous figure emerged from the kitchen to my right. This Ashay person was no more than five feet tall but easily weighed over three hundred pounds. The voice was feminine but not the persona behind it. The woman wore some kind of light brown canvass blanket that covered her from head to foot like an Indian teepee. Odd symbols and strange lettering were splattered all over the garment.

The woman stomped over to Rollie. A pair of limbs that looked more like gnarled black rubber tires than arms emerged from the bizarre dress. She grasped Rollie by his collar and yanked him to his feet. "C'mon you old fool. Get up," she said. It was not necessary. Rollie was up an instant after Ashay's hands had seized his neck. The troll was slightly taller than the strange woman who gripped him but dwarfed by her bulk. Without another word Rollie was hauled away.

"You alright, Rick?" Harry asked.

Surprisingly enough, I was. My head felt almost normal and the crackling pain in my neck seemed to have disappeared. "Uh, yea," I said.

"Is that Rollie guy gonna be okay?" I asked the witch.

"Yes. He will be fine. It is good of you to ask," she said but her face retained what seemed to be a permanent glare. "Now it is time to deal with you two idiots," she said.

I didn't like the sound of that. From the look on Harry's face he didn't either. I could tell from his expression, though, that he was ready to bolt for the door. The same urge was quickly developing inside me.

The witch arched an eyebrow in my direction and then at Harry. "Stop being stupid, both of you!"

That statement jolted us; it was as if she could read minds. It alarmed me. Just what on earth had we stumbled into here? We might have still made a dash for escape but just then Ashay stomped back into the room, every step vibrating the floor. I could feel it through the recliner. She positioned herself in front of the living room door like a cement truck. We weren't going out that way.

The witch looked at Harry, then me, and then back to Harry and pointed at him. "Now that both of you idiots are awake tell me what you were doing out there. We will start with you, Idiot Number One."

Harry's eyes rolled over to me as if to confirm what he was about to say. "We got lost; then we saw this light and came here. All we wanted was to find out where we were. Where are we anyway?"

"You know exactly where you are you little fool," the witch scolded.

"Well, I kinda know," Harry started, but before he could say anything else the witch commanded him to SHUTUP! He did.

She turned to me. "And what is your story, Idiot Number Two?"

"Uh, same as his," I said. "We got lost."

"And the cause of your predicament? The reason you ended up lost?"

This question seemed to be directed at both of us. Under most circumstances Harry could concoct a convincing tale, a believable lie could spring from his lips like a grasshopper. Present circumstances, however, had stymied his abilities. Just the same I could tell his mind was working – and that worried me, too. The witch had already seen me before and I didn't think a deception would work with this woman. I decided to beat Harry to it with the truth.

"Okay, ma'am," I decided the polite, and honest, approach was best. "We were up to no good over there in the park. We, well I, stole some beer but we got caught. They chased us into the woods and we got lost out there."

My little speech seemed to satisfy her. She pointed at Harry. "Well?"

"Yea, that's right," he said.

"And what were you doing during this theft?"

Harry stammered on this for a bit. He opted for a close to the truth answer. "I was swimming."

"Swimming! Hah. You were running around with no clothes on weren't you?"

"Okay, yea I was skinny dipping," Harry admitted. At this the giant Ashay standing by the door let out a snort of laughter. The witch silenced her with a glance.

"So I have a thief and a skinny dipper in my house. Such distinguished guests. But you are not guests. You are trespassers. Why exactly did you attack my house?"

"Attack?" Harry and I both asked at once.

"Yes, you idiots! There is a mark on my house where you, Idiot Number Two, rammed into it with your head. Why do something so stupid?"

By now Harry had recovered his wits. "Oh that," he said. "That was just a boned headed mistake, pardon the pun. We were sort of sneaking up here and I fell down. Rick fell over me and collided with your home. He's got a pretty hard head. We'll repair any damage."

The witch rolled her eyes and pointed at me. "You have wounded my home and my friend." She pointed at the tree troll who had by now stumbled back into the living room.

"Sorry," I said. I asked the troll if he was alright but his grunting mumbling answer was unintelligible.

"What did he say?" I asked the witch.

"He says you're an idiot."

"Of course."

At this point the kitchen door opened and another extraordinary figure entered. I say entered but what he actually did was duck. The guy had to be seven feet tall. Long, stingy brown hair hung over his shoulders and bordered a startling beard that looked like a tar colored hedge. He wore an old boony hat and some kind of ragged sweater that hung down to his knees. The garment terminated just above a pair of white, boney knees and cut off blue jeans.

"Ain't no one else out there," he announced. I thought the voice sounded weak for a man of his size.

"Thank you, Stosh," the witch answered. Stosh nodded and twitched his nose in our direction. The witch understood. "We are trying to get a semblance of honesty from them," she said.

Stosh pulled back his head in exaggeration and rolled a pair of eyes every bit as black as his beard. The message of distrust and disgust was clear. Harry and I looked at each other. He had to be thinking the same thing as me. This Stosh character might be as tall as an oak tree but he had the constitution of an overgrown weed. We could take him. The grotesque female by his side, however, presented a more formidable challenge. Even if she did nothing more than just wedge herself in the doorway she'd be impossible to move. What to do? What to do?

Harry spoke up. "Ma'am, we're not arguing. Me and Mike were wrong in the way we approached your home and invaded your privacy; and like I said, we'll pay for the damages." He paused briefly for effect. "Can we go now? My old man's gonna be getting worried. I gotta get home."

The witch stared down at Harry and her eyes narrowed into crevice like slits. No doubt about it now. She meant us harm. But then she did something completely unexpected – she smiled. And I don't mean a grimace of a wicked grin. Oh no, this was a genuine happy face smile. What a change! In less than a second she'd changed from a demon to a fairy godmother. Then she broke out laughing – and transformed back into a demon. This woman didn't laugh. She shrieked.

Her bizarre laugh provoked guffaws, giggles, and sneers from the witch's audience. Long, tall Stosh produced a flemmy wheezing filled with whatever atrocious waste filled his lungs. Ashay giggled like a school girl and shook like the proverbial bowl of jello. The troll named Rollie pointed his finger and slapped his legs in delight.

"They want to go!" the witch screamed. "And even before they know why they came here!" This statement brought on even greater gasps of breath stealing laughter from the awful trio. Even the witch was shaking now. Harry and I weren't laughing at all. The night had gone from amusing to suspicious to downright frightening. I was genuinely scared at this point but even more when I looked at Harry. His face was white and his eyes wide as hubcaps.

"What shall we do with them, Stosh?" the witch asked.

Stosh pursed his lips and rubbed his black beard thoughtfully. "Mmm..the fire seems good." He motioned with his head toward an empty fire place.

"Ashay, what do you think?"

The monstrous woman opened her maw into a hideous grin. "The fire is a good idea, no doubt," she said. "But I am also very hungry."

The witch now turned to Rollie. "And your opinion, Rollie?"

Stosh and Ashay had quickly replied with their horrible solutions for our fate but Rollie struggled. "Well, let me see," he began and knelt down in front of me. He leaned closer and I caught a scent of fish soup. Looking directly into my eyes he said, "This one spit soup on me."

"Yes," said the witch. "That he did. So what is your decision?"

Rollie paused and grimaced. "Drown him," he said at last.

"What about Idiot Number One?"

The troll snapped his head toward Harry as though seeing him for the first time. He looked back at me and then back to Harry again. "Bury him alive," he said decisively.

The witch pulled Rollie away from me and took up a position between me and Harry. She looked from one of us to the other. "Mmm…fire, water, earth, food. Which do you prefer?" She pointed at me.

"Uh…water," I said. To this day I don't know why.

She pointed at Harry. "And you?"

"Water," he mumbled.

The witch actually appeared pleased by this. She raised her hands up toward the ceiling. "Fire it is!" she yelled. "Take them outside and burn them!"

At this command Ashay and Rollie grasped us by the back of our shirts and yanked us to our feet. Stosh took up a position to our front and moved towards the living room door.

"Into the fire! Into the fire!" the witch screeched over and over. Stosh raised his hand above his head, made a dramatic swooping gesture, and grasped the door knob. Ashay and Rollie dragged us forward. I could feel the torture even before I saw the searing flames. I could see my flesh bubbling and peeling away from my body and smell Harry's long locks burning in the flames. And then I couldn't.

Still dangling from Ashay's grip the witch was suddenly in our faces. "There is something I want you two idiots to do," she growled. "Stop acting like young idiots and find a way to live useful lives."

With that Stosh swung open the door and we were pitched out into the night – the very cool night. With adrenaline soaked fear we sprang to our feet like cats and tore off into the forest. Behind us cackles and gales of laughter echoed. It was a night, and advice, we never forgot.

The Idaho Sandman

I'm an environmental super star. Awards from numerous state Fish and Game Departments, Colleges, and the US Department of the Interior. Oprah left a message on my phone the other day and there's even talk of a nomination for a Nobel Prize. All nonsense, of course. You don't garner those kinds of accolades when you are deemed to be insane so I'm writing all this down before I disappear for good. I doubt anyone will believe it anyway. Hell, sometimes I'm not sure I believe it. But I am me and despite my doubts a man sees what he sees and hears what he hears. And smells what he smells. There's a bit of reality that's hard to deny.

The study I was conducting was certainly in the realm of reality, as was the four thousand dollar grant to observe the western harvester ant. These guys cause a lot of damage in some states gobbling up crops and crop seeds. They can be a significant agricultural nuisance. The little buggers have quite a bite, too. You wouldn't think a critter just a quarter of an inch long could pack such a wallop. My research was part of an effort to stop them by inventing a technique that did not include bombarding the area with insecticides. It's politically and environmentally unpopular these days, not to mention danged unhealthy. Sure, I'm down with that but four grand for a month of watching ants crawl around? I'd do that for free! Most of the time I do anyway; I love the little beasts.

My study was centered in a brush covered prairie a couple of hours outside of Boise, Idaho. The land is a combination of enormous flat open spaces bristling with knee high creosote bushes occasionally broken up by steep, rocky hills. On the surface it looks like an endless kingdom of sand and scrub but the terrain is deceptive above and below. Idaho may be a quiet bastion of prairie and potato farms now but in days past it was a riot of fire and brimstone.

Wandering around alone in a place like this with nothing but the wind for a companion probably sounds pretty boring to your average human but to me it's bliss. Most people only see endless stretches of endless stretches as they zoom past in their cars and trucks. Can't blame them. It takes time to get to know the surprising life bustling around all that sand and scrub. But it's there. I've already mentioned the ants; they're out here in the billions. And so are snakes, lizards, prairie dogs, ground squirrels, voles, moles, mice, badgers, deer, coyote, hawks, crows, ravens, magpies, feral goats, wild horses, owls… I could go on but you get the idea. The point is that there is a lot to see out here, actually more than anyone knows – far more than anyone knows.

I left the hotel at my usual time that morning with my basic load of lunch, water, camera gear, note books, canvas roll, knee and elbow pads. Working with ants you tend to spend a lot of time on your hands and knees or stretched out on the ground. Timing is important, too, and not just by the clock. For insect observation temperature and seasonal time of year are key, especially for ants. Too cold and the little guys are hunkered down and barely moving. Too hot and they'll do the same thing. Nice, warm weather is not really the answer either. Ants are quick, relentless bundles of activity that spread out all over the place – and that place is likely to be up your pant leg biting every exposed square millimeter of exposed flesh. Trust me on this. Nope, the best time is early spring with cold mornings that gradually rise into a sunny warmth. That way you get out early, pick your spot, focus the camera, position the notepad, and watch the colony blossom to life. As the little ladies (which most ants are, by the way) begin to go about life you can pick out the workers, the scouts, the soldiers and observe their individual habits before they pick up too much steam. My job was to observe the insects over the period of a month and see if I could find some chink in their habits that could be exploited in order to control them naturally. Introduction of foreign predators in cases like this had turned out to be disasters for the most part so that was off the table for now.

A chilly wind blew down my neck as I settled in for my twentieth day of observation. So far I hadn't garnered anything that had not already been observed and reported on but that did not dim my enthusiasm in the least. If I was not here lying on my stomach observing ants in Idaho I'd be someplace else doing it. The morning was overcast and a bit chilly so I knew my little friends wouldn't provide me with much entertainment for a while. Oh well, like I said, there's always something else to see out the Idaho plains. With rucksack on my back and camera in hand I began a leisurely stroll about the surrounding countryside. When the weather warmed up to acceptable standards I'd plop down and observe one of the thousands of ant mounds in the area.

My time was not wasted. As I meandered about I snapped some respectable photos of ravens, ground squirrels, a badger, and an assortment of mice and voles. Probably due to its isolation but relative proximity to a roadway, this area is dotted with small piles of trash, old furniture, and occasional mounds of deer carcasses where hunters have dispose butchered remains. It's not something you'd easily see from the highway and the debris is not enough to ruin the scenery. Actually, these small piles of trash are a bonus for photographers like me. Rodents, reptiles, and a huge variety of insects make their home in these tiny dumps. I've spent many hours turning over chunks of cardboard, plywood, and discarded pieces of furniture and I have been rewarded with some remarkable sights. But none as remarkable as the one I was about to see.

I'd meandered on for a couple of very peaceful miles until I was well out of sight of the highway. The terrain out here is quite pristine so I was surprised, and a bit pleased, to see a small couch overturned on its back amidst the sand and brush. Someone had gone through some extra effort to dump trash this far out, and the lack of tire tracks signaled that this discard must have happened some time ago. I approached in anticipation just knowing there'd be some intriguing wildlife hiding under the old sofa. Camera in hand I grasped the thing and attempted to turn it over. The thing didn't budge. Okay, I thought, it's a bit heavier than usual; must have some weird backing or something. I slung my camera around my neck and gave the couch a good two handed yank. It moved but not much. I approached from the other side, bent down, dug my fingers under the back of the sofa, and yanked again. The thing still would not move. But with this last effort I discovered that the back of the sofa was attached to something beneath the sand. I stomped my foot on the ground. It sounded hollow.

"What the hell you doing!?"

I jumped and whirled around at the gravelly voice bellowing from behind me. To say I was startled would be an understatement - this was a real excrement mover! To make matters even more frightening I saw no one standing behind me. Then the voice spoke again.

"Leave my damned house alone!"

There are rare times in a man's life when he is faced with something so extraordinary, so bizarre, so unusually freakish, that immediate reaction is impossible. The mind struggles desperately to make sense of something for which there is utterly no point of reference. Shock is the initial overwhelming emotion; often followed quickly by horror. Such was my situation. Has a talking head ever popped up out of the ground near your feet? Probably not, so I will elaborate.

When I first spun around to confront the voice I was duly startled. After all I had seen no one around me from horizon to horizon for several hours. But even in that moment I was preparing an apology. Obviously, my wanderings had ended up on someone's property and the owner had approached from behind while I worked to overturn the abandoned sofa. My eyes, however, were greeted by the same empty horizon to horizon Idaho prairie. That was concerning. Was I losing mind? I know I had heard a voice. The next utterance, however, was infinitely more roiling.

"What are you, stupid?"

There was no mistaking it – the voice had come from the ground. And there it was, about six feet away from me. The head was covered with beige sand but I could see the features very well. Long, sand colored hair hung over both sides of it and well over the ears. Shaggy eyebrows covered squinting, angry blue eyes. A sand colored beard hid most of the rest of a chubby red, oddly speckled face. I conjured the only explanation I could come up with. Of course, this had to be some kind of trick, a bizarre robot doll made to look as real as possible. I looked around for the hidden camera destined to make me a joking sensation on YouTube. But as I backed slowly away that rationalization blew up. A pair of stocky arms protruded from the sand followed by a very human torso and two very human legs covered in ragged jeans. The being stood there for a moment staring at me. And then it spoke again.

"Find what you were looking for?"

"Uh, no," I said.

"So what were you looking for?" he demanded.

"Mice, voles, lizards, snakes. Anything I can take a picture of," I explained. "I'm a biologist out here doing research." I held up my camera to reinforce the point. "I didn't mean to disturb you. I'm sorry." The words rolled out of my mouth but I remained in a state I can only describe as stupification.

The strange man took several steps toward me and stopped. Despite the fact that I estimated myself to be about three feet taller than my bizarre adversary had he come any closer I would have run. His appearance coupled with the whole weird situation was just too much.

"What kind of research?" he asked, an obvious suspicion in his tone.

I explained the whole business about the harvester ants and the grant I had been given to study them and why. I then added in the reason why I had wandered out here taking random photographs instead of observing insects at that particular time.

The odd fellow's hard face softened. He nodded in agreement. "Okay, you sound legitimate. But what are you going to do now?"

"Go back about my business," I said. "It's warming up; the colonies will be coming to life."

"That's not what I'm talking about. I'm talking about me. What are you going to say when you get back to town? Are you going to run your mouth all over the place and tell them you saw the Idaho Sandman?"

"I hadn't even thought about it." That was surely the truth; I was still coming to grips with the present. "I assume you'd prefer that I keep our encounter a secret?"

"Yes. It don't happen very often but I've been spotted once or twice before. Then the whole place gets run over with a bunch of punks thinking they're going to find some kind of a midget prairie sasquatch or something. It's a real pain in the ass."

Much to my surprise I was beginning to feel at ease. But I was still perplexed. "You live out here?"

"Yep. And that's my home you been stompin' on." He pointed to the ground I had been standing on moments before. "At least it is for now," he added. "I shift around quite a bit."

"Uh…my apologies. I had no idea," I stammered. At this point I'm in a total quandary, and not ashamed to admit still unnerved by this encounter. Had the guy been a normal sized man maybe I wouldn't have been so dazzled. But the diminutive stature of what I faced added to the unreality of the situation. I seriously considered running back to my car.

44

But the little fellow did not approach. Being shirtless, shoeless, and barefoot it was obvious that he held no weapon. Curiosity and sympathy began to overtake fear. Was this guy really living out here in some homemade underground bunker? If so, why? Was he forced into this life? Or maybe he was just like the thousands of homeless cases in big cities, only with a prairie country spin. I wanted to find out more – and whether or not I was losing my mind.

"Sir," I said. "Do you mind if I ask your name?"

"Just call me Idaho for now."

"Okay, Idaho. My name's Bill Covell. Pleased to meet you." The sentiment was sincere but I did not offer a handshake.

"Okay, Bill Covell. I would appreciate it if you don't mention our meeting to anybody; like I said it tends to cause me problems. All I want is to be left alone. Besides, I could do a lot for you in return, mister."

"Really?"

"That's right," he said. "You said you're a biologist sent out here to study ants, right?"

"Yes, that's right."

"Have you found out what you're being paid to find out?"

"No I admit I haven't. But I've got a couple of more weeks to go." My reply sounded weak even to me.

"Well, let me tell you something, Bill. I live out here with these animals. And I mean live. I mean 24/7 and in the exact same habitat. I've been doin' it for quite a while now. I'm no college boy biologist but I can tell you things about what goes on around here that you'll never get close to with your academia outlook."

It was an irritating accusation but I decided not to argue the point. After all it's pretty hard to top the observations of a man who actually spends his entire life in the dirt with the animals. If that was true, of course. And it's not wise to argue with a madman no matter what size he is.

"Well, Mr. Idaho I won't say I disagree with that. If you really are out here as much as you say you must have seen an awful lot. So what can you tell me?"

"I'll tell you a lot. But not out here. I've been out too long in the open." He looked over his shoulder and then back to me. "Let's talk in my place."

"You mean underground?"

"Scared are ya?"

"Well, I…uh…it's just that…" I stumbled for an answer. I sincerely didn't want to hurt the little guy's feelings, but to crawl underground with him? "Uh, Idaho, I appreciate the invitation but I'm over six feet tall. Isn't that a bit much for you, I mean, your place?"

I thought I'd come with a sound excuse to refuse the invitation but Mr. Idaho was undeterred.

"I got eyes, big fella. I can see how tall you are. Yea, you'll have to squat down a bit but we'll manage. Bottom line is you're scared ain't ya? Hah! Here you are so big and brave lookin' down at a bunch of little ants and takin' pictures of squirrels and shit but when it comes to really getting' down to the heart of things you back down. Face it. You're scared of my home, you're scared of me, and you're scared of lookin at things from a completely different view."

I threw my hands up. How the devil was I supposed to answer that? What made matters worse was that this strange man was right. I was scared! I was totally creeped out by the whole situation. But here I was facing a chance to delve into the most unique situation in my whole life, if not the world. In the midst of this mental turmoil Idaho walked up to me. He looked angry, too.

"Okay, Mr. Bill Covell, Biologist. Or should I say Doctor Covell, biologist, which I'm sure you are. Go on, get outa here. I thought you were different from the rest; I thought you had a genuine interest in things. Go on, keep lookin at the world your way and learn nothin that ain't been learned before. You'll never find what you're looking for. And don't come back here lookin for me either. I'll be long gone by then." He turned way.

I watched as he shuffled away, taking note of his bare back and ragged cut off blue jeans covering his stubby legs. Well, if he had a weapon I certainly could not see one. And he had been close enough to use something if he did have something hidden that escaped my observation.

"Wait, Idaho, wait," I called. He turned about slowly, head cocked and lips frowning.

"Yea?"

"Okay, let's go into your place and talk."

Idaho did not reply. He simply beckoned me to follow with a wave of his hand and continued to walk back toward his "home." I fell in behind him wondering if I'd just made the stupidest decision of my life. When we got to the entrance I was pretty sure I had.

Idaho stopped at the sandy hole he had emerged from. He turned around and slipped in feet first. With just his head poking out of the earth he looked up at me. "Ready?"

"How am I supposed to get in there?" The hole hardly looked bigger than the entrance to one of the many badger burrows that dotted the area. I couldn't believe it.

He snickered and shook his head, apparently finding humor in my bizarre predicament. "Obviously my humble home was not made for the likes of you, Bill. So here's what you gotta do. Just grab the plywood here, lift it up, and then slide in like I did. You can manage that, can't ya?"

My burrowing friend waved his hand by his ear indicating something just behind his head. I got the picture quickly. Idaho's burrow was actually ceilinged by a large piece of plywood heavily covered in sand and rocks. I'd been so busy trying to overturn the sofa before on top of it I had not noticed.

Still prickly with suspicion I bent over to do as instructed as Idaho disappeared into the burrow. I grasped the edge of the plywood where his head had been and pulled. Covered in sand as it was the thing did not come up easily but I managed to raise it. I could only get the thing up to about waist high, though. Feeling utterly ridiculous I stood there struggling with all my strength to make further progress but it was impossible. Then I heard Idaho's muffled voice.

"That's as far as she'll go. What you gotta do now is turn around and go down to your knees and let the roof come down on your back. Then you can slide in backwards like I did."

Unbelievably, I did exactly that. The "roof" closed with a thump over my head. To my extreme exasperation it also cracked down on my camera and broke the lens since I had not managed to pull it out of the way. Stupid! Oh well. I rolled over, got myself into an upright sitting position and rubbed sand out of my hair and face. I opened my eyes to an incredible sight. Illuminated by the dim light from the hole behind my head sat my diminutive host, several feet away from me sitting on his haunches with arms folded. Next to him was a tattered sleeping bag and what looked to be a mini refrigerator. A single wooden chair was tucked under a small table pushed against the dirt wall to my right. A large round tunnel that vanished into darkness decorated the other side of the place, and as my eyes adjusted I noticed another tunnel behind Idaho.

As I was adjusting to this bizarre domicile a soft gurgling growl caught my attention. It seemed to be coming from the little man himself but Idaho reassured me. "Don't worry," he said. "The little guy's just a bit upset. You're only the second human he's ever seen. And you have to admit we are pretty different in appearance." Idaho reached down and picked up the still grumbling animal.

"I don't believe it!" I exclaimed. "You tamed a badger?"

Idaho smiled with obvious pride at my reaction. "Well, tame might be too strong a word. He's calm enough, though. As long as I keep him fed. I found him a few weeks ago. He was real emaciated, just wandering around out there. I figured something happened to his mother so I took him in. Couple of feedings and pretty soon the little guy is treatin me like mama. I call him Sparky."

"Idaho that is fantastic!" My admiration was sincere.

He waved off the complement. "Oh, I've got better surprises for ya. But before I forget my manners let me orient you to my home."

"Please do," I said. This had to be interesting.

Idaho stood up and placed Sparky down on the spot where he'd been sitting. The little badger curled up and sat still; apparently very content but did not take his eyes away from me. I had no idea how to break the ice with a badger so I decided to keep my distance. Idaho leaned over behind the refrigerator, picked up an object, and set it on the table. It was a lantern. He pushed a button and light blossomed with an electric glow. The entire dirty domicile came into clarity. The burrow was about four feet high, kind of square in shape, maybe six feet by six feet. With the light on I could clearly see the outline of the plywood ceiling above.

Idaho pointed to the tunnel behind the resting badger. "That's the latrine. Go ahead if you gotta go. Just cover it up good with dirt when you're done. There's a little shovel in there; I think there's a bit of paper left."

"That's okay, Idaho," I said. "I'm good." Thank god.

"Sure. Help yourself anytime you feel the urge."

He pointed to the other tunnel. "That's kind of an escape hatch; it goes back a ways."

At this point my fear had transformed into insatiable curiosity. I couldn't hold any longer. "Okay Mr. Idaho, you got me. How did you end up here? What made you live like this? How long have you been here? How do you manage to live? I mean this is unbelievable!"

"It ain't that hard. You've seen the trash out there? It ends up being my fine furniture in here." He opened his arms as if to proudly display it. "These hicks out here are always dumping stuff."

"But what do you do for food and water?"

"Food is easy. This prairie is loaded down and crawling with squirrels, mice, and a hundred other small animals. I eat lizards for a change in protein source; sometimes snakes. Sparky there has become a pretty good hunter, too. We've learned to share. Water's just as easy.

This place has hidden wells all around. I know just about all of them."

Idaho sat down on the chair near the table. He wiggled a bit pushing the wooden legs firmly into the dirt. He looked down for a moment as if trying to decide what to do, then raised his head and planted his hands on his knees.

"Alright, alright," he said. "I suppose I ought to give you some background. To begin with – do I look normal to you?" His fingers accented quotation marks around the word normal.

"Well…no," I said. This guy sure had a talent for asking awkward questions.

"Okay, at least you're honest about it. Most would spit out some fake sympathetic nonsense to that question."

"But, Idaho," I said. "Aren't there a lot of people out there with your, uh, your condition? I mean I've seen TV shows and stuff."

"No. There ain't that many people like me, not many at all. Why else would they make a TV show about people like me?"

This was getting uncomfortable. I searched my mind for some "kind" thing to say but I had the feeling that no matter what I said it would sound stupid and phony and get thrown back in my face. The little man, however, relieved my tension.

"Forget about that," he said with a wave of his arm. "It's just a small part of how I came to live out here. No pun intended." He actually smiled at this. I returned the expression and he continued.

"Oh yea. Right from the beginning I was different. I was different from everybody in my family. School was a real pain in the ass and I have no pleasant memories about it at all. But I didn't want to be part of their normality anyway. My parents tried to get me into sports and all that crap, tried the whole self esteem bit despite my height, you know, on and on. I don't blame 'em for that. What else could they do? My older brother and sister were normal kids. They obviously weren't prepared for me. They weren't prepared for just how different I really was – and still am." He added that last with obvious pride.

Once again I struggled for an adequate response. "Well, it still must have been hard for you. Your parents, too."

"That ain't the point. I was different in ways much bigger than how short I was."

"You got my attention, mister."

"It was the things I was interested in, you see. Just one thing, really. And that one thing took me over. I didn't care about all their school crap, sports, literature, or all the other nonsense that's supposed to make you normal. It just didn't interest me in the least. God love my parents. They tried, they really did. But I was beyond their understanding, way beyond. Finally, they gave up and just let me be. I was making their life miserable anyway."

Idaho shook his head at that last statement. It was not gesture of sorrow, however. His expression looked more like one of relief from a bad situation.

"So you left home and went your own way, right? I can certainly relate to that, Idaho. In fact, we have a lot in common when it comes to school and stuff. All I ever wanted to learn about was animals, mainly ants. Everything else I had to force myself to put up with."

For the first time since we'd met a big, genuine smile lit up the face of the Idaho Sandman. He pointed his finger at me. "And that's why I invited you in here, Bill. I suspected that about you."

"Really?"

"You don't think you've been wandering around here all this time unnoticed do you?

"I should have known," I said in a laugh. What a blinding flash of the obvious! Idaho had been observing me observing ants for the past several weeks.

"That's right big guy. Your ant obsession is similar to mine."

"But I don't live underground," I answered, urging him to go one with his story.

"Nope," he said. Your desire to know isn't strong enough. Mine is."

"C'mon, now. You got me down here to tell me you live like this to study ants?" But at this point I was pretty much expecting the blathering of a mentally disturbed loner.

"Nope. No. My concern is a bigger, a lot bigger. Life, Bill. I had to learn about life. It's the only thing I've cared about since I can remember."

I had not expected that. "Okay…care to expand on that?"

"Where does life come from, Bill?"

Now I knew what he was angling at. "The earth," I conceded.

"That's right, my friend. But it's only half the answer. The sun is the other half. The sun and the earth give rise to life. I can't very well live in the sun, can I? The earth, however, is open to anyone who wants to know its secret. So here I am."

Yep, I was dealing with a lunatic; an interesting lunatic, but a lunatic just the same. To be on the safe side I decided to humor him a bit more and then be on my way. Besides, the place didn't smell that great. "There are other ways to study life, Idaho. I'm sure you're aware of that."

"Try not to condescend to me, alright? Sure there's other ways. There's your way, for example. And what have you gained so far? Fact after fact after fact. You know a lot about ants, their physiology, their behavior, etc. Maybe more than any scientist in the world. But you still don't know ants like I know them. And ya never will."

At this point the little guy was getting worked up, his agitation was obvious. And my discomfort level was rising accordingly. It was time to end this bizarre meeting. "Okay, I'll accept that. Now I really have to get going; I have a job to do. Maybe my methods are not up to your standards but the university pays me and expects me to do my best." I got up into a kneeling position and positioned myself toward the exit. Idaho then said something that stopped me.

"Don't you want to know how to stop the ants?"

I turned back around. "Stop from what?" I said but the little guy saw right through me.

"Oh knock it off. You know what I mean. The college didn't send you out here on a grant just to count ant antenna nodules. You want to know how to stop these harvester ants from taking over farms and such. If you lived out here you'd know how. It's a simple trick, really."

"You got me, Idaho. What's your method?" He had me again.

"Rocks," he said.

"Huh?"

"This ant we're talking about, the western harvester, hates a certain kind of volcanic rock out here. Grind some up and spread it around; the ants won't go near it. It helps to wet it down a little, too. Something about the moisture interacts below ground and a kind of fungus builds up. The ants hate it. It helps to run a steam roller over parts of the property, too. These ants don't like hard packed earth."

In all my research I had never even thought of volcanic rock as an ant repellant. I didn't totally buy the idea but it did have potential. There were several types of volcanic rock in the area and there were sporadic patches out here completely devoid of the insects. The fungal network made sense as well. I sat down again. "I have to admit, Idaho. That sounds like it's worth try. But what kind of rock are you talking about."

"I'll show you," he said. "But it's just a tiny part of a bigger picture. It's hardly worth discussing."

"It is to the farmers and ranchers around here." I offered. "And me."

Idaho sighed. "Shit…they know less than you and you know less than I thought."

The little guy had a talent for cutting remarks; no surprise considering the life he'd led, but it was definitely time for me to go. "Alright, pal. I understand. You've had a rough time of it in this life and you picked an alternate route." I wanted to end this discussion in the most humane way possible without upsetting this strange man. Besides, my butt was starting to bother me. Try sitting underground for a while in hard damp sand pebbled with small rocks.

Idaho was oblivious to my discomfort. "You just don't get it." he said.

The remark annoyed me to respond. "I'm sitting underground talking to a man who lives in a dirt tunnel in the middle of an Idaho prairie. And you say I don't get it. Gee, how could that be? I should understand this intuitively, of course. But I only run into situations like this rarely." I could lay on a little sarcasm myself when the occasion called for it.

He leaned forward in his chair. "I ask you again – where does life come from?"

"I thought we covered that, Idaho."

"Stop trying to be a smart ass and answer the question. Where does life come from?"

As much as I tried to prevent getting dragged into this insane conversation I couldn't seem to stop myself. "Alright, alright. As we discussed before life comes from the earth with the sun as the trigger."

Idaho rolled his eyes. "Once again, only half an answer; not even that actually. What is it about this earth that allows it to constantly bloom life, Bill? You see, you're so busy staring at your little arthropods, and yes they have a fascination, that you ignore the most important question. Why are they alive to begin with? Answer me that, will ya?"

Well I had to admit that I'd never even considered the why of their life. I was not, however, about to let that stop me. "Oh c'mon, Idaho. There are many theories about the origin of life. You know that. Some say it came from a meteor; some say deep sea ocean vents; some say it started from a lighting strike. Of course, some claim it came from God in just a few days."

"So you're telling me that you and everyone else doesn't know, right?"

"I concede that. I do not claim to have the answer to the origin of life."

"Well I've studied every single one of those theories and not one of them provides the answer, Bill, not one of them. And you know it. This earth we're sitting in is a constant explosion of life from core to surface – and nobody knows why."

"So what is the answer, Idaho?"

"That's what I'm down here to find out. How much more do you think you could learn about your ants if you could shrink down and actually live inside a colony for a while? If you could hear their language like they do, smell their scents like they do, feel their emotions, have the same sense of body. Think you'd learn something, then?"

"Yeeeah."

"That's right! And it'd be a lot more than any lab experiment or outside observation, wouldn't it?"

"And a lot more impossible." The expression of condescending sarcasm on my face surely penetrated the tone of my voice. "Even you're not that small."

To my relief the little man ignored the tasteless joke. No matter. Now it was really time to go. In addition to the knowledge that I was underground with a mentally unstable representative of his kind I was getting terribly uncomfortable from my cramped position and my damp backside.

But once gain the little guy seemed to sense my emotions. "Alright, alright," he said as he held up both hands. "You need a little more background, Bill. Just sit tight for a little bit longer. Can you do that for me? Please?"

The sudden change of tone from haughty know it all to humble requester was a surprise yet I remained suspicious. I placed my hands on the "ceiling" above my head and pushed. It gave way easily enough.

"Don't worry," he said, noting my motion. "There is nothing at all keeping you here except what I have to tell you. Hang with me for just a bit longer, okay? If I don't get out what I know it'll all just die here with me. For obvious reasons I can't come out and do it myself. It has to be somebody like you. Can you imagine how quickly I'd be put in a nuthouse if I decided to go downtown looking like this and began telling people about my life?"

He surely had a point there. I agreed to stay a while longer. But I told him that was as far as I could go; I had real work to accomplish and real results to produce or suffer the consequences. A look of genuine relief came to the man and he resumed the narrative of his life.

"Now, remember when I told you that I was different even from very young age?"

"Yea."

"That difference came to me early in life, and again, I'm not talking about my size. Although that might have had something to do with it, it's really irrelevant. As a kid I loved all kinds of animals. Just like you, right, Bill?"

"That's for sure."

"But I liked plants, too. I liked everything that was outside of the house. I used to go off into the nearby woods and prowl around there for hours just in awe of the bursting life around me. I got lost quite a few times, though. Once for a couple of days. That was too much for my parents and they forbid me to go out in the woods alone. My dad went out with me a couple of times after that but it just wasn't the same. In fact, whenever somebody else was with me, even my big brother who I loved, it just wasn't the same. I didn't get that big sensation of awe that overwhelmed when I was by myself."

I had to agree with him there, too. I preferred solo expeditions as well. Whenever I went out with a friend or research comrade they seemed to spend too much time talking or doing other things that disrupted my concentration. When alone I could pause and silently observe at great length anything that caught my interest.

"So, cut off from the woods, what did you do?"

"That's the real irony. I couldn't go out alone in the woods but I was free to go out in our backyard by myself as long as I cared to. We had a big, fenced in place out in the country but my brother and sister preferred to visit friends a lot. Naturally, I was left out of these social engagements but that was okay by me because I enjoyed being alone and away from all the teasing and such. So I spent time rolling around our backyard looking at trees, grass, and stuff. Of course, there wasn't much to see after I'd trekked around the place for a few days. But then one day I turned over a large rock on the side of my mother's garden. I was astounded!

"A hundred different little things were squirming around under that rock. Centipedes, pill bugs, spiders, different kinds of worms, ants, and dozen other creatures I couldn't identify! I sat there entranced. The awe I'd felt in the forest seized me again but this time like a giant ocean wave. From then on I turned over every rock, log, piece of wood, trash I could find no matter where I was. And that's when it hit me. There is far more life hidden away inside the earth than there is above it. We see trees and think how beautiful they are but the real action is going on underground in a gigantic maze of roots, fungus, and biochemical reactions that pull life from the earth. In fact, every living thing on this planet is pulling life from the earth in one form or another. I became obsessed with learning the secret of that life force."

The enthusiasm of Mr. Idaho as he related this unique story of his life was contagious, and once again he'd given me something to think about. I'd been studying insects for the better part of my life but I'd always been concerned with their behavior. I'd just taken the fact that they, like every other animal on earth, were alive for granted; that they pulled energy from whatever they ate, absorbed into their bodies, and got on with their lives. Exoteric, metaphysical questions about the origin of life? I had no time for that. Yet here was giant chunk of obviousness I'd never considered. There was an enormous amount of life living just under the very surface of the earth. I shifted my numbing backside and stretched my cramped legs in order to get more comfortable. Now I wanted to hear more.

"And that's what drove you into a life underground, correct?"

"Exactly," he said. "I call it the 'subsurface,' that area just underneath the stuff we see every day. But those things living in the subsurface are just an indicator, a symptom of a far greater mystery. I knew I had to go deeper."

"Then why out here in this particular prairie, Idaho? There's a lot more ground life in other places; why'd you end up here?"

"Partly by accident; partly on purpose. My family moved here after living in other parts of the country. Some places are too wet, some too crowded with humans, and some too crowded with big predators. A couple of years ago I was out here wandering around, kinda like you, and decided this would be a perfect place for my studies. Came out here one night with a shovel and started digging. By morning I pretty much had what you see now not too far from here. From then on it was just a matter of adapting."

This was amazing. "But still, why do you have to live underground? Why live like this?"

He shook his head. "Alright. I knew you wouldn't pick up on it right off the bat. Let's take an example." He pointed to his badger friend, Sparky. "If you stayed out in the field observing this guy day and night, night and day, for a year you'd probably know a hell of a lot about badgers wouldn't you?"

Another point on which I had to agree.

"And if you could somehow find a way to actually live like a badger, get right up close to them, you'd know even more, right?"

"That's right," I said. It was the "live like an ant" lecture, this time with a mammalian slant. But the little guy was ahead of me again.

"We've established the fact that you're too big to live like an ant or a badger. And, believe it not, so am I. But ants and badgers are sideline, minor issues so forget about them. You don't have to shrink down or change shape to fit in the earth. It has plenty of room. So here I am – learning the secret of life by becoming part of the thing that produces it."

With that last intriguing sentence hanging in the damp air Idaho leapt from his chair and raised his fists over his head. He was positively beaming with pride and I had the distinct impression that he'd been waiting for a long time to tell someone this. How long had he endured the dark isolation of these earthen burrows? He was certainly insane. Even if he had been living like this just for the past couple of months instead of years as he claimed it had to have taken a toll on his mind. Crazy as he was, however, the man was sincere. Of that I had no doubt. I asked the obvious question.

"Alright, then. What is the secret of life?"

Idaho's eyes lit up. He dropped his arms and leaped toward me in a single, startling motion. "NOW you're starting to get it, Bill! NOW you're starting to get it! But like the storyteller says – show, don't tell. Besides, I couldn't describe it anyway. Come with me and I'll show you." He beckoned toward the tunnel that led away from the main room of the burrow, the one he had called his escape hatch. Without waiting for my reply he snatched the small lantern from the table and headed into the tunnel.

To say I had reservations about following my diminutive friend into this black tunnel is another gigantic understatement. The idea was positively unnerving. Idaho, however, took no notice of my hesitation. He stomped into the dark hole. Judging from the distant sound of his voice he was a bit of a way in before noticing that I was not tagging along. "C'mon, Bill," he yelled. "There is absolutely nothing to be afraid of and a world of knowledge to be gained. Literally!"

With Idaho out of sight this was my chance to jump break through the burrow ceiling and escape into the blessed lighted world above. That would be pretty rude, of course, not to mention downright cowardly. But to crawl though the dirt following an ostensibly insane midget into a dark cave? Seriously?

In the midst of my hesitation Idaho emerged from the tunnel, the lantern producing a weird array of shadows on his face. "Bill, you don't have to go in very far, it's a straight tunnel, no curves. I'll be in front of you all the way so they'll be nothing in your way if you decide to turn around. I'm telling ya, this is something you have got to experience!"

For several long, uncomfortable minutes I just sat in place staring at my strange new friend. Imagine yourself in my predicament – sitting underground with a sand covered, half dressed, shaggy haired, miniature person who is begging you to crawl further underground in order to discover the secret of life. What would you have done? Well, I'll tell you. You'd have let out a scream and bolted faster that you'd ever done in your life. No, not to the sunlight above but right directly toward Idaho and his tunnel. Which is exactly what I did. And you would have done the same thing if an angry badger had jumped on to the back of your neck. One startled scream later and I was on my hands and knees just inside the entrance of the mysterious burrow. From my new position I looked up and came face to face with Idaho. He was laughing to the point where he was having difficulty catching his breath. A wave of anger replaced my initial fear. I sprang up only to slam my head into the sandy rock soil over me and was left sprawled on the dirt. Fear, anger, and confusion jolted my entire body as I scrambled completely around, this time determined to escape. I had not moved more than a foot before coming face to face with three more badgers, each fully grown and fiercely growling. I halted in place. Behind me Idaho continued his exasperating laughter.

"Call them off, Idaho!" I yelled.

"You'll have to give them time to calm down a bit, Bill," he answered between spurts of giggles. But his voice seemed a little further away than before.

Cautiously I backed away from the little carnivores facing me. They ceased their growling and did not advance. Feeling somewhat relived at that I turned around again. Further down the tunnel I could see the light of the swinging lantern and Idaho's loping silhouette on the dirt walls. "C'mon, Bill," he called. "I promise that this will be the experience of a lifetime."

I turned around again. The three little monsters were still in place. They advanced and began growling again. I backed away. My retreat calmed them down again. Follow Idaho or risk mauling by the badgers? It was a miserable choice. Yet as rattled as I was by the badgers, I presumed that an attack on my unprotected butt was the lesser unpleasantness than having my unprotected face ripped apart. On hands and knees I began to follow my small tormenter. Idaho, I thought, this better be one hell of a show. As soon as I made this decision, however, another equally unnerving situation presented itself. Idaho was nowhere in sight. The only thing that prevented me from dropping into sheer panic was the glimmering illumination that still shown from the burrows main entrance. Well, I thought, perhaps he had just gone on a bit further than his lantern light could project. If he did not appear soon I vowed to go back and escape even if I have to battle a dozen badgers. It was then that the ground beneath me gave way.

I'm not sure how far I fell. I only recall falling into a cascade of rocks and dirt that swept me like a small river and suddenly dumped me into an open area. At least it felt open. The total darkness made the outlines of underground trap impossible to make out. I lay motionless, covered in dirt and fighting looming panic as I waited for the crushing pressure of the cave in. After several long moments I pushed down with my hands and raised my head up into the dark. Cautiously I rose to my feet and stood to full height. I had not been buried alive!

As you might guess, though, my comfort was short lived. Yes, I was alive, and no, I had not been crushed in some kind of an underground nightmare. But the darkness was absolutely, utterly, complete. I had not the faintest concept of where I was or how to escape this black, opaque prison. I tried to orient myself. What position was I in when the collapse occurred? On my hands and knees. Mmm... The rush of dirt had seemed to propel me forward, so considering my current posture, the way out must be behind me. But then I seemed to recall being spun around during the descent. I bent over and felt the dirt pile in front of me. The pile was rising. That told me that I must have cascaded down from that direction. I took a couple of steps into the rise. Then a couple of more, and a few more. A rush of soil and small rocks rolled down with every step. I was going nowhere.

Fighting panic I turned about again and chanced a few cautious steps. To my shock I stepped into another pile of dirt and rock rising in that direction which began to cascade down just the other side had. I dropped to my hands and knees again and felt all around. To my horror I realized that I was trapped at the base of an enormous pile of sand that rose all around me. Coupled with the total darkness the effect was terrifying. In my entire life I had never fainted. I had heard about people passing out from fright. That had never happened to me either. Today was different. I collapsed.

I recovered quickly but remained utterly bewildered at my inky dark and cold surroundings, thinking I was recovering from an awful nightmare. I was fully awake, however, and reminded that the nightmare was true. A surge of adrenaline began to well up inside me as the renewed horror of my situation returned. I tried to stand but collapsed again. This time, however, I hit the ground hands first. To my surprise the earth felt very warm; an unexpectedly pleasant sensation in my cold prison. I dug my hands deeper into the soil and felt increasing warmth. My spirits rose with the discovery and cleared away more and more of the earth until I had made a shallow kind of a burrow for myself that I nestled down into. The uncontrollable panic that had gripped me just moments before oozed away as the soil's warmth oozed into my body. I crossed my legs and leaned back putting as much of my body into contact with the earth as possible. All the emotion of terror that should have encompassed me in this situation abated. I felt totally at ease; the kind of feeling you have when everything is right with the world, when you are without the slightest worry and about to take a well deserved nap. I would have taken a nap, too, but another sensation overwhelmed me. And this even more wonderfully pleasant than the first. It started as a dull, soft vibration underneath me that crept into my entire body and suddenly I was engulfed in the most beautiful emotion I have ever felt. It is nearly impossible to describe so wondrous was this event. Try to remember a moment when you heard a musical melody so beautiful that it overwhelmed you to the point of tears. That was my state, only multiplied many times over.

I was in the midst of this incredible euphoria when a dim light slowly blossomed into brilliance. Suddenly Idaho was standing over me grinning.

"Sorry about the trick with the badgers, Bill but I knew it was the only way to get down here. Forgive me?"

"Yea, sure" I said. But I was actually so engulfed in the odd pleasure of my predicament that I was kind of sorry to see him show up. It threatened to ruin the moment.

"Now you see what I mean when I said I couldn't describe it," he said. "The way out from here is easy; that path I came in from leads back to the surface. You can't miss it." He swung the lantern around so I could see the opening behind him between two huge mounds of earth. Total darkness remained above. As I grappled for a response he placed the lantern on the ground beside me. "Take this, Bill, and guide yourself out. Don't worry about me. After a while you don't need light to find your way around."

With that he turned and walked off into the darkness. I called out to him several times but the only answer I heard was a very faint reply of "You're going to be fine now."

I reluctantly got to my feet, and I sincerely mean reluctantly. The intensely pleasurable sensation I had been bathing in oozed away as I stood. Overall, though, my emotions remained calm and peaceful. With lantern in hand I stumbled along in the direction Idaho had indicated following his footsteps and oddly confident in the entire enterprise. A while later I came upon a dim light gleaming ahead of me and stepped out of the dark earthen tunnel into a cave like area of black volcanic rock that reflected a light from above. I climbed up and emerged into a glowing, sunny afternoon. Since I had no idea where I was I headed for the nearest hill to get my bearings.

Well, I got my bearings alright. I had travelled almost a half a mile from the point where I first entered Idaho's burrow. No none had stolen my car so I drove back to the hotel and loaded up on some supplies. I was not yet as ready for underground self sufficiency as my little mentor. Eventually, however, I managed it. Once you learn the trick this place is loaded with food and water. It's been about a month now of this sub surface life and I have learned a lot. I have lived with ants in a way that no other human (except maybe one) has ever lived. I've crawled about in their burrows, gathered food with them, fought their enemies, and shared their life. And yes, I have done the same with badgers, and squirrels, and mice, as well as millipedes, spiders, centipedes, and a host of other subsurface creatures. The experiences are incredible! For the first time in my life I have truly come to know these animals, actually experienced their life – felt their lives. Yet there is so much more to learn. There is something deeper, much deeper; an intense wellspring of life that I had felt before in a meaningful but superficial way. And now, here I am like the Idaho Sandman before me, delving deeper and deeper in the quest for that ultimate secret. Perhaps someday our paths, or tunnels, will cross. I'll fill you in on what I have learned but I'll have to show you. This is something that must be experienced!

DERWIN GLASPER
John M. Regan

Dinner was over and coffee served. I love that petite pleasure derived from the aftertaste of an excellent meal; followed by rich steaming coffee it is a small daily delight of a civilized man. But my mood shifts to dubious as I reach for the remote control knowing that the mere flicker an invisible blip of infrared light brings my television to life, and what comes to life is most uncivilized. The evening news is my nightly compulsion, however; a compulsion nearly as strong as my attachment to after dinner coffee. Hardly as civilized or peaceful as my domestic stimulant, but we all have our vices. I only raise this coffee and news business because that used to be the time the telephone rang for Derwin Glasper. The calls have stopped now. But after dinner coffee still reminds me of Derwin.

We were new to the area and rented a small house while we searched for more permanent, hopefully larger, quarters. This particular place is the type usually referred to as "rental property." A great deal of humanity had lived and departed the suburban shelter identified as 1609 Iron Oak ST prior to our arrival. Just the same it was a nice little place and my wife and I were content enough for the interim.

Anyone familiar with this kind of arrangement surely recalls the occasional misaddressed mail that flow to the current residents. But mail is not irksome. It makes very little noise and can be disposed of instantly. Something significantly more peculiar plagued us on Oak Street, though – a phone call. Phone calls are a different category of nuisance. They make noise, a sound no easier to ignore than a knock at the door, and sometimes just as difficult to dispose of.

But after a month or so these unwanted communications usually dissipate. Friends, relatives, and even bill collectors of the former tenant eventually realize that the person in question has taken up residence elsewhere. Such was the natural course of events in our house, with one persistent exception: Derwin Glasper.

Every couple of days for several months a woman would call and ask to speak to Derwin Glasper. She sounded like an older lady and conveyed a normal tone of voice until I explained that Derwin Glasper did not live here. At that she would sound confused and anxious, apologize and hang up. The calls usually came between six or six thirty at night. The name Derwin Glasper was so distinctive, and the ritual repeated so often, that any time the phone rang at that hour my wife and I would look at each other and say "Derwin Glasper."

One night, exactly on schedule, the phone rang. I grasped the instrument and restrained myself to a closely normal "hello," just in case it was a legitimate call.

"May I speak to Derwin Glasper?" Same woman, same request. It was exasperating.

"Ma'am, there is no Derwin Glasper here. Whoever he is he has not lived here for months. I don't know what it takes to convince you, but I wish you would stop calling. Derwin Glasper DOES – NOT – LIVE - HERE." I did my best to amplify my irritation by adding a few vulgarities, an easy effort thanks to the volume of beer I'd been drinking.

There was a brief silence and I thought I heard a silent crying, like air pressed out of tightly constricted lungs. There was a deep, shaky inhale; the woman apologized for calling and hung up. I felt a bit loutish, then perplexed. What on earth was the woman's problem?

"What's the matter, dear?" my wife asked. I realized I was staring at the receiver I still clutched.

"Well I don't know exactly. That was the Derwin Glasper woman again. You heard me tell her that these phone calls are getting a bit ridiculous, right? The woman got all upset. I think she was crying."

"Crying about what?" Cindy peered at me over the top of the couch. She looked suspicious.

"Because Derwin Glasper isn't here I guess."

We discussed the trivial mystery for a while, concluded the woman was an eccentric of some sort, and vowed to change our phone number. Minutes later we were engrossed in one of those natural history television shows I love. The woman and Derwin Glasper were quickly forgotten. We passed the remainder of the evening without further enigmas.

A phone call like that, bothersome though it may be, is a terrific conversation piece. At work the following day I mentioned it to several friends. I'm a cook in a large hotel and the people I work with have been together for quite some time. We enjoy each other's company and often go out socially, too. Such co-workers take a true delight in the trials and tribulations they share. We look out for one another. The Derwin Glasper thing was a gem. Everyone was engrossed and numerous theories were put forth. From the comic to the macabre, it was the topic of the day. I milked the whole thing for quite a few laughs.

But an odd thing happened while driving home that night - I was overtaken by guilt. I felt sublime when I got into the car, and then a slow depressed emotion welled up inside.

It took a while to understand. I had shamed some old lady and then spent the day snickering foolishly over this poor soul's tragedy. I shrugged off the feeling. This is stupid, I thought. The lady is obviously mad. Nothing I do will make the slightest difference. The melancholy persisted, however, like the beginning stages of a cold or flu.

When I got home Cindy was in no better spirits. Usually she is there to greet me, asking about my day and inquiring about my appetite. Instead she sat solidly on the couch staring straight ahead, her eyes red rimmed and wet.

"What's the matter, Cindy, what is it?" I could not have possibly imagine any incident capable of putting her into such a state. Cindy does not cry with ease. There must have been a death in the family or some horrific incident. I felt a surge of adrenaline. I prepared myself for the worse. "Cindy speak to me. What is the problem?"

She dabbed her eyes and face with tissue. When she at last spoke her voice was cracked, full and ragged. She had been crying for some time. "I'm sorry Lewis."

"Sorry about what?" My voice, and my concern, were rising. Whatever had occurred was surely bad. I was certain of an immense tragedy.

Cindy held her face in her hands. "I'm pregnant."

You can't be!" I exclaimed. How many men in my situation have uttered the same doltish words?

"I am," she answered, "and please don't talk like an idiot. I feel badly enough already."

After several moments I recovered, somewhat. "OK, you're pregnant. But this hardly qualifies as a tragedy. Why are you so upset?"

"You know damned well we can't have a baby now." There was an angry snap in her voice as she stood and turned her back to me. "This is the worse time, we just can't afford it...but...well, it happened."

"Alright."

My relief at finding there had not been some accidental death was being replaced by a new, perhaps even more terrible anxiety. This was unexpected. We had certainly taken the proper precautions. One more of life's nasty little surprises.

"There are alternatives, you know." I let that slip out sheepishly, more to test her reaction than a concrete proposal. I realize now it was the coward's way out, throwing the decision onto her. We had agreed before about what to do in this case. We both had careers, futures, plans; children would come along only at the proper time. We had to establish some sort of life for ourselves first, didn't we? The remainder of that night was an uneasy discussion debating about a course we had already decided upon. The discussion was pointless. We would not have children, not yet.

A brilliant sun lit up our small bedroom the next morning. I awoke after a foggy, restless night still worried about Cindy. How would she react today? My apprehension dissolved when she peered up at me and smiled. The decision was made, there was no more need for worry or tears. One great thing about Cindy, once her mind is made up to something you can bet she will follow through. Conviction brings peace of mind.

Just to make sure I called into work and told them I wouldn't be in. That would give me a three day weekend with Cindy. She began a new job on Monday and this would be our last real break together for some time. The tourist season was beginning to crest and that meant a lot of work and a lot of money to be made. Now we had another matter to attend to as well. It would be best to be with her now.

We snatched up our standard bundle of supplies and a newly acquired giant sun umbrella, dumped the whole works into the car and settled in for a soothing drive. Rock music, the highway, a three day weekend, and the beach. If that's not a formula to forget your troubles then such a thing does not exist. We have a pet place for these minor escapes, a little outcropping of land called Libby Island. It juts out into the Atlantic from the south coast of Georgia. It's a scruffy little tourist town, definitely not for the wealthy, but out of the way and difficult to find. Therein lies its charm.

The beach that day of our escape was even more perfect than usual. Warm, blue curling waves arced in precise rhythms and sliced along the shore. An insignificant sprinkling of people walked the sand ensuring that ours would be a day of privacy and solitude. We parked along a narrow strip of blacktop nearest the beach. In a well rehearsed procedure we unloaded the car and trudged to a spot of sand that just suited Cindy's fancy. Cindy always selects our beach locales with a precision I find baffling. Why eight square feet of sand is so peculiarly appealing compared to the billions of others I don't understand, but I learned the futility of debate in these matters early in our marriage. Today she claimed this singular piece of real estate so I obediently went about setting up shop.

With all in order we went for a swim. Libby Island has a unique geography and unusually high tides that makes swimming and strolling the beach an exceptionally interesting experience. Running the length of the shore are troughs of various depths completely exposed during low tides as long, narrow pools of translucent water. At one point a rock jetty thrusts out into the ocean. A flat beach lies on one side while the other is a fascinating moonscape of hundreds of little round tide pools and sand bars. Each is miniature world filled with sand dollars, blue crabs, and fish of all description. We like to swim, body surf, and then, after devouring a bit of lunch, do some exploring in the tide pool land.

The water was perfect as we splashed in. We seemed to have nearly the whole shoreline to ourselves and for about an hour we played like carefree children, catching fast waves that sent us careening to the shallows, only to swim back out as quickly as possible to repeat the exhilarating process. The waves that day were meant to ridden. Like seals we caught one after another, our heads protruding from the front of each cresting current as we soared inland. Later, when we dropped our tired, bodies onto the blanket, we were laughing and content.

It was still early and the sun was gentle. On one elbow I turned on my side and admired Cindy. She always looks magnificent in a bikini. Gleaming wet, with her breasts rising and falling heavily, she was irresistible. Children? I couldn't bear the idea. Even the thought cast gloom into my mood.

"We will have children someday, won't we Lewis?" It was as though she was telepathic. Her sudden question landed like a punch.

"Cindy don't bring that up now, please. Let's just enjoy the day, can't we?"

"Sure." When you get that monosyllabic reply, trouble is very near.

"What do you want me to say? We're broke, you're starting a new job Monday, the car is not in exactly pristine condition, and now you want a kid?"

"I didn't say that." She used a tone that warned me she was about to begin sulking. When Cindy starting sulking she could remain quiet for hours, sometimes days. Normally this would bring out my nice guy act, an attempt to persuade her that everything would be alight; but this business with babies all of a sudden was vexing. We having such a great time and she has to bring up that. Damned broke as we are and she wants kids? And we had agreed that there would be no children until we were ready.

In an instant I was in a foul pique. She had turned a wonderful day miserable by bringing up a very sore, supposedly closed, subject. I was not going to be dragged into fatherhood at my age, I wasn't even twenty three and she wants to start making babies when we can barely afford the rent. Foolishly determined to further display my anger (thereby increasing her guilt) I got to my feet and stalked off into the water.

For some time I made a half hearted attempt to swim but our argument kept replaying over and over in my thoughts. I invented new replies, argued passionately, argued logically, threatened to quit my job; and succeeded in aggravating myself even more. Finally I decided that something had to be done about this pregnancy before it was too late. I concluded that the best thing to do would be to confront her right here and now and make her commit to ending the pregnancy. Before we had only agreed. This time we would set a definite date - and it would be next week, job or no job.

As I strode purposefully out of the surf I realized that the current had caused me to drift several hundred yards from where I started. So swept up in my frustration and anger I hadn't even noticed. A large number of beach lovers had gathered by now and were walking aimlessly around in that lazy manner the ocean seems to encourage. I was striding quickly and with determination. I didn't care who knew I was mad, in fact I wanted these carefree strollers to sense my anger. I stomped through the hot sand heading straight for our picnic place with a rehearsed lecture in mind. Cindy was going to hear what I had to say like it or not. I knew that when she caught the full stature of my displeasure she would apologize and agree with me. My teeth and fists were tight when I reached the blanket - and saw that it was empty.

Most of our picnic gear was still laying nearby so I surmised that Cindy had also decided to go for a swim. Wasn't that just like a woman? Here I was full of righteous indignation ready to pour it on her like a storm, and she's gone. Fine. I would just sit and wait and get angrier. So I sat and waited, and waited, and waited...and waited. And got worried.

An hour passed. Then another twenty minutes. From my position I could see our car still parked in the same place. I walked over and inspected it. No sign of her. I returned and stood by the blanket anxiously inspecting the shoreline for her familiar outline. I saw nothing but milling, unfamiliar strangers. Her blue and white beach bag lay against our cooler, untouched. The towel Cindy had used to dry her hair sat in a wrinkled heap precisely where she had earlier positioned it to rest her head. I unfolded it and found it was still damp. Inside I began to tighten with apprehension, a hollow feeling low behind the throat. Why had I been so stupid? Where was she now? Surely she wouldn't have attempted to get home by herself? Perhaps she decided to walk around and linger through the tourist shops, I thought. It wasn't beyond reason, and far less terrible than several other assumptions I was beginning to imagine.

Lined up along the narrow parking lot were several bars that overlooked the beach front. Cindy would not be indulging her sorrow in booze, I was sure of that, but she could be sitting somewhere sipping a soda. I poked into three or four of these places without result. The last was a weathered, yellow, two story building on a street corner that bore the uninspired name of The Playful Dolphin. The first floor harbored the typical kitchy souvenir shop while the top floor was a bar with an open balcony that offered a great view of the beach. Cindy was not in either one but I kept the bar in mind because of its excellent view. If I had no luck in the other little shops I'd come back to here for one last look up and down the beach.

I exited the store and took a left on the sand splashed street that led back into the city. Libby Island is a scruffy, diminutive copy of most beach towns with a small main street lined with tasteless tourist attractions. But the town comes alive from time to time with wandering beach bums, tourists, and an assortment of odd looking strangers. I surely appeared odd looking as well, hurriedly dashing about with strained worry evident on my face. I wound my way through every nameless arcade, boutique, bar, and novelty shop on the strip. I could see Cindy clearly in my mind but I didn't see her in person anywhere else. Several times my peripheral vision would pick out a glinting piece of familiar clothing or shape. Each time my elation rose, then fell. After two hours of this my anxiety transitioned to fright.

I was close to giving in to despair when I decided to go back to the Playful Dolphin and attempt another look from the balcony. This was my last hope. I considered the police but I could imagine their reaction at my story. You storm off and leave your pregnant wife and now you wonder where she is? She's out looking for a lawyer, kid. She ain't lost. A well deserved lecture that I was not ready to listen to. My clothes were perspiration drenched as I bounced up the stairs leading to the balcony lounge of the Playful Dolphin. Oblivious to anyone I rushed to the veranda.

The beach spread out before me in a huge hazy blue arc. Hundreds of faceless people meandered around in the same carefree disorder. Nowhere did I see anyone resembling Cindy. My God, I thought, I hope she just got angry and found some other way home, although that possibility held little comfort. Well, if Cindy was trying to teach me a lesson it had worked. And that must to be it, I told myself. There was no sign of any struggle, she hadn't taken her beach bag, and I couldn't remember if even her pocketbook was missing.

I returned to the beach and sat down on the blanket. Nothing was changed, not a single item had been removed or touched. She had not come back while I was gone and all of her personal belongings remained in place. That was odd. If she had tried to go home she would have taken some something. Maybe it was time to notify the police.

"Excuse me, are you Lewis Daley?"

The voice came from behind startled me but I knew immediately it had something to do with Cindy.

"Yes I am. Did something happen to my wife? Did you find her?" It was a patrolman, tanned and stocky, dressed in shorts.

"She's alright, Mr. Daley. A doctor found her. Apparently she passed out somewhere down the beach." He pointed to the jetties where all the small tide pools were. Cindy must have gone for a walk after I left.

"She described you when she woke up, right now she's pretty woozy, still in the doctor's office. If you'd like I can take you there."

"Please,... oh yeah, please!" I was so relieved yet so surprised by this sudden explanation I stammered mindlessly. "Should I walk? I mean is it better to drive?"

The patrolman understood my predicament. He offered to help me gather up my belongings and haul them over to my car, saying that it would be better to drive since we wouldn't have to walk back in the hot sun. My mind was not exactly functioning at top efficiency and I would have obeyed any instruction at that point. We dumped the entire sandy mess into the back into the trunk.

"You OK to drive Mr. Daley?"

"I'm fine," I assured him, "just pretty anxious about my wife." The cop's patrol car was parked alongside mine. He jumped in and I trailed him back through the town. We went to the main thoroughfare, took a left turn, and continued on until the tourist shops gave way to residential and rental homes. About two or three miles out from there, but still close to the water, we turned onto a dirt road that directed us back toward the beach. Here the road dead ended. Amidst an isolated pocket of dunes and sea oats on the right stood a weathered, two story Victorian home overlooking the shore line. The officer walked with me to the house. Before we even knocked the door opened. A sun bronzed man with a silver speckled beard and thin, grey hair smiled at us.

"Hello, Doctor," the policeman said. "I found Mr. Daley." He nodded in my direction. "Right where his wife said he'd be."

The doctor reached out and gripped my hand. Please come right in, your wife is fine. Just a little too much sun."

We both thanked the policeman several times for his help and he in turn told us not to hesitate if there was any further trouble. As soon as he left the doctor led me into his living room. On an oversized couch, with a small wet towel covering her forehead, was Cindy, still contentedly asleep. I took her hand and sat beside her. With slow effort she opened her eyes, smiled at me and blinked.

I slobbered through several renditions of "Are you alright?" mixed with numerous "I'm sorrys." She weakly assured me that she was fine and just needed a little rest. The doctor agreed.

"Let's just give her another half hour or so to let her stomach settle, then I think it will be okay to take her home." Cindy vaguely nodded her head before her eyes limply shut again.

"I sure hate to bother you like this, sir." I said.

"Oh please don't think about it," he replied, holding up his hands, "It was a boring afternoon and I do like company."

I began to think of more practical matters. After all this guy was a doctor. "Look doctor, I don't live around here so I'll to write you a check before I leave."

"No, no don't worry about a thing. I really didn't do much and there is no charge anyway. Let's just see that she gets back on her feet and well."

"How did you find her?" I asked.

"I happened to be out watching the surf. Your wife was walking around among the tide pools. I thought she had simply fallen down, but then a group of people gathered around her so I walked over to see if I could help. That gentleman from the beach patrol helped to bring her here since there is no real hospital on the island. My practice is in Savannah. This is my little weekend getaway and most of the locals know me. If there's a problem, chances are I'll hear about it."

I looked back at Cindy. She appeared completely relaxed but I felt uncomfortable standing in a stranger's living room while I waited for my wife to recover. To make the situation more embarrassing I knew I was responsible for the entire mess. The doctor seemed to sense my discomfort.

"Lewis," he said, "please sit down and relax. It's alight. And by the way, I apologize for not introducing myself," he held out his hand, "My name is Dr. Glasper, Derwin Glasper, and please call me Derwin."

"Well I'm pleased to meet you Dr. - Did you say 'Derwin Glasper?'" I asked.

"That's right. You act as though my name has some significance."

I was not sure how to begin. "This is a really strange coincidence, Derwin."

His face expanded into a warm smile. "Really? Please tell me more"

I related to him the story of the mysterious phone calls.

He frowned and slightly turned his head away. "Tell me, just exactly where do you live in Atlanta, what's the address?"

"1609 Iron Oak Street." I replied.

"What does the voice sound like?"

"Sort of an elderly woman," I said. Noticing his reaction I was a bit hesitant to say anything further, but I figured it was too late anyway. "The last time she sounded like she was crying."

Derwin closed his eyes. He looked thoughtful, and somewhat pained, as if some disturbing memory had unexpectedly jarred him. There was an awkward silence while I waited for him to speak.

At last he pursed his lips and slowly let out a long expulsion of air. He looked at me with an odd smile. "That woman who calls you, Lewis....is my mother."

I remained thoroughly puzzled and Derwin knew it.

"Please try to forgive her, she is at an age where her mental acuity is not what it used to be. We lived there when I was very, very young. My father left us and, well, there are some other hard memories associated with it. From time to time she forgets my telephone number and make random calls looking for me. I have stopped her previously, but this is the first time I have actually met the people she is calling. And what a coincidence! I promise you Lewis, I will make her stop."

His explanation expanded my curiosity further. Other hard memories. What did that mean? Obviously it was not something a total stranger had the right to know or ask about. I decided not to ask.

"Don't worry about it, Doctor," I said, "It's really not a big problem; it's just that she sounds so upset sometimes. I hate to hurt her feelings."

He smiled, thanked me, and assured me again that the phone calls would stop. He did not appear terribly upset about the incident; mildly embarrassed would be a better description. What could I say? Sometimes elderly people do things like that. At least now I had an answer; strangely coincidental though it was.

As if to reassure my doubts he added, "Mother forgets where I am occasionally. I have to call and remind her. I live

96

so far away it's hard to visit." His brimming smile returned. "Hey, let's go check on your wife."

Cindy reacted as though she had heard us mention her. With clumsy effort she sat up. I took a seat beside her and pushed the hair from her face. She was pale and drained, her eyes still only half open. She said she was beginning to feel better, at least not as dizzy. Dr. Glasper told her to remain at ease, there was no rush. With effort she propped herself up in the corner of the couch and began to breathe deeply.

"Honey," I said, "You'll never guess who this is." I pointed to the doctor. Cindy blinked at me, unsure of what to say, or even what I was saying at all. "This is the doctor who took care of you when you fainted. His name is - Derwin Glasper!"

It took a while to register. Her voice was no more than a murmur and thick as tar. "You mean the phone calls?"

"Yes, isn't that a coincidence?" I said, anxious to hear her response. But all Cindy did was melt into the old chesterfield sofa and fall asleep again. Dr. Glasper paced to her side and felt her pulse. He placed his palm on her forehead and examined her slumped, lifeless eyes. "Nothing to worry about Lewis, she's fine. A bit more rest is the answer." He stood up and walked to an ancient, mahogany cabinet on the other side of the room. With a soft squeal he opened tiny liquor cabinet. After splashing a generous amount of amoretto into two brandy glasses, he turned and offered me one. "Lewis, it is alight for you to relax. Cindy is fine. I am a doctor and I really do enjoy the company. This is not an imposition."

I took a large gulp of the sweet liquor. Almost instantly I felt the alcohol climb into my brain, the exertions of the day speeding its effect. glasper raised his glass to me in an odd, silent toast, and fixed me with his fatherly smile. "She's pregnant isn't she, Lewis?"

I stared at him, unable to speak.

"Oh come now, young man. I keep telling you I am a doctor!"

He dumped another generous portion of the spirit into my glass. "You and your Cindy are quite welcome to spend the night here. You will have a large room completely to yourself and the quiet rolling of the surf as a lullaby. I suspect that the two of you are in some need of quiet reflection after a wrenching day. And it is two and a half hours of traffic back to Atlanta."

I pondered the invitation. Less than an hour ago this man was a total stranger. Then, at the mention of a name, he becomes a weird coincidence intimately connected to me by a mysterious recurring phone call; a flashing paternal smile follows and he's a gentle Good Samaritan full of wisdom and understanding. Now I saw Dr. Derwin Glasper as just what my parched mind needed - a cool glass of knowledgeable water. Despite the liquor in my glass, of course.

"Lewis, let's step out to the veranda while your wife rests. There is a marvelous sight I hate to miss." Derwin led the way to his enormous front porch and we settled into comfortable chaise lounges with oversized cushions. "Is all your furniture designed to make people fall asleep?"

He laughed. "I make humble efforts at comfort. After all this is my little get away."

Derwin wanted to witness the sunset. He claimed there was enchantment and contentment in the process for those willing to understand. On Libby Island it did not take much understanding to feel either. Because of the peculiar geography of the island and the location of Derwin's summer home, the sun appeared to set in the ocean, a sight denied to most on the east coast. It glittered in brilliant orange fading to purple. To our right the sky was already like black milk. The sea blazed in silver and wiggled the new moon's light. The tide pools were small glaucous gems slowly disappearing with the rising tide. Enchantment was the word.

"Do you understand now, Lewis?"

I hadn't the vaguest notion of what understanding he referred to. "I understand the beauty of this, if that's what you are talking about."

"Part of it. There are such great joys here." His face gleamed in the liquid light, accenting his silver hair and robust complexion.

"Cindy and I love this place," I said. "We come here quite a bit but I admit that I've never seen it like this before."

"Someday you will understand."

"Understand what?" I don't like strange conversations, particularly with people I have just met.

The doctor said nothing for a while, just sat there musing silently and rubbing his mouth, coiling and uncoiling a grin.

"The show is over here, Lewis. Now I have something else for you to see. But I warn you. It will require open eyes....and an open heart."

I began to think of excuses to leave. This father figure had metamorphosed again. This time with the shadings of a nut case. Was this Glasper one of those crazies you see in the movies? A movie which Cindy and I were about to have the ill fated starring role? I could simply go, I thought. The only problem would be rousing Cindy's inert body into the car. It would be awkward and embarrassing, of course, but better than a night with a lunatic. Maybe he'd given Cindy some kind of drug. But then again, a cop had brought both of us here, hadn't he?

"Lewis, I understand. If you want to go, that is perfectly fine. I'll help you get your wife into the car. But there is much to learn if you stay, at least for a while longer."

"Learn what for God's sake?" He had pricked my ego and my curiosity in one stroke.

"About the things troubling you." He spoke paternally, patiently, and in the tone of someone who feels sorry for the ignorant. Now he really had me curious. I considered the situation. At six foot one and two hundred pounds of primary young muscle I could break this old man in half if I wanted; three or more pieces if I felt like it.

He stood up and beckoned me to follow. I did.

To the right of the balcony a wooden stairway built into the outer wall of the house lead to the second floor. It produced horrendous squeaks and groans as we ascended and the outer railing reminded me of those breakaway things used in old TV westerns, yet we made it to the top without calamity. The stairs opened onto another balcony that surrounded a dome like roof. At the top of the dome I noticed a circular pattern of large sky lights, partially exposed.

"It almost looks like an observatory," I said.

"Very good, Lewis. That's exactly what it is." He swung open a large door that squarely faced the seaward side of the dome. "Please come in."

I stepped inside and Derwin shut the door. The windy open air of the sunset changed abruptly into unmoving, quiet darkness. I could just discern the shape of numerous panels surrounding the interior. In the center was a large easel that I almost knocked over in the darkened room. I heard a loud snapping noise and the murky room came to vivid life. It was the aerie of an artist – a great artist, too. The circular interior of the room was laced with a circular parade of panels, each a beautiful painting about two feet wide and three feet high. Color, people, life, burst from the paintings, emanating like living motion pictures. Another magical hue in the baffling aura of Dr. Derwin Glasper.

"I give you my life," he said, "from beginning to end. This, Lewis, is a celebration!" The calm demeanor vanished, the voice roared and he exuberantly threw out his arms.

"Dr. Glasper," I said, "it's fantastic; it's beautiful!"

He beamed and threw back his head. "Of course! What did you expect? This is life!"

Fear and doubt became wonder and reassurance; I felt foolish for my private dispersions of a while ago. This was a man who could create beauty and mystery and share it with fulminous zeal. Perhaps I did have much to learn.

"This way, my friend. We must start over here."

Derwin led me to a panel next to the door we had entered. I recognized the painting instantly. It was the house in which I now lived.

"Look familiar?" he asked.

"Absolutely," I said. "It's awfully good, Derwin; better by far than it looks now. And you did say that you used to live there." I wished Cindy could see this.

"Yes. Many years ago. With my mother as I said."

The tiny house in the painting was new, brighter and happier; like a story book home. A knee high fence painted robin egg blue bordered a perfectly green little green lawn. A slender oak was just beginning its long silent life. "That tree is still there," I said, "Grown to a giant now."

"Indeed," Derwin said.

A long haired young woman was visible in the painting, standing in front of parted curtains behind the big bay windows of the front of the house. Slightly bent at the waist her rounded hands are pushed against her eyes. Behind the woman, on a drab couch, I could see a baby. It seemed to be crying. The front door next to the where the woman stood was partially open and oddly canted as though someone has abruptly left and neglected to close it. The painting did not give off a feeling of happiness.

Derwin must have sensed that I understood this. "It was hard but we got by. My poor mother."

We moved to the next panel which I guessed to be a kindergarten graduation. Small, serious looking boys and girls formed a wiggling, impatience line while a large bald man, probably the principal, called them forward to receive their prize. The audience to the front was composed of proudly grinning parents. One frail looking woman stood by herself holding a handkerchief to her face. I knew whose mother that was.

Painting number three was a beach scene. Libby Island jumped out in pure bright sunlight. A young boy in a red bathing suit was constructing a sand castle of considerable achievement, his hand reaching to carefully position a colorful shell on a sandy turret, the brown structure starkly outlined against an azure sky. Gracefully draped over the boy and his mighty fortress lie the shadow of an unseen woman, hands held high, clapping in praise.

The fourth panel was of skinny, determined looking lad hurling a baseball from a pitcher's mound. Derwin's face was unmistakable under the protruding cap. The ball was an arcing blur as it left his fingers on its flashing journey toward the tense batter. The bleachers were jammed. I swear I could hear the frenzied cheers of encouragement and hope. And there again, conspicuous by her detachment from all the others, was Derwin's mother, her face a picture of utter delight as she watched her growing son.

On and on the panels went. A true celebration of the life of a man. The commonplace maturing of an infant into an adult portrayed as a fantastic mystery on a circular wall. I saw Derwin's childishness disappear into the confidence of young manhood. I watched his mother's worried, pretty young face become mature, proud, and peaceful. And finally beautiful again. Baseball, high school proms, graduations, part time jobs...so mundane yet so divine here on the colorful murals. A degree as a doctor! A lovely young girl, marriage, children; the frail lady becomes a serene grandmother, elevated through the years from despair to delight. The simple life of one person as the cause for so much happiness.

"Do you understand now, Lewis?" Once again the nagging riddle.

"Dr. Glasper, I'm afraid that I'm still not sure what you wish me to understand other than the fact that you seem to have had a great mother whom you made very proud. You have obviously accomplished much with your life. Doctor, painter, writer, beautiful wife and children....your father missed more than he will ever know."

"Yes! You begin to comprehend, young man with so much on your mind."

He walked silently to the easel in the center of the room. It was shrouded by a dull, red velvet cover with black fringe. Derwin placed his hand on the top of the easel and gripped the cloth.

"I have one more painting to show you," he said.

I centered myself in front of the stand. The other panels had provoked so much pleasure and surprise I knew this must be his masterpiece. All else had dealt with the past. Now he would reveal a vision of the future. In pleasant suspense I prepared for more mystery and wonder.

"Lewis, you have correctly surmised that my father left when I was quite young, and therefore did not share in a single one of my life's tragedies or triumphs."

A quick turn of his fingers threw the cover forward. It slid down the front of the easel and onto the floor revealing a stark black panel. The wooden frame was black. The canvas beheld no lovely vision of what was to be, only a thick coating of flat black oil paint. In angry contrast to the colorful panorama of life in the room, this ugly portrait of darkness could only represent one thing. It was unnerving.

Derwin stepped behind the easel and positioned himself so his head was on top of the black painting. He placed his long, pale fingers on the carved borders of the pitch frame. The fatherly smile of wisdom and patience was gone, frighteningly replaced by a crooked, misshapen grimace full of pain and anger.

"This is what you must understand young fool." The voice pulsed with disgust and passion. "No my father did not share in my life, Lewis. Nor did my mother, even though her anguished voice still calls for me. Nor did anyone on this earth. My life has been nothing more than this black hopeless hole before you. A life not allowed to be a life. People used to call it something different back then. I believe it is referred to it as 'reproductive rights' today.'"

Derwin growled the last sentence. I reeled backward and fell, colliding against the wall, frantically trying to regain my footing and make it to the door.

Our little girl is almost two years old now and she loves to play in the tide pools. Sometimes when Cindy holds her they share an expression of such serenity and delight...I saw that look once before.

BONIFACE THE ANONYMOUS

Richmond Hills on a summer night soft and heavy. The Waverly household is a pleasure. Well groomed, exquisitely stocked, a testament to good taste. Being associated with this dimension of elegance infuses me with serenity. It is simply impossible to convey the splendid way this abode, and others like it, nourish my soul. Yet even in this silent bliss ironic recollections sometimes occur; unpleasant, murky hauntings from another life, hapless days of sordid pettiness and miserable associations; habits ingrained from the stain of life's sewer.

Ah, but that servile existence is thankfully past. Like Socrates' illuminated man I have emerged from the cave; emerged an extraordinary man of remarkable components: shepherd, protector, artist, lover of culture, devotee of beauty; the refined hallmarks of a service that provides an elevated class of living to me and an anonymous blessing to my clientele. I have emerged clean and pure. Call me Boniface, unseen servant, doer of good. Boniface the Anonymous!

No, I am not a braggart of wealth and power. I do not measure my professional accomplishments on gross scales of volume and value. That would be an injustice to me and an absurd mistake as well. Excess and ostentation are the fool's elixir, ingredients for disaster. I have loftier criteria: loyalty, justice, beauty, clean culture.

Let me explain. As the realtor reminds us, location is critical. One cannot experience the values I have set for myself in the shabby establishments of the middle class. Their throwaways would starve a pauper and their excesses are laughable. Even the so-called upper tier of that group cannot approach my requirements. That is not to denigrate, mind you. If you wish to remain in the median land of accomplishment then by all means inhabit it. Mine, however, is the realm of excellence; the abode of people that you lust to be while denying your envy. My clients cast away more on an impromptu dinner party than you gross in a year. The price of one of their automobiles could purchase your home several times over. They do not travel first class – they charter, they own.

To understand these environments is to live a life nestled in acres of diamonds. But to know it as I know it and to live it as I live it demands far more. It takes a dedication of ferocity and god like awareness, talents I possess in abundance. An internal barometer, sensitive to the minutest shift of my surroundings, curls around my heart. A serpent does not feel the vibrations and movements of its prey with more acuity. Want to know the time and location of Mr. Randle King's business trips? Ask me. Want to know when Mrs. Albert's personal hairdresser is due to arrive? Ask me. How about young Jenny's tennis lessons or Jack's equestrian class? What about Edna Albright's fertility, or the timing of her doctor's vacation? There is one who sees all and knows all.

But back to the business at hand. The Waverly's, bless them, have not changed their habits since my last visit. A small window over the bathroom sink of a second story guest room is unlocked and possesses no alarm. An overhanging branch of a giant oak tree provides easy access to the roof. Executing some minor acrobatics I position myself and slide quietly through the window, gliding feet first over the sink, avoiding the occasional cup and glass. (If I were not what I am I could be a gymnast or a jockey.) I arch my back, rest briefly on the edge of the sink, then duck my head and curl in under the window ledge. I am a shadow. Invisible poetry.

There is such an exquisite suspense about entering a home in this manner! For a short, wondrous moment I luxuriate in the stillness and feel the gloom, each breath precipitates a rolling titillation that seeps into my spine and floods my loins. The intensity of this sensation, the beautiful enhancement that elevates it to a nearly erotic thrill is this simple realization - within feet of where I stand the inhabitants of this home slumber in peace, blind to my presence. I stand for a while and inhale the moment; it is an occasional excess I allow myself.

There have been times, purely for the joy of the sensation, that I have knelt at the very bedside of my clients, so close that I could feel the soft gusts of their exhalations on my cheek. I watched a television program once about a peculiar insect that preys on ants. The creature is able to disguise its scent so thoroughly that it can invade an ant colony and pick off the little workers one by one in the darkness of their very own tunnel. You might say I am the human form of that amazing beast. A far more refined and gentle form, mind you, and. Please do not misunderstand my motives!

I glide into the hall, silently descend the stairwell and pause in the kitchen. Mrs. Waverly is a gifted cook and her mouthwatering efforts linger into the night. Something else lingers as well - a trace of lilac and jasmine. I know this delicious scent, too. It is the sweet perfume of an amber haired, emerald-eyed teenager blossoming into extraordinary beauty - young Dawn Waverly.

But is she still out on her date at this hour? Two a.m. is no time for a young woman to be out and a young man of proper decency would not entice her into such behavior. I make two quick mental notes. First - Dawn may come home unexpectedly. I'll be on the alert for that. Second – I may have to protect Dawn and her family from this crude fellow. My clients demand ceaseless vigilance and the good shepherd is always ready to defend his flock.

The dangers are many - young fools bent on vandalism, the odd crook, occasional drug addicts, random cat burglar, etc. These are easy. Turn them in anonymously to the police, deliver a darkly worded threat, or treat them to a series of "accidents." Youngsters are especially superstitious. Puncture the tires on their cars a few times, leave a menacing message. They scurry like rodents. I consider it pest control.

Sometimes a more direct approach is required. Take the episode with Eddie "Fast Fingers" Fuller. The work and methods of Fast Fingers were well known to me from previous days. He was a smash and grab crook, a vulgar vocation whereby the modus operandi is to demolish a car or storefront window, seize whatever is handy and run. Operators like Fuller, no matter how quick, are certain to be caught. They are too obvious and blind to continue undetected, and no matter how ego swelling the crime, bragging from a prison cell is a futile exercise. Fast Fingers Fuller was of this ilk but he possessed a sliver of ambition in his makeup, however. Unfortunately for him he selected Richmond Hills for his program of self-improvement.

By lucky coincidence I was living in the unseen folds of the McGonigle house at the time. The arrangement was profitable for both of us. Lady McGonigle lived by herself in a large mansion in a quaint older section of town. The venerable gal was the single inhabitant of a mansion of enormous proportions, a throw back to a time when a million dollars was real money. Solidly into her eighth decade, this blue haired blue blood of the old school was then a mere shadow of her former magnificence. Even less remained of her eyesight and hearing.

Living unseen in a mansion alongside a nearly blind and deaf elderly woman is not a feat requiring Houdini like talents. The attic alone was immense and here I often spent the bulk of the day resting in quiet slumber after a night's work. In the evening, if not actively engaged, I prowled the home, eating, reading (she has a wonderful library), watching television if the mood struck me. Naturally I have the good grace not to overstay my welcome, I take residence in several homes.

This surprises you? Do you expect me to live in some squalid tenement and commute to work? It would be unseemly to accept accommodations beneath that of my clients. I therefore reside in places neither better nor worse than any in Richmond Hills. Some homes are more suitable than others, of course. The good lady McGonigle's was one of my favorites.

And a fine thing it was on that early Thursday morning. The moon had just achieved full blossom and I had returned from a wonderfully profitable night. The Rierson's daughter had celebrated her sixteenth birthday and doting relatives had showered her with a variety of jewelry, much of it obviously unsuited for a young lady. Knowing her parents to be discriminating guardians, I assisted them by removing several of the offending items. From that single foray I could have lived quietly in some Central American hide away for a year. When you do good work the reward is returned many times over.

But I have a heavy sense of responsibility to Richmond Hills, and that is a good thing. I counted my profits for the evening, secured them safely, and settled into the McGonigle library for another reading of Don Quixote. (There are certain books that a cultured man should read several times in his life.) The natural quiet of the home had barely reasserted itself when I heard a distinct thumping sound coming from somewhere on the first floor.

I doused my reading light and slipped into the hallway. The McGonigle residence has a marvelous spiral staircase that rolls from the upper reaches of the home like a great oaken waterfall before expanding into an enormous parlor. From the top of this edifice I noticed an intruder moving among the furniture. I immediately recognized the awkward bulk of Fast Fingers Fuller. I was angered and chagrined at this invasion! The clumsy gall of a smash and grab proletarian like Fuller invading my clientele was as offensive to spirit as it was to professional ethics.

He proceeded directly to an antique buffet that stood conspicuously large in the living room. The beam of a tiny flashlight winked, whirled, and refracted around the cabinet. Fuller's reaction would be interesting. The collection in the buffet was not sterling silver dinnerware. What glinted back at Fuller from dark glass shelves was Lady McGonigle's seashell collection.

But my eccentric host, as in every aspect of her life, did not have a normal seashell collection. Lady McGonigle's conches were composed of hand painted, antique china, ivory, and jewels. The collection was worth a fortune, but it was a fortune not readily apparent at first glance. Fuller, though, had an eye for value I had not expected to see in him; surprisingly quiet, too, as he deposited the collectibles into his bag. He'd probably lined it with feathers. It's an old trick, but effective. For a guy like Fuller, though, it was like upgrading from a typewriter to a computer. I had to admire him for that.

Yet however admirable his technique I could not suffer this pest in my garden. A brute like Fuller would attract the single commodity I must live without - attention. Just one or two of his jobs would destroy every profitable business relationship I had taken so long to establish. Publicity of his thefts would spread quickly. A swift chain reaction of increased security, extra police patrols, updates to burglar alarm codes, purchases of large dogs, and a cascade of secondary effects would follow.

But my unwelcome friend presented other complications. Fuller didn't suffer from an overdose of intelligence, but you couldn't classify him as exceptionally stupid either. He wasn't going to be frightened off by teenaged ghost stories, and I doubted that I was here first reasoning would enlighten him to the error of his ways. He had unpleasant friends, too, acquaintances capable of sending me into a painfully premature retirement. So as Fuller looted the cabinet I considered my options. Swift action was imperative, but the situation called for prudence and caution, an open confrontation under present conditions might not succeed.

My tactical instinct for caution proved correct. After pawing through the last drawer Fuller appeared to hesitate. I knew what he was thinking. Even with a sack full of valuables he just couldn't help wondering what other treasures abounded in the place. As if he had suddenly made a decision Fuller headed straight for the back door nearest the kitchen, the one he had entered from. He returned without his bag and headed for the stairs. I retreated to the dark and waited. At the top of the landing he turned left and crept straight for the master bedroom where old lady McGonigle herself slept. I slipped into a hallway bathroom. Fuller entered the bedroom. I listened but I did not detect any sign of struggle. Assured that he had not molested Mrs. McGonigle I waited for him and set my ambush. Fuller soon emerged, now clutching a fist full of McGonigle jewels in his right hand. His left hand covered a pad on his stomach where he had secured another cache of gems rolled into the front of his shirt. Lovely. I allowed him to advance several steps and then fell in behind him.

Just at the crest of the stairway I expelled a breath, about the force required to blow out a candle. Fuller's reaction was instant. Remember this if you ever happen to be caught in the same situation: if someone unexpectedly blows into your ear while you are burglarizing a home do not stop and turn around. Move quickly forward - away from the exhalation.

The memory of Fuller's face still makes me chuckle. I have never seen eyes so wide! His look of shocked terror could not have been more pronounced if I had been a genuine poltergeist. To prolong his horror would have wonderful amusement, but such luxuries are the realm of James Bond villains. I must practice a more efficient professionalism. With his back to the stairwell I speared him full in the throat with a bent knuckled thrust of my hand. I felt and heard a satisfying crunch as his Adam's apple and associated anatomy collapsed.

Fuller landed in an undignified heap at the base of the stairs. But he was made of stern stuff! Muttering and groaning he attempted to rise to his hands and knees. Well, as my father used to say, you can't have everything – where would you put it? Using the banister for leverage I stomped down on his neck and broke it. That stopped his muttering and groaning.

I arranged the body so that Fuller's head protruded between the wooden spokes at the base of the stairs. The people from the maid service found it in the morning and called the police. Those fine public servants concluded that some inept thief had attempted to rob the house, and - in what is commonly called a freak accident – had fallen down the stairs and broken his own neck. After identifying the body as none other than the notorious Fast Fingers Fuller their theory was confirmed. Case closed. Richmond Hills could relax. I doubt that the good Mrs. McGonigle is aware of the incident to this day.

Of course, I'm not naive. My clients aren't all lily innocents. The things I've seen! Wife beatings and husband floggings, illicit trysts, rapes, masturbations, lies, language that would make a sailor's devil cringe, thefts on a grander scale than Fast Fingers had ever contemplated; it is a long black list of sins that depresses me to think about. I could make a grand living on blackmail alone.

But blackmail is not in my nature. By my soul I am a lover of beauty. That which is ugly I am driven to improve. Like the artist who brings the ugly clay to brilliant life, so do I strive to raise civilization's occasional beastliness to sacredness.

As proof I offer the case of Mr. Marcel Cardine. In the externals Mr. Cardine was an exemplary picture of hard earned wealth - an exceptionally respectable, card carrying representative of the species. He was a thirty-five year old, nattily dressed manager of a financial planning concern. In case you aren't familiar with financial planning then let me set you straight. Mr. Cardine's profession is a lot more difficult than mine. He worked hard! And for his efforts he was exceptionally well compensated by the corporation, very exceptionally well compensated. It is no exaggeration to say he was headed for even greater rewards. I had high hopes him. But Mr. Cardine had a distressingly subterranean current boiling beneath this virtuous sheen.

Each day began in like fashion. After kissing the beautiful Mrs. Cardine, a lively blond goddess, Marcel would then kiss and pat the heads of the cutest little stop and squeeze 'em in the supermarket, tow headed twins in all of Richmond Hills or anywhere else for that matter. He'd then slip behind the controls of a sleek BMW. Framed in the rear view mirror he'd see a two story, many roomed, beige brick dream house with swimming pool and an extra wide driveway for his wife's Lincoln Navigator, not to mention the bass boat that could go on E-bay right now for fifty grand plus. I'd go on about the tennis court, swimming pool, etc., but you get the picture. Marcel Cardine is the man you dreamed of becoming in your post college years.

The Cardines were vacationing when I visited. Alas, I was disappointed with furnishings, a common problem with the newly rich. They have not had the time and seasoning to garner the items of taste, culture, and value that are the hallmark of the truly refined. Information is sometimes more valuable than gold, however. I probed Mr. Cardine's computer files.

Now I am sure there are those who might call me a sinner, but as I peered into the history of my host's pornographic cyber world I realized that alongside the loathsome Mr. Cardine I am the most insignificant of venial offenders. If the clergy speak the truth, and I believe they do, then the name Marcel Cardine is written below even the ninth rung of the inferno. To relay specifics of the flickering horrors I witnessed on that screen would serve no worthy purpose. But I will tell you this. The pictures were of subject matter illegal in all fifty states and abhorred by the decent everywhere.

I suspected that a man of such perversion would be equally base in his financial dealings although it gave me no gratification to find out that I was correct. Every twist and click of the mouse exposed business practices of staggering corruption, layer after layer, file after file of financial evil, vile reflections of his mental and spiritual degradation.

In the midst of this revulsion my mind conjured an even more painful image – a visage of the beautiful Mrs. Cardine and her lovely children. Reeling with shock as I was, my disillusionment would pale next to the monstrous emotions that wonderful family would one day have to endure. The situation screamed for justice. And justice prevailed. It prevailed the very moment that the brakes on the Mr. Cardine's sleek BMW failed and plunged off the side of a steep, rocky incline on his way to work.

You expected otherwise? Haven't I stated that I am devoted to beauty and fearless in confrontation of the ugly? The man of honor does not shy from duty. I consider Marcel Cardine my finest achievement. Instead of a mortified family shattered by knowledge of paternal wickedness, the remaining Cardines have instead a legacy of loving memories, plus a generous insurance settlement that will allow the blond suburban goddess and her children to continue the life they are accustomed to. And in this newfound status they will acquire the taste and culture that will someday repay their unknown benefactor.

Back again to the business at hand. I move further into the home and inspect the living room. The Waverly's are a well-traveled family, insatiable collectors of memorabilia, and more often than not it is an expensive little bauble, too.

It's another one of the things that makes a visit to their home such a pleasure. Miscellaneous pieces of crystal, jade, onyx, statues, memorabilia, and knickknacks of jewelry fairly encrust every room. Particularly prized items are stored in red mahogany cabinets that outshine any comparable collection in Richmond Hills. The cases are so loaded that they have to move things to the rear with each new acquisition. I help them rotate their stock.

Here's a lovely little jade dragon hidden behind several other glittering pieces. Seems absurd, but I have seen one like it in a jewelry store priced at over five hundred dollars. Half the price will make the night worthwhile, but as the good poet says, I have miles to go before I sleep. Several other items look extremely promising as well. But before I can make a prudent selection the beam of car headlights flashes in the dark. Young Dawn Waverly has returned from her date.

I hear footsteps heading for the rear entrance; two sets of footsteps postured as though trying to be quiet. Dawn's beau is with her? Perhaps they will linger in the starlight for a while.

I peer out a window and see them. Dawn's fellow is Ricky Knapp. I'm familiar with Knapp, his family inhabits a less well to do section of town. This coarse featured, hirsute football star, while outwardly respectable, is unhealthily fond of female conquest. Ego problem I suspect. Dawn's father, like me, a man of well-bred discrimination, senses the flaws in Knapp's character. "Something about him," he is fond of saying, "reminds me of a sex mad Eddie Haskell."

He is neatly right about young Knapp. The overly polite young man has only one thing in mind for our fair maiden and her youth is too preciously short for derailment by the likes of this. The situation, though, presents a dilemma. My present position is untenable. I could slip into the night, but Ricky may cause the Waverly's a disturbing problem. Ah, well. Once again duty to my clients outweighs personal interest. I return to the guest room and exit back out the bathroom window. Like ink in shadow I make my way around the house and creep to the side of the swimming pool bathhouse. From here I have a fine view of their tryst.

Despite my misgivings about Knapp I am momentarily distracted by the innocence of this adolescent attraction. Dawn is wearing a swirling summer dress that accents her youth and blossoming sensuality. Knapp's sleeveless tee shirt advertises his physique and virility. Cradled in soft summer and the illusion of endless youth, they embrace and kiss. A charming picture of young love! As yet unaffected by strife of the dollar and worldly cynicism, aware of nothing more than the presence of each other and the swirling lusts of their bodies, they cling to each other in timeless emotion.

The tennis court and the lovers are suddenly snared in harsh light. In bathrobe and pajamas Mr. Waverly appears. His stride is quick and angry and when he reaches the couple his words are as harsh as the light. The young man raises his open hands and begins to walk away. Dawn clings to him and remonstrates with her father. Mr. Waverly becomes more agitated; his voice rises. Dawn begins to cry and screams words I can barely believe I hear. Her father is struck into silence.

Mrs. Waverly now joins the fray. She is understandably distraught, and paler than her white robe. Mr. Waverly repeats Dawn's proclamation to his wife. Suddenly there is silence and all four walk to the house. Just outside the window of the living room I hear Dawn repeat her intention to marry this muscled charmer. The Waverly's have another view for the course of their daughter's future and production of future Knapps is not it. I heartily agree.

Their argument escalates. Voices and passions rise. Dawn is becoming hysterical. Knapp repeats meaningless clichés of his devotion. Mrs. Waverly is trying to remain calm, but she clearly sees the danger. As for Mr. Waverly, normally a gentlemen of great composure, the vision of his daughter forgoing college for a future as hausfrau to this over muscled, under brained jock is sending him into heretofore unknown realms of anger.

Just as I am certain that the situation will get dangerously out of hand Dawn bursts into a fit of uncontrollable tears. Mrs. Waverly immediately embraces her. Mr. Waverly retracts his outburst. Even the doltish Ricky Knapp understands that it is time to pull back from the brink. The crescendo of invective ceases, replaced by soft whimpering and sobs.

This is, however, a mere respite. Nothing has been resolved. Young Dawn will continue to pine for her big-armed, intellectually deprived cavalier. If her parents allow the attraction to continue chances are extremely likely that their beautiful daughter will soon ruin a brilliant future. If they forbid the romance to blossom further, a prospect as likely as stopping the moon from affecting the ocean tide, chances are extremely likely that their daughter will soon ruin a brilliant future.

Knapp is leaving. He bids a tearful farewell to his intended. Frosted silence follows him out the door from the mother and father. He walks to his car and stands for a moment, head down. He appears genuinely upset. Have I misjudged him? But as he opens the car door the dome light flashes and illuminates the gleaming smirk on his face as he reaches for his cell phone.

I had hoped to make another stop tonight but this matter must be brought to a close. Leaning against the open car door young Knapp has his back to me as he jabbers on his cell phone. He does not realize that I am just several feet away now and overhearing every word he speaks. I can even hear the replies from the person he is peaking to; the voice sounds feminine.

Knapp giggles almost maniacally. To my disgust he proceeds to brag about the distress he has caused the Waverly family! "They'll never recover from this, Lilly!" he says. I clearly hear the laughter from the receiver of this revolting announcement. "And I've only just begun. I've got things in mind that'll screw these pompous Waverlys but good." As the conversation proceeds the meaning of it becomes perfectly clear. The entire seduction of Dawn Waverly was an act. Knapp had no intention of marrying Dawn. His actual intention is to draw her into some highly immoral act of sexual degradation with the person he is addressing on the phone. There is talk of video and blackmail as well.

My urge, as I'm sure you understand and agree with, is to do immediate physical harm to this odious oaf. That would certainly be a pleasurable course of action. But I have a better option. At some time in the extremely near future an important law enforcement official will receive a phone call about Knapp. The call is sure to cause the gentlemen some distress but the subsequent investigation will reveal material in Knapp's car even more distressing. I will not go into the sordid details but the material they will discover is illegal in all fifty states and abhorred by the decent in countries around the world.

I had hoped for a more productive evening but the welfare of my clients always takes precedence. It is time to return to my current abode and work out the details of the Ricky Knapp issue. So keep this in mind should you decide that Richmond Hills is in your future – Boniface the Anonymous is watching.

MAMMOTHS BY THE SQUIRRELY BROOK

A squirrely brook is just the best description; it's
what he always calls it. A corkscrewed, twisted stretch of
bubbly water in the middle of a northern prairie burning gold
in the glow of fall. The stream rolls in gentle rhythms
through swaths of beige brown rushes tipped with lifeless but
still red flowers that beckon like tiny Christmas lights as a
line of quaking aspens rattles in the sunny breeze. Several
ancient oaks tower over the stream on the other side. Later in
the day these giants will block the sun like a solid wall but
for now the light shines warm and direct on Marty's face as
he lays back on his favorite knoll; a hazy perch of solitude
lost in an endless rolling landscape. It takes a while to get
here but he doesn't mind. The journey is purifying and the
end is bliss.

Ah…the wonders he has seen! The awe he has felt!
Reptiles of colors so intense they remain in his dreams,
insects as bizarre as aliens, enormous hyenas on the run,
black beavers so big a man could float on the animal's back
as it swam. He's seen monstrous birds, boulder sized
hedgehogs, and gigantic lions. Little tree dwelling shrews
have jumped once jumped into his outstretched hand as a
giant sloth tore down their home and one ton armadillos dug

up the earth. Marty's eyes water at the memories. A spectacular cascade of life that grips him in iron bands.

But mammoths are what he really comes to see. There's a truly magnificent beast for you, a vision worthy of the most soaring imagination. But don't delude yourself into thinking you can just stroll out here and expect to see them. Oh no, no, no. These guys have their own rhythm and mysterious drummer; they resonate to a tune far more ancient than young Marty. Even after all this time of chasing after them, after all the arcane mental exercises and driven discipline – even after all of that – it is still a rare day that he is treated to the sight of the great beasts.

The giants are felt before they are seen. Rumbling vibrations drift up from the earth in a soft, powerful hum. The sound is quiet at first, so faint that it cannot be described as a sound at all. It is a feeling actually; a creeping awareness that grows as slowly and quietly as a sunrise on a cloudy day. The sensation then builds into a penetrating throb; a powerful, distant symphony. Before long the earth vibrates in earnest. Trumpets and bellows roll across the prairie and the entire ensemble plays in thunderous tunes. A pungent bovine odor that some might find disagreeable precedes them. But not Marty. To him it is an aroma of power and beauty and mystery. It is the scent of an ancient secret life other humans will never fully know.

So that's why he is here against an outcrop of boulders west of nowhere near a squirrelly brook under an impossibly blue sky and waiting patiently. He knows they will arrive today. He feels the tingling shiver of excitement in the knowing, the emotion rolling over him like an ocean wave. His fists clench and every muscle goes rigid. The feeling passes and the shivering stops almost as soon as it begins. The aftermath of that fleeting is exhilaration and a calm beautiful sensation.

And there it is! The deep, earthy rumble seeps into his back and chest. His senses arouse and sharpen to a peak. They are coming! The great beasts are coming! Every action now is extremely important; a single misstep, the slightest aberration of posture or attitude and the giant pachydermial comrades will scatter. You would not think a six to seven ton animal with the appearance of shaggy city bus could disappear so quickly. But it happens and he must be careful. It's a matter of the right attitude.

The earthy rumble grows. Completely motionless, not daring to look up, he pulls the sensation into his heart. Once centered properly like this the experience will blossom until it is nearly impossible to stop. The rolling vibration increases steadily, stronger and stronger, until it is an actual sound instead of a dull, amorphous throb. The single indistinct mesh of soft rumbling soon becomes a heavy thunder of distinct footfalls. This is the moment he has prayed for. It is now safe to rise. Mindful about spooking the wonderful beasts he pushes himself up to his feet. Slowly, slowly… his eyes rise in cautious rhythm with his upper torso. Fuzzy tipped shoots of prairie grass and the sparkling burbles of the squirrely creek in the noon sun blur his vision. The bank on the other side of the creek is slightly higher than the one on his side so he lifts his eyes to the rim of it, and then to the lilting prairie ocean beyond. Marty knows the exact protocol.

Can anything compare to the sight of a mammoth herd? It is truly regretful that we have only meager words to share it. The soft sway and stroll of these beautiful ancient elephant ancestors accent the sheets of brown wool hanging from their sides. The herd numbers about thirty animals. Two enormous males border the left of the herd some distance from the group. Tusks over ten feet long and a foot thick roll out from their massive heads like smooth, alabaster tree trunks. On the right a truly gigantic specimen screens the herd, his tusks even more magnificent than the males opposite him. That giant bull is one to be watched. Even Marty has never seen a mammoth so enormous. In between

132

these monsters walks an extended mammoth family of sisters, cousins, maturing calves, and newborns all following a dominant matriarch.

The animals rumble, trumpet, and snort in a symphony of elephantine noise more beautiful than any human composition. The sounds are enhanced by the ceaseless soft and powerful thunder of mammoth footsteps and the silent hidden rumble of their sonar language, a mysterious communication known only to the great beasts themselves. Marty dreams that perhaps someday he'll learn their secrets. As yet he is too much of a neophyte.

The rumbling, boisterous herd approaches ever closer but Marty is familiar with this phase of their behavior. The magnificent beasts will come to the edge of the squirrelly brook and remain on that side of the water; the bank is just a little too steep for them to chance a crossing at this point. Like modern elephants they are extremely careful about each step. They will then follow the meandering creek upstream to a point where the bank eases down into a mammothly acceptable slant and flattens out into a wide pond.

They enjoy the water. Not so much as modern elephants, of course – these guys have a lot of wooliness to contend with – but they love it just the same, especially on these warm days. The adults will frolic about throwing gouts of silvery spray over their backs while the young ones wrestle and play in the pond until the entire pool is a muddy mess. What a joy to behold!

At this point, though, the herd is still a few hundred meters away. But the experience is fully entrenched; it has transcended Marty and nothing can stop it. The wonder of the sight is not to be denied. A herd of beautifully gigantic mammoths strolling along a sun filled prairie. Ah yes, the vision is firmly in control.

The herd drifts ever closer. The animals pause from time to time as the tips of their trunks rip patches of grass from the earth and stuff it into their great maw. Out of habit they occasionally scrape the sand with long sweeps of their tusks. There is no need for this, of course, the snow has long since melted away. But occasionally the beasts pick up pieces of the earth that they have uncovered and pop it into their mouth. Some type of mammoth mineral supplement? They are rather particular about it. The young ones fumble cutely with their appendage. It will take weeks for them to acquire the muscular control to feed themselves, and a lot longer to achieve real dexterity with it.

To the left and right the enormous bulls march along behind the herd, further down the creek. They are not ready to mate right now; if so at least one of them would be actively intermingling in the herd or fighting with one of the other males. For now they seem content to follow and linger alongside the herd. The cows, too, are at ease. They would not be as nonchalant if one of the great bulls was in musth or if one of them were ready to mate. The herd continues its leisurely pace. With every step the long, rangy rolls of woolly shag dance and sway in gentle rhythm. It is wondrous, awe inspiring, and peaceful at once.

"You enjoy them as much as I do, I think."

The sudden voice is startling. Marty whirls around to brown eyes set above high cheek bones that gaze beyond him to the mammoth herd. Marty is over six feet tall but this barefooted female nearly matches him in height. Her sleek physique is browned, polished from the sun, and sparely covered in beige deer skin. A luxurious waterfall of raven black hair cascades beyond her shoulders and down her back.

She turns her eyes slowly to him and smiles. The effect is tongue tightening. Marty is sure she is an illusion, until she speaks again. "I have seen you here many times," she says. "So I know you love them."

"You have?" he asks. It's a dumb response and his choked voice makes it sound even dumber. He grapples with the information his eyes are conveying to his brain. A breeze billows her hair to one side and she sweeps it back with a quick movement of her hand. Smooth muscle glistens with the motion.

"Oh yes, I have." Her tone is oddly wistful, almost sad. Her gaze returns to the ambling herd, yet her lilting voice clears his mind enough to compose a rational thought; her reality has penetrated.

"Why…haven't I seen you until now, uh, before?" Marty forces himself to stop before a torrent of questions pour out.

"I've not had the unity until now," she says. She looks down at her hands and clenches her fists.

No idea what her answer means. "Unity?"

"Later," she says. "It is, well, it is too difficult right now."

He nods as though he understands. "Okay. My name is Martin, Martin McGinnis, but everyone calls me Marty." He out his hand and she takes it in hers. Her grip is strong, soft and warm.

"I know you well, Marty McGinnis, but I prefer the more proper Martin. Do you mind?"

"No, not at all." How can I mind? And you know me how?"

"I know you well," she replies. "I know you intimately."

The enigmatic answer only adds to the puzzle. Marty gets the feeling that no matter how he phrases the question of her origin he is not going to get a straight answer until she chooses. He can live with that. This lady is so overwhelmingly beautiful that she'd have to do a lot more than give evasive answers to annoy the young man. Quite the contrary, he is afraid she will disappear at any minute. He must choose words carefully.

"May I ask your name, ma'am?"

The wonderful smile again. "Call me Maya," she says and takes his hand again. "Come Martin. Let's walk with the herd."

He'd almost forgotten about the mammoths. During the distraction the animals have approached the other side of the creek. Meandering along they ignore the humans. Marty had observed this behavior before; as long as he remained on the far side of the creek they did not treat him as an object of danger or even of interest. But this was the first time he had shared this side of the stream with a gorgeous Indian maiden. At least that was his best guess of her origin at the moment.

The walked upstream, their pace matching the relaxed tempo of the ancient animals on the other side. Maya did not speak and Marty was so unsure of what to say to this vision of beauty, so fearful of disrupting the spell, he remained silent as well. They stole glances at each other and exchanged periodic smiles, but no words. Marty resolved to keep his thoughts quiet despite the fact that he was exploding in curiosity.

"Martin, would you like to ride one?" she asked.

"Ride? Ride what?"

She paused and tilted her head as though dealing with a child. "One of these beautiful animals you love so much. Would you like to ride one?"

His response to the odd question was immediate. "Absolutely!" he said. "Uh, I presume you've done this before?"

"Oh many times. It will be much more fun riding with someone else, though."

"Of course."

That pleased him immensely. He did not know how such an incredible woman could be lonely, but maybe she lived out here alone. But how could she live alone on the prairie? She had to be part of a tribe or something.

She put a finger to her lips. "Don't ask, Martin. I can see it in your eyes and I understand. But the time is not right, not yet. All will become clear soon."

"Okay, it's just that I don't meet a goddess every day," he offered.

Marty was pleased with his remark but Maya ignored the compliment. "I am just as curious about you, Martin. But for now let's just enjoy our shaggy friends, okay? You will love the ride, I promise."

He bowed his head. "Oh, I'm sure of that, Maya. But how do we do this? Mammoths are not little ponies waiting to for a saddle."

"You'll see when we reach the pond."

They ambled on for a quarter of a mile or so, keeping time with the herd and sharing a spare dialog. Marty maintained discipline about asking or even hinting about Maya's origin and she offered nothing further along that line despite the fact that she must have known his curiosity was reaching criticality. Wherever she came from, however, one thing was certain – she was incredible to look at. Her physical presence made it a bit easier to keep from asking questions; a lot harder to watch where he was going, though. Maya swayed with an easy, fluid grace. Every movement displayed sleek muscles that jumped, clenched, and relaxed; her legs gleamed taught firmness and her hips rolled in sensuous rhythm.

"Here we are," she said.

Marty's mind returned to earth and discovered that they'd come to the downstream boundary of the pond. The body of water here was actually a small lake. Wondrously clear and vibrant with aquatic life, the pond was fed by the brook and a cool underground spring as well. The mammoths seemed to sense the beauty of the water as keenly as they did. They paused at the edge of the water as though prolonging the pleasure they'd derive from plunging in. The animals gathered by the water's edge bellowing, trumpeting, and waving their trunks. Suddenly they were silent and still. Were they waiting for a signal? Indeed they were.

"Come! Come Nehanyala!" Maya waived her arms in a beckoning gesture. The reaction of the mammoths was instant. In the middle of the herd the huge matriarch let loose a bellow that ripped and echoed across the empty prairie. The other elephants followed suit. A second later the water erupted from the unstoppable force of thirty charging mammoths. Water flumed and sprayed upward into a thousand flashing rainbows. Rolling waves rushed like an ocean storm. The little lake was deceptively deep, however. Several of the adult beasts dove in and disappeared beneath the surface. But they soon bobbed up again amidst long waiving strands of mammoth hair that stood out like garlands of auburn seaweed.

Marty had seen the animal's play before, but never an aquatic spectacle like this. The scene was simply overwhelming; his eyes watered at the sheer wonder of it.

"How on earth did you that, Maya?"

Maya demurred, but she was obviously pleased at this exclamation. "Martin, Martin. So many questions." She laughed.

He glanced at the carousing herd and clapped at their antics. "And you said that you would answer me at the water's edge. Well here we are!" He had to shout above the noise of the splashing herd.

"And I will keep my promise," she said. "But I promised you a ride, too, and I always keep my promises. Are you ready?"

"I've never been so ready for anything in my life!" The statement was not an exaggeration. The emotions exploding up and down his body had volcanic power. It took enormous will on to keep from screaming in joy.

All over the water the beasts frolicked madly, reveling in the cool glade like children released from school onto a new playground. Trunks thrashed back and forth, long curling rolls of ivory battered the water into spray, and great volumes of clear pond water rocketed toward the sky as the mammoths rose up and threw themselves down. It was a prehistoric scene of magic!

Maya's joy matched his own. She clapped and giggled at the antics of the elephant ancestors. "Is it not beautiful, Martin? Is it not beautiful?" she cried.

"Yes, yes!" he yelled in return.

It took a while for the wild enthusiasm of the animal to subside, but gradually their raucous play calmed. One by one they sauntered back to rim of the shore and stood knee deep, pulling at water plants and tufts of grass that grew nearby as water dropped like sparkling rain from their wooly hides. All the while the great matriarch kept careful watch over these proceedings ensuring that no animal left the safety of the herd. The water of the lagoon stilled and cleared. A silence spread.

Maya held out her hand. "Now it's our turn."

"Turn for what?" he asked stupidly.

"Time for us to swim, Martin," she teased. "Do you think this water is just for the use of these lovely elephants?"

He paused awkwardly at the water's edge but his beautiful companion displayed no such reticence. With graceful ease she kicked her moccasins onto the grass.

"I wait for you in the water," she laughed. She took several swift strides and plunged into the translucent pond.

For a moment he stood transfixed and watched as the heavy sunlight descended though the water and rippled over her. Each stroke took her deeper and farther away. An instant later he was tearing off his clothes and flinging them onto to the shore behind him as he raced into the water. Marty was a strong swimmer himself and quickly caught up to her fleeting form.

He reached out and grasped Maya's ankle. There! He'd caught her. The idea of her wonderfully warm flesh pressed against him raced through his body. But no sooner had that lovely thought entered his head than it was dashed by a powerful stroke of Maya's leg. Her ankle broke free of his grip. He had a fleeting underwater glimpse of her as she wriggled away like a beautiful silver fish. Undeterred, he burst to the surface for a gulp of air and continued the pursuit. Swimming just as powerfully for the opposite shore Maya remained submerged.

Marty's lungs were straining for air when he at last felt soft earth beneath his feet. He stopped swimming and regained his footing, standing in water just below chest level. Maya stood about ten feet away close to the other shore, her body and raven hair gleaming in the sun. with a sudden twisting motion she broke the spell of erotic hypnosis she had put him under. A splash of water and a fleeting spray of rainbow hued drops and she disappeared again. Marty instantly followed and engaged in this maddeningly exciting game of tag. Finally, with Maya in the lead, they pulled their exhausted bodies to shore.

Marty was still laughing and gasping for air when he suddenly became conscious of the closeness of his beautiful companion. Maya simply stood with her hands on her hips. Was she enjoying his discomfiture or physique? He stepped to within a foot of her fighting the urge to wildly grasp this glorious woman, his desire almost uncontrollable. Maya remained motionless, smiling at him. Suddenly the matriarch of the mammoth herd bellowed; a shattering sound that jolted Marty. The frightening sound was followed by an even more ominous noise – the frothing explosion of water as the giant mammoth exploded out of the water and onto the shore and directly in front of Marty. An instant before he was flattened into a blade of prairie grass Maya barked a command at the beast. The mammoth stomped up to Maya's side, flared her ears at Marty and bellowed another ear splitting warning. The message was unmistakable: one false move, buddy, just one, and you'll be worm food. It's tough to be heroic when you're near naked, but it is absolutely out of the question when similarly attired and in the face of an angry, fully grown mammoth. Marty did the sensible thing and backed up.

Maya raised her arm to the animal's trunk. The gigantic appendage was restlessly twitching and alternately thumping the ground making a sound like a hollow eight inch wide PVC pipe. Probably the tune she'd like to play on my head, Marty thought.

Maya turned and faced the animal. "Easy, Nehanyala, easy. Quiet, quiet, girl. The man is our friend." She rubbed the mammoth's enormous trunk and the animal rumbled and the twitching finally stopped.

"It is alright, Martin. Come now. It is time for our ride. You can put your clothes on."

With one eye on Maya's giant woolly pet he slipped his jeans and shirt back on as Maya stepped back in to her moccasins. Marty cautiously knelt down, pulled on his socks and tennis shoes, and laced them up despite the uneasy feeling that that the trunked monster examining his every move would step forward and squash him while in this vulnerable position. Yet Maya controlled the ancient elephant as easily as one commands the family dog.

"Down, Nehenyahla," she said gently. "Down, girl."

As Marty watched in awe as the mammoth pushed itself back with silent, powerful grace and sank down to the soggy earth. Her forelegs pushed deep impressions into the moist surface as the great prehistoric beast lie flat on her stomach. Maya placed her foot on one giant limb, grabbed two fistfuls of mammoth fur, and pulled herself up onto the animal's back. She moved up to a position just behind the great domed head and then looked down and beckoned Marty to follow.

He stole a quick, anxious glance at Nehenyahla. But animal did not appear distressed or angry; no twitching ears, restless trunk, and no furious trumpets, thank god. Whatever elephantine transgression he had committed in her point of view had apparently been forgiven. He glanced up at Maya. The sight of her astride this ancient creature was stunning. He took another look at Nehenyahla – just for insurance. Even in this prone position she was monstrous. Her back rose well above his head, a mountain of light brown fur that blocked the sun. Her tusks rolled out like ivory roller coasters and pushed wide impressions into the mud. He wondered how she supported the gigantic things while upright. Would those muddy imprints be here a thousand years or so from now? Would some nameless paleontologist from the future wonder at the meaning of what had occurred here one day at the side of this squirrely brook? The enormity of the situation suddenly overwhelmed him. He went light-headed.

"Why are you waiting, Martin?" Maya called. "Jump up here! Nehenyahla won't hurt you."

"I'm just…well, never mind," he said. "I'm coming aboard!" He pulled myself together. Mimicking Maya's actions he placed his right foot on top of the mammoth's foreleg, grasped two handfuls of the beast's wool, yanked for all he was worth, and swung himself up. After a bit of adjustment he was seated behind Maya, and surprisingly comfortable, too. The thick mat of fur provided a mattress like cushion.

"Hang on," Maya said over her shoulder. With her feet she gave the animal a slight nudge behind its flapping ears and voiced a command. "Up, Nehenyahla, up!"

The mammoth pushed backward off its forefeet and they were rocked backwards. Maya's body pushed into Marty. Just as suddenly he was jolted forward into Maya as Nehenyahla brought her rear legs up. Seconds later they were off. The mammoth strolled gracefully back into the pond pushing the water ahead of her in a great bow wave. The deepest part of the pool where Marty had gone completely under the water barely made it beyond Nehenyahla's chest; their toes were not even in danger of getting wet.

The huge beast lumbered up the opposite bank, each step producing a feeling of rising gently into the air. Nehenyahla walked directly to her herd and bellowed. Her roar was followed by deafening chorus of obedient mammoth replies and off they went, strolling across the vast prairie perched on top of the largest animal on land. Nehenyahla rolled and rocked in an easy, unhurried shamble while the rest of the herd followed. Never had Marty experienced such exhilaration. Maya's warm body arched against him and his hands rested on her thighs. The sweet soft sensation of her hair wisped against his face. Two youthful bodies melded together on a soft cushion of mammoth fur, rising falling time to an ancient prehistoric rhythm. From fourteen feet in the air he felt like an teenaged god with his goddess, fearlessly touring their kingdom.

"Maya?" Marty asked, desperately attempting to maintain a modicum of composure. "Where are we going?"

The beauty did not even turn around. "I thought you might like to see my home, Martin," she said.

"Yes, I'd like that a lot." The tight constriction of his throat almost made his voice croak. "How long will it take us to get there?"

She twisted half around and paused as if considering the question. "At this rate," she said, "about two days."

"Will we be resting at some point between here and your home?" he ventured.

"Oh, of course, Martin," Maya said. "There is no reason to travel for two days without rest."

He was relieved by her reply. It was already past midday. In a few more hours the sun would begin to set; darkness would creep in. They'd have to stop and prepare some kind of a camp of course. But that thought made him realize something quite obvious.

"Maya, you mean we'll pause somewhere for the night, right?"

"That is correct."

"Are we going to sleep on the ground? I have nothing but the clothes I'm wearing and you're not exactly dressed for a cold night on the prairie. Do you have some camping gear stored nearby?"

"There is no need to fear the cold, Martin."

That remark kind of touched his male pride. "It's not me being cold that bothers me, Maya. I'm worried about you. You can't sleep on the ground."

Maya seemed to find his concern amusing but stifled her giggles. She reached back and patted the side of his leg. "Martin, Martin. There is no need to sleep on the ground for you or me. We have all the warm bedding we need. Don't you see?"

"No, my dear, I'm afraid I do not."

Maya half twisted around again. "Look around you, sweet boy."

The remark confused him but he turned around as directed. He saw nothing but a trailing herd of woolly beasts trampling the prairie grass, and beyond that nothing by more rolling grasslands. A pleasant enough sight to be sure, but nothing whatever to do with the subject at hand.

"Can you see our bed now, Martin?"

"Maya," he said. I have no idea what you are talking about." But suddenly he did. It was right there behind him – and under him - the wide back of Nehenyahla.

"This will be an experience, Maya."

"It certainly will, Martin." Her suppressed giggle sounded especially mischievous. Marty glanced at the sun. It would not be long until he found out what he was in for, and he was delighted at the prospect.

He turned his attention back to the immediate present. What a sight we must make, he thought! He imagined the two of them as some kind of prehistoric royalty; a surrealistic Adam and Eve. It might not be Eden but this northern prairie suited him nicely, thank you. And if this is what Adam went through with Eve he was a damned fool to allow himself to get kicked out of the garden.

Their conversation meandered along inconsequential tidbits. Maya remained vague about her origins and how she had acquired her skill with the mammoths but Marty did learn that she had possessed such an uncanny talent since she was a child. She'd always had a fascination for animals and they in turn seemed to be charmed by her. "Fortunate by birth," she called it.

"Will you ever tell me all of your secrets, Maya?" he asked.

"Will I ever know all of yours, Martin?" she countered. It was maddening.

"Alright, now, Maya. I've been coming to the squirrely brook for a long, long time. It is rare that I see the mammoths, but I have seen them on several occasions. Never once have you been with them on my previous visits."

"Are you so sure you have not seen me before?"

"I most certainly would not have forgotten the sight of you, my dear." He saw her amused smile and persisted. "You say you have seen me before, Maya. When was that? And where were you?"

"You must have patience, Martin. Our time is soon."

"I am the soul of patience," he pouted, "but I would not be a man if I did not have a man's breaking point. My curiosity is almost unbearable; as is being this close to you."

She giggled. Too mischievously this time, he thought. Devilish was probably the more accurate term. "You could sit back further," she said. "There is plenty of room on our transport you know."

"Just the same I think I'd like to stay up here with you."

She sighed, raised her head to the sky, and wagged it back and forth. "Only if you behave."

"You have my solemn vow."

"Good," she said and removed his hand from her thigh.

Moving away from Maya at that point was the last thing in the world he wanted to do. It was bad enough that he was in a frenzy of emotion; he was in a frenzy of curiosity just as intense.

She twisted around and smiled. "Now just stay right there," she said. Maya returned to a posture of looking forward over the mammoth's head. Then, with the same impish grin, she turned back again and pointed a forefinger at him. "It will all be clear soon, Martin."

"That's what you said at the pond, Maya."

"It was; you just did not see it."

"You are speaking in riddles, Maya. I have no idea what you mean."

She sighed. "Sometimes, well…sometimes it is the only way. There are things that must be shown instead of explained. Don't you see?"

"No."

"It is like describing the taste of a wonderful food or the wind. No matter how hard I tried it would be inadequate."

"But Maya, I'm not asking for a description of an unknown something. We are together here – right now. I want to know about it and I want to know about you."

"My dear, Martin. Please be patient. Very soon you will. For now you must calm your thoughts. Think and feel the experience; live in it. Don't question it, please don't."

He tried to puzzle her words out, the way she accented please. There was something, just something, that struck him. The words felt oddly familiar; sad but sweet. The lightheadedness returned. Everything in front of him dimmed and he had this bizarre feeling that he was about to leave his own body. And then Nehenyahla trumpeted. Her bellow brought Marty back to reality, bothered by the sensation he'd had, but back to consciousness.

The mammoth paused, raised her trunk, and scented the air. She bellowed and the rest of the herd answered her.

Soon there was a deafening symphony of mammoth roars and trumpets.

"What's up, Maya?"

"Nehenyahla has scented something, something that's caused her great concern."

"And that would be?" He had to yell over the racket of elephantine uproar.

"Only one other animal out here makes the herd act like this."

"A saber tooth?"

Maya listened and studied the herd. "No, much larger than that," she said.

He mentally scrubbed his knowledge of the big prehistoric mammal predators. There was a giant bear, larger than the saber tooth and presumably just as ferocious, and another giant cat. But judging from the herd's reaction it had to be something even more ominous. A group of giant carnivores?

Maya squinted in the direction of the mammoth's upraised trunks. "Over there," she said and jabbed her finger in the direction of the setting sun off to our left.

I squinted into the sun but saw nothing more than a line of trees on the distant horizon. "I can't see anything but a tree line out there, Maya. Is there something I'm missing?"

"Oh yes, there's something you're missing. Just wait."

By now the herd began moving again, at a slightly faster pace than before. Something was clearly agitating the mammoths, although Marty could not see what. With Maya's encouragement Nehenyahla move the herd steadily along. To their right, and perpendicular to their path was a steep sided rocky cliff. Responding to Maya's prodding Nehenyala led the herd toward the cliff where it came to an abrupt end. From here the terrain led downward, leveled off, and then rose again onto a wide boulder strewn path of greater elevation than the prairie they had been marching on.

Marty looked again in the direction of the animal's distress. This time he did see something different. The tree line appeared to have moved closer. His first thought was that the advancing tree line was a trick of the setting sun, but as he looked closer he saw that the trees seemed to strangely bob in a kind of up and down motion. They were not oaks or pines or anything he was familiar with. These trees had no branches or leaves, just a kind of stalk growing from a very bulky base. Long limbs sprouted from this oversized base and appeared to waver or something in the distance. There was an unusual quality to the motion of the trees and he concentrated on distinguishing the movement, but between the setting sun and the rolling motion of Nehenyahla it was difficult to make out anything except that the forest was coming closer at an alarming rate.

The realization of what he was seeing finally struck with the force of an earthquake. It was a living forest alright, a forest of gigantic animals; animals so huge they might as well have been trees. Even from this distance he could tell that they were monsters. No wonder the mammoths were alarmed.

Marty nearly lost his balance and fell to the ground when Nehenyahla suddenly swerved to the right. He had a brief, but alarming, idea that she had panicked and Maya had lost control of the animal. Maya and Nehenyahla, however, possessed more awareness than he had given them credit for. She had found a natural bridge that arched over an open gorge. The pass was relatively narrow for an animal the size of a mammoth, but Nehenyahla must have known it would support her weight and the weight of her herd. The passed over the gorge easily and the rest of the herd followed close behind.

The path then rose gradually until it crested the top of a plateau. The entire mammoth herd clambered up. Once she was assured that her extended family had made it safely to the top of the plateau Nehenyahla bellowed loudly. As if on cue every mammoth in the group turned and directed their attention to the giants approaching from the west. By now they were close enough to truly understand their immense size. And the sight was astounding.

Until that moment Marty had always thought that mammoths were the largest mammals ever to walk the land. The beasts that slowly paraded in front of them, however, actually made the giant mammoths look small by comparison.

"Good God!" he exclaimed in a hushed whisper. "They are monsters, Maya!"

"That they are, Martin. "We don't often see them this close. The mammoths are careful to avoid confrontations with them."

"They're plant eaters aren't they?"

Maya nodded. "Oh yes. They aren't aggressive, but they are so big they'll just inadvertently stomp over anything in their way. Nothing like them exists anywhere."

"I'll say."

Despite the fact that they were standing a hundred feet away from the monsters atop a plateau separated by a canyon the earth rumbled and shook; a feeling similar to that when a fully loaded semi truck barrels down the highway. Only this time there were dozens of the big trucks – and they were actual living creatures. The outlandish monsters strolling along in front of them made even Nehenyahla, the largest mammoth in the herd, look that small in comparison.

The air in Marty's lungs involuntarily whooshed out; for many seconds he stopped breathing entirely. The sight was simply too overwhelming for his senses. Zoological enthusiast that he was Marty's first thought (when he finally recovered that faculty) was that he was looking at a herd of brachiosaurs or diplodocus, some of the biggest dinosaurs that ever lived. Many were well over twenty feet long and looked to be in the range of thirty tons by comparison with the mammoths. But the body type was not right for a dinosaurian. Despite their gargantuan bulk the beasts had long, relatively slender legs supporting their barrel shaped bodies. Their necks were stout; thicker than an elephant's and ten feet long at least. Stubby tails were held upright as they walked. But the most astonishing feature of all was the fact that these animals were covered with fur – these monsters were mammals!

The beasts were utterly colossal; so huge Marty felt vertiginous as they passed. It was like the earth itself was passing before him. A constant dull rumble vibrated from the ground into my feet and throughout is body. The mammoth herd seemed equally affected. Every one of them stood perfectly still and silent as they watched the incredible procession pass by.

"God, Maya," he whispered. "I had no idea! What are they?"

For several moments she did not answer. Maya, too, was captured in the majestic spell of the sight in front of them. "We call it the God Beast," she said without taking her eyes away from them. "It is a rare and wonderful thing to see them so close; it is like a blessing, Martin."

"There cannot be another sight like it on earth," he agreed.

He pulled his eyes away from the parade of titans and looked at Maya. The setting sun illuminated her in soft golden light; black hair and beautiful eyes gleamed against bronzed, glowing skin. She did wear an expression of childish wonder as if a religious awe had enveloped her. And indeed it had. Marty knew because he knew precisely what she was feeling at that moment. He, too, was in rapture, enthralled in an emotion impossible to describe.

He took her hand and squeezed it. Maya returned the gesture. With natural and perfect ease their arms entwined and they embraced. The slow, soft sun continued its inexorable slide to other side of the earth. Colors turned rose and gold. To their rear the great mammoth herd stood still as

159

if they felt the rare perfection of this moment. The moment was too perfect. The light headed dizziness returned, this time stronger than ever.

"Martin, Martin…Martin Doyle."

He woke to the giggles of the rest of the class and Mrs. Sennich standing by the side of his desk grinning. "Thank you for joining us, Mr. McGinnis. Now, perhaps you can attempt to answer the equation on the board?" She pointed to where a long chemical equation stretched out in white letters on a green background.

"Yes, ma'am. Give me a minute," Marty said and groped for his pen and pad. He really did not know if he could deduce the answer. But he now had an answer to the most important question on his mind. And he didn't like the answer. Well, maybe he could go back and see Maya again someday. Qualitative analysis chemistry was boring enough to provoke a return visit and that was on the schedule for the next hour as well.

OVERHEARD AT HAPPY HOUR

I've seen the type over and over at this hotel and usually at the "Manager's Reception." (Which the rest of the world calls Happy Hour.) The two typicals in this case are sitting at the table across from me making an obvious show of their laptop computers, charts; excel spreadsheets, and other pretentious crap. The guy with gray white hair is draped in classic business attire. White shirt, black tie, and suit coat with all the appropriate creases. He's clean shaven and has that smooth skin look that tells you he doesn't do any real work. Probably some financial bean counter or digital geek. The guy across from him is doing all the talking and doing it in rapid fire, too loud dialogue, as though he wants to be overheard. He's an open collar man and sports the currently popular "I shaved three days ago" beard. Dark and sallow skin, heavy eyebrows, and shaded eyes. I'm reminded of a hyper little squirrel. They're seated at a table behind me to my left. From my seat at the bar I can hear every word and see every expression.

Why these people come here I don't know. Anchorage is a man's domain, especially so during hunting or fishing season; the reason I'm here. Oh well, I suppose somebody has to handle all the twerpy little business details. I'm just glad I'm not one of them. That kind of work turns a man soft to the point of being girly. I get a morbid fascination out of listening to them, though. It magnifies the contrast between me and these little twerps as much as my callused hands and busted knuckles do. Makes me glad I'm the man I am. Being the hunter that I am I pride myself on keen observation, though. I practice picking up on details wherever I am. So I order another Amber and settle in for the geek show. These two had obviously had more than the two complementary drinks; they'll prattle on for a while and I'll have a great time telling the boys about it when we linked up in the morning.

Squirrel man is all nonstop talk. "I'm from the Northeast, you know, I guess it's part of me I like to get things done. That's how I hire people, Ed. I suppose we all do, right? We hire people in our own image." Bragging about what kind of people he hires; typical superior management talk bullshit. Ed nods dutifully. You can tell he wants to say something, but motor mouth is not giving up the oxygen. I knew he was from the Northeast before I heard him say it from that goofy accent and pansy clothes.

"I hired this Nancy, see?" Squirrel points to one of the charts as though it's some big deal that he hired this woman. "I put her in charge of a number of projects and she takes off like a rabbit. Sales up almost overnight and bringing in in new business from day one. That's what I like." Squirrel man takes a breath, probably to let the genius of his decision sink in. This guy Ed sees his chance for a few words. "I have to admire you Sig; you are a mover." Sig? What kind of fairy name is that? Sig is drinking in the complement with a nose browner than a dog digging up a mole hill.

"Like I said, that's the way I am. I worked for Ralph Molly once. You remember him, right? Had the western territory?" Ed nods. I can tell by his expression Ed knows the story before he hears it.

"I guess I moved too fast for Molly. I'm pulling in clients so fast Ralph can't keep up. I mean, it's making him look great – but the workload is just overwhelming him. Can you believe this? He asked me to slow it down! 'Take it a little easier, Sig!' he tells me." Sig throws his hands up in the air to emphasize the incredibility of the situation.

Ed shakes his head. "I can't imagine you working with Ralph Molly, Sig. What a pair! Molly was a good man, don't get me wrong. I've known him since the company started. But let's face it; Ralph was never the kind to make fast moves."

Ed and Sig share a laugh. Ed finally has a chance to break into the conversation, though, and he's not about to let it go. "So where is Molly now, Sig? You got his territory I heard before you took over the eastern gig?"

All of sudden fast talking Sig slows his voice. "Hell, Ed. I don't know. I just whacked the lazy bum. Wasn't my job to take out the trash, right? A couple of hired pros took care of that. No idea where they dumped him."

Ed nods sagely with puffed out lips. "I understand. Can't blame ya, either. I had a similar problem with Cookie Jones when I took over. The organization's simply got no room for snails and slugs these days; too much business. You should have seen the look on his face when we fileted him. Of course it didn't last long!"

At this remark the both of them break out laughing – and look up at me. I quickly decide it time to leave the bar. Then on the way out I hear something that really pisses me off. It's a remark from the Squirrel. "Hah! Did you see the look on that goon's face, Ed? Wait'll we tell Ralph about it!" I could still hear them guffawing by the time I got to the elevator.

RANDOM ATOM

Absolutely no doubt. The bronze hair had thinned a bit, spouted some silver and had strayed fashionably over the ears, but the vivid, intense face illuminated by strange fires never left the memory. Even shrouded by a magician's cloak and the space of fifteen years I knew it was Henry J. Houlihan instantly. So here he is, calling himself "Random Atom - The Amazing Chameleon." How appropriate; how perfectly appropriate.

Hank had a philosophy and he liked to lecture. I'd heard it so many times I remembered it to this day. "You can't recognize the possibilities because you're all too frightened; too frightened of change and consequence. Every one of you is a cause and predictable reaction drill, a polarized process of thought, behavior, and blind, stupid obedience. You have no more concept of freedom than the sheep on the other side of the border."

His exact words, and the exact last sentiment I heard him speak until this moment. I still had the journal I wrote them in and quoted from the day we first discerned that First Lieutenant Henry J. Houlihan was missing. They were the same words I wrote in the investigation report, too. Captain Rosenberg, the battery commander, didn't find the quote insightful or moving - just exasperating - like everything else

1LT Houlihan did.   "Did he say anything else, Tom?" he asked

"No, sir. I wrote it down because Hank was acting so weird that night, weird even for Hank. He came in to the dayroom bar Wednesday night, had a beer, made his speech and left. I figured he went back to his apartment, but the next morning he was a no show for PT."

CPT Rosenberg squinted at the ceiling and shook his head. With his thick glasses he looked like a slightly overweight, nearsighted hedgehog but he was the most knowledgeable artilleryman I knew. And he took care of his soldiers, a rarity in those days of the border patrolling 11th Armored Cavalry Regiment. I hated to bring him news like this.

"And nobody has any idea where he is?"

"No, sir."

"Two days away from border duty and I've got to tell the squadron commander that one of my lieutenants is AWOL. Super.

"All right Tom. I'm going over to see the old man. I want you to keep asking around and see if anybody has seen or heard from Houlihan. But for right now I want you to write a statement and stay near the phone. Colonel Washam will want to talk to you."

Fifteen years later I'm still annoyed about that. 1700 hours on a Friday night and I had a statement to write and a cross examination that was probably going to take two hours. CID would get involved because Hank had a Top Secret clearance and access to nuke codes. My weekend off was history and I had a month of border duty starting Monday. Houlihan, I cursed, where ever you are I hope you're miserable.

But I was better off than CPT Rosenberg. Situations like the Houlihan caper made you glad you weren't the commander. Washam did not take the news well. He ranted and raved and blamed the BC. Hell, it wasn't CPT Rosenberg's fault that one of his lieutenants was loopy. Maybe he wasn't even AWOL. Perhaps he was hurt in an accident somewhere, maybe even dead. Maybe he went crazy and bugged out. He wouldn't be first soldier to do that. All that was crap, though. I knew real deal. Hank Houlihan was AWOL, deliberately AWOL. And he wasn't coming back.

And now, fifteen years after the Cold War and the East German border, I'm watching Hank Houlihan, a.k.a. Random Atom, perform magic tricks in a theater in Kansas City. Unbelievable.

And that suddenly annoyed me a hell of a lot more than the weekend he'd cost me.

My wife noticed me shaking my head. "What's the matter, Tom?"

"You don't recognize 'Random Atom'?"

"He looks familiar."

"You remember the lieutenant that disappeared when we were in Fulda? That's him. That magician is Hank Houlihan."

"You're kidding!" Lisa said, then leaned forward and narrowed her eyes. "Good lord, you're right! It's him! What on earth is he doing here?"

"Enjoying the fruits of his desertion from the Army," I replied.

For a while we watched the act in amazed silence. I'll say one thing for Houlihan, he might not have been the greatest soldier in the world but he had developed considerable skills as a magician. His act was based around transformation; changing people and things; of himself, his two gorgeous assistants, animals, and objects; a non stop razzle dazzle of flashing movement, colored smoke, lasers, explosions, dramatic gestures.

Change, it was all about change. "Random Atom's" flashy show biz suits alternated in color and style in seconds. Tigers turned into lambs and lambs into lions. Blue and gold macaws became shimmering displays of floating orange feathers. He performed a variation of the saw your assistant in half routine that had the audience gasping. Sawed both of them in half and mixed up the torsos. They not only emerged wearing each other's clothes - but with their heads on backwards. Several razzle-dazzle cape flashes and wand waves later both craniums were restored to the correct azimuth. By any standard it was a performance.

I marveled with the masses when my old colleague executed a particularly clever feat, transforming a deck of cards into a twinkling flutter of butterflies. The coruscant cloud alighted on a white sheet held by two female assistants. A slight pause prompted the audience to erupt into applause, until a snap of the sheet caused the colorful insects to dissolve into a vivid rainbow. The applause became an amazed gasp followed by an explosion of claps and whistles. I might be repulsed by knowledge of the man's history, but the talent Houlihan displayed under the auspices of Random Atom transcended performance - it was art. Houlihan had found his place in the universe.

The frenzied spasm of applause had barely ceased reverberating throughout the theater when Random Atom called out for a volunteer. My hand waved in the air like a second grader with the correct answer.

"Tom, stop it!" Lisa scolded.

"It's an irresistible moment, dear."

"Tom, sit down! You're going to make a scene!"

Exactly my intention. Our front row seats gave me the visibility I needed. The beautiful assistants approached. I gave Lisa a last sly look before being led to the stage.

The girls directed me to a short stairwell at the side of the stage. I mounted it and walked directly to Houlihan. As thousands of people clapped I grinned in anticipation. I knew he'd recognize me. Would it derail the act? I hoped so. Random Atom might do his most amazing transformation of the night, I thought. His display of show biz confidence would turn to staring disbelief. And then - who knew what? He had nowhere to go. He had to face me.

I readied myself for the confrontation but I was unprepared for the brilliant lights that assaulted my eyes at center stage. Houlihan threw an arm around my shoulder. "How do sir? What is your name?"

The unexpected thrust of the microphone and the booming, acoustically enhanced question surprised me. The lights made everything difficult to see. A sudden, awful awareness of the enormous number of human eyes beyond the stage lights disrupted my concentration.

"Your name, sir?" he repeated. "I assume you have one." The audience snickered.

"Uh, Tom Miller," I stammered. The mike stayed pointed at my face while Houlihan directed his attention to the audience as though I were a mere stage prop.

"Mr. Tom Miller, thank you for agreeing to be part of my humble act. Valerie, Jeanine, take the gentlemen's jacket if you would." Houlihan manipulated me so that the stage lights glared even more directly into my eyes. Did he see me? Did he know who I was?

Valerie, a statuesque redheaded construction of cleavage and sequins, moved quickly to my front and deftly unfastened the buttons of my sports coat. Her nimble fingers had no sooner clipped the last button than the unseen Jeanine slipped my coat away. Houlihan, his back to me now, continued to address the expectant audience, explaining the principle of the amazing transformation of which I would be an integral part. I tried to think of a way to position myself in front of him but Valerie grasped my arm and pulled me to the left. Jeanine, meanwhile, directed two men onto the stage pushing a tall, rectangular glass box.

If Houlihan recognized me he was doing a masterful job of disguising it. He continued to work the audience with the same aplomb he had displayed throughout the act. "How many of you," he asked the hushed audience, "would like a new life? A life of drama, intrigue, and romance?" The emphasis on romance provoked feminine tittering.

The house lights darkened and a silky blue spotlight gleamed directly on Houlihan. Valerie held my left hand while Jeanine clutched my right. We were bathed in red. Houlihan continued in a breathy baritone and the audience leaned into his words.

"How many of us yearn for the touch of magic? A flash of sinister danger? A mystery beyond ourselves and the mundane lives we lead? It is possible you know - so very possible.

"I invite you to watch as we give Mr. Tom Miller the magician's caress; a breath of the fantastic - a TRANSFORMATION! Listen to me. Change is for all of us. Change is good. YOU CAN CHANGE IF YOU WANT TO! Witness Mr. Tom Miller!"

Houlihan swirled his cape in my direction. At the signal Valerie and Jeanine hustled me into the rectangular box. With great flourish they closed the glass door and sealed me inside. The murmuring sounds of the stage and audience vanished. Houlihan, still drenched in the shimmering blue light, approached the box. His cape arced and a sharp flash of red satin glittered. There was an explosion of smoke and a brief stab of stark green light. An electric, cobalt blue face glittered for an instant, glaring at me through the glass. The floor of the box became empty space. As quickly as gravity determined I plummeted downward and collided with a slippery sheet of metal angled like a giant sliding board. I rolled and slid helplessly down the smooth slope and tumbled into a cushion of pillows in a dark room.

I sat upright, one hand on the metal sheet, aware of dark silence. My thoughts struggled. This must be part of the act. Any minute now Valerie and Jeanine will appear and whisk me off to a secret entrance to complete the "transformation." It had to be quick, too. The audience could not be kept waiting much longer.

No such thing happened. The darkness and silence continued. I wondered if something had gone wrong and Houlihan was delivering an outlandish explanation to the audience. Maybe I wasn't supposed to fall down here. Any magician's stunt can go bad. Then I remembered the face outside the box just before I began my unexpected descent. To say the least I felt uneasy but in the near total darkness of the place I was in caused me to sit motionless. There had to be a reasonable explanation for this. Minutes ticked by in silence.

A sudden, rapid ripping sound startled me. Yellow light filled the room as a set of heavy curtains parted. Hank

Houlihan stood in a small room smiling at me. "Sorry about the fall, Tom. I trust the pillows broke your fall."

"Lieutenant Henry J. Houlihan," I said.

"That's something I haven't heard in a long time." He laughed merrily.

"Where have you been for fifteen years, Hank - besides playing Harry Houdini?"

"A journey, Tom. Very long journey. Europe, Australia, Asia mainly; learning, trying to figure it all out. And you?"

"I've spent my time fulfilling the oath we took."

"The Army certainly holds grudges."

"Houlihan, stop the crap. What in hell's going on? My wife, not to mention several thousand other people are waiting for me to reappear so let's stop the games."

"Tom, don't even concern yourself with that. You were the grand finale of the act, the most amazing transformation of the night, you should be proud. Of course, I had to use a stunt double to complete your mystical journey, but the audience was amazed anyway. You know how people believe what they see and hear."

"And what about my wife?"

Hank grinned. "Naturally she didn't believe what she saw, Lisa knew it wasn't you. She did, however believe what she heard, that you had a minor injury during the stunt. Valerie distracted her for a while but she's bringing her back here now. You know I'd never do anything to hurt Lisa, Tom. C'mon over here to my dressing room, we've got a lot of catching up to do." He waived me over.

"And why are you going through all this?" I asked as I approached the room, trying to contain my anger.

"I really didn't want to Tom. But I've been watching you in the front row and you appeared agitated. I thought I had better get you up on stage where I could keep you under control. Believe me, it was for your protection not mine. The Army no longer wastes its time tracking down those who left the service on a 'personal' time table and the stage hands would have thrown you out if you made a scene or tried to get backstage. You might have even been arrested; there's a lot of cops on duty out there."

"Personal time table. You mean desertion?"

"Call it what you will."

"You deserted Hank. You left me and a lot of other good people wondering if you were dead or gone over to the other side."

Houlihan removed his cape and smiled broadly. "Tom, I feel no compunction to explain anything to you, I don't live that way. But of all the people I knew back then you were the one man who displayed the greatest glimmer of understanding. You weren't free then, or now, yet you possessed the most potential for it."

He spoke behaved as nonchalantly as if he'd bumped into an old Army buddy and simply wanted to catch up on the old days. What he said was true, however. Even if I returned immediately to the post and reported him to the Provost Marshall nothing would be done. MPs no longer actively pursued AWOLs and deserters, the new strategy is to wait for them to fall into their hands through income tax evasion, a traffic violation arrest, or some other minor irritant. The idea is to let the civilian police force do the leg work.

Hank continued. "I can't give you an apology Tom. Apologies require regret, and I have none."

"Hank, we graduated from the Academy, remember? Four years side by side. Sure you had some crazy ideas, but you were imaginative, soldiers responded to you; I admired you. Why does a West Point educated, intelligent young officer decide to disappear without telling anyone? How can an officer of your intellect and supposed integrity betray the trust of his friends and country and desert? I'd like to know that Hank."

"Fair enough. I'll explain, but I warn you - I may say some things that are disturbing, plant some thoughts that are like an insidious infection, lurking unseen in the body and suddenly coming full bloom at an unexpected moment, just as it did to me; a philosophy I'm not sure you're ready to hear, Tom. Can you handle such a danger?"

Still the Hank Houlihan of old. Mysterious, intellectual, provocative. Fifteen years ago on cold nights overlooking a grim East German border layered in bluish snow Lieutenant Houlihan would voice similar colloquies, his breath hanging in the moonlight. The enlisted men thought he was strange. Most of the other lieutenants did, too. His superiors knew he was working in the ozone. But we all used one common adjective to describe him - intelligent. That was not my opinion at the moment. Disgust would be a far better description. Despite my growing anger I decided to play along, at least until my wife showed up. But with a trilling, leaky drip of suspicion behind all of it.

A knock at the door interrupted us. "Come in Jeanine," Hank said.

Jeanine entered balancing a small tray with two tall, glistening glasses of beer. Like Hank's other companion she was a spectacular sight, a brunette version of sequins, cleavage, and legs; her presence filled the little room. Jeanine's smile was as long and sensuous as the rest of her. "Hello, Mr. Miller," she said. She put the tray down between us, smiled again and left.

"Something to see, isn't she?"

"No argument there."

"Suppose you could have a woman like that Tom, anytime you wanted."

"I would find it rather difficult to face my wife."

Hank lifted his beer and made a motion of a toast.

"Of course," he said. "It's what I'd expect you to say. But what if your lovely wife could never find out, or if she did, what if she was perfectly happy with your rendezvous? Suppose that there were absolutely no adverse consequences, physical, mental, or emotional. Nothing whatever that could bother your overdeveloped conscience."

"Hank," I said. "I don't see how pandering to my fantasies has anything to do with why you deserted the Army."

"It's a metaphor for desire." He raised his glass again and peered into the gold depths. "If you, or most men, could have such a dalliance, without consequence, you would probably succumb. At the minimum, the prospect becomes extraordinarily attractive. You must admit that much."

"Admitted. And your point?" I puzzled as to where this line of reasoning was headed but Hank Houlihan always pointed heresies in a logical direction.

He continued. "I notice Tom, that you still like beer. Most men do."

"Absolutely."

"Then what is it that stops most men from becoming alcoholics?"

"Consequences again."

"Exactly. The cost to job, family, health, is too high. And as much as you like money, you won't rob banks to get it. You'd rather work your entire life rather than steal. It's a matter of morality and consequences."

I could only nod and agree. Hank hadn't said anything I disagreed with so far, but that other shoe was hanging heavily in the air. He stood up and began a directionless pacing about the room, picking up objects at random, regarding them intensely as if they contained some key to his thoughts, then suddenly spinning about into a few quick steps to reach for something else. His mannerisms had changed very little over the years, and as much as I hated to admit it I actually was somewhat intrigued by the discussion.

Hank Houlihan was the only person I ever knew who talked like this. And just like the old days Hank Houlihan had a lot more to say.

"The point is this, Tom. Practically the whole of humanity is animated and driven by these pleasures. Money, power, sex, having the proverbial good time - the entire gamut of sensuous humanity. But the ancients clearly understood that we could not live in a perpetual state of these pleasures, the consequences would be horrendous. Hence morality was born out of consequence. Tell me about conversations with God all you want, the fact remains that there are consequences for all actions, and I believe that holy men understood this above all, regardless of their concept of God.

"So into our world was given morality. And what does morality do? It allows us to pursue these same forbidden pleasures yet do so in a manner that is the least harmful to our fellow humans. Morality is nothing more than the science of consequence dressed up in spiritual language."

"Hank, you've lost none of your talent for articulation," I said. "But I disagree. Spirituality is the foundation of morality. It's real."

He seemed pleased at my rebuff. "Tom, I've missed our conversations in the German snow! Most men would have simply agreed or been too dull to even discuss the concept.

"Morality is the science of consequence, but you are right in that it is the link to spirituality. As you correctly perceive, man is a spiritual being in a world of physical appearances. But we have concentrated so much of our effort on the science of morality that we have become trapped by it. Layer upon layer of rules to live by! The tyrant of consequence has robbed us of our freedom. You must have a job, you must have security, you must have a nice home, you must have clean thought, the list is endless - and stifling.

"Such rules are fine for small children but not for thinking, spiritual adults. We cannot live according to an endless protocol of cause and effect, perceived proprieties and improprieties. Consequences will befall us no matter what we do. But this is the real issue." He shook his index finger to emphasize his point. "Morality without spirit is still a groping struggle for the forbidden fruits, you are enslaved by desire, enslaved by the consequences for giving in to that desire, and enslaved by the consequences of not giving in to the desire. But the truly spiritual man is free, totally free! He embraces consequence, he does not fear it."

Hank looked at me as though I should have grasped some elementary point in his logic.

"So when did you come to this revelation?" I asked. "Was it the morning you committed treason?"

He ignored the jibe. "No, that's when it became too difficult to ignore. My entire life up until that point had been a search for that one truth, Tom. The truth about pure, elemental freedom. It's the thing I've always wanted above everything, even though I could never understand it or articulate it. This unnamed yearning roiled and consumed my thoughts as far as I can remember. I went through high school, West Point, jump school, ranger school, and the Officer Basic Course believing and fearing the morality of my actions. This is good - do it. This is bad - don't do it. I lived like everyone else I knew, precisely as I thought I should.

"As long as I was working or studying or otherwise actively engaged I could live with the underlying despair. But those long nights on the border, standing by an absurd wire perimeter that consumed so many lives, so much time, and energy, forced me to think. There had to be something else. Then I saw the elephants."

"Elephants?"

"It was a night after we had returned from some training exercise. A small circus had come to Fulda and I walked into town to see it. The elephants, those poor, magnificent beasts, were the catalyst that finally pieced it all together. I sat very close to the center stage. I was amazed by their size and power. There were five of the giants, doing all of the usual tricks, standing up, dancing, skipping around the ring. And in the center was a man with a stick in his hand. He wasn't a large man, just an average sized fellow in a spangled blue suit. But he easily controlled five of the most powerful creatures on earth.

"He controlled these beasts because they were afraid of what would happen if they disobeyed. And what would happen? The man would hit them with the stick. That little pin prick of pain, that sudden uncomfortable consequence, filled these enormous monsters with fear, an irrational fear. Any one of them could have squashed the man into pudding the instant it felt like doing so. They possessed tremendous power, yet it was confined and inhibited because they were afraid of a little man and a stick.

"It was the perfect metaphor! We have such potential, such incredible power, amazing abilities, but we are so consumed by the terror of consequences that we do as little as we can to get by. We are trapped by our desires and enslaved by the morality that dictates how we will achieve them.

"Watching those elephants I was seized by a ferocious anxiety. I had been wasting my one precious life drowned in the confining rules of a world that had forgotten the spirit and remembered only the process. I resolved to conduct my life according to my own priorities. The trap was sprung open."

"Doesn't your word mean anything, Hank? As I recall we all took an oath of loyalty. We swore to uphold and defend the constitution of the United States, and we signed a contract with the Army to do exactly that for a specified period of time. A lot of people depended on you to stand by your word. I was one of them. For all we knew you went over the fence and gave the East Germans every one of our defense positions and who knew what else. Are you trying to tell me that your pursuit of personal fulfillment allows you to scrap any kind of commitment simply because you have other things you prefer to do?"

He narrowed his eyes and looked at me for a moment before answering. "Tom, I understand what you're thinking. I have pondered this for twenty years and you've not had twenty minutes. Yes, I raised my hand and swore an oath just like everyone else. But unlike everyone else I kept thinking and asking questions. Would you honor a business agreement if you found out that your partner had withheld vital information?"

"That's not the same thing and you know it Hank."

"You're right Tom, it's worse!" he shouted. "We were asked to give more than money. We were expected to give up our lives and limbs. Since kindergarten we were fed an elaborate illusion of expectations or damming consequences. By design or ignorance, it makes no difference. The result is the same - people robbed of a destiny of happiness and freedom, manipulated into a half life of crippled potential.

"You stand here now with your rank and prestige and education as if it's some great accomplishment. All that shows is that you've obeyed the rules and reaped some rewards. It doesn't mean you're free. You have no concept of true freedom or reality, and probably never will. You get out of bed day after day and do what you think you have to do. Not because you take great joy in it, but because it makes you feel good to think you are accomplishing some higher purpose; serving some great honor. But YOU are the higher purpose, Tom! Try serving that and see what happens.

"The day I learned that simple truth was the day I began to live in true awareness. I have complete responsibility for my life and unlike you Tom Miller I blame no one but myself for the consequences of my actions. And do you know what the consequences have been? I am absolutely and utterly content for the first time in my life. A claim you and the millions like you cannot make."

I suddenly realized Hank's game and that brought me to my feet. He actually was trying to transform me; transform me into what he had become. I was not about to play his game. "You tell me with a straight face that your own selfish priorities outweigh the trust of friends and family? And you actually attempt to explain desertion by some egocentric philosophy of self fulfillment? I'm not impressed, pal. This crap about 'true freedom' is nothing more than pure selfishness; probably cowardice." I was yelling now. "Your philosophy has nothing to do with freedom. From what I hear the whole idea is very simple: screw everybody, Hank Houlihan has things he'd rather do."

"Selfishness has nothing whatever to do with it, Tom. But life, and living it with every cell of your body, does. You said you could handle this and now you make accusations because my life interferes with your preset, hand me down protocols about human behavior. Humans were meant to be happy Tom; supremely, joyfully happy. Not miserable, half awake, settle for what we get stumblers hoping to win the lottery or get that next big break on the winds of chance. We control every bit of the action. Anything you don't like or agree with you can change. That's what I've done with my life. I've changed it according to my prerogatives and I accept full responsibility. No one's been harmed by any of my actions. They may have been infuriated, but brother, I've long since given up on trying to placate egos. I'm the only one who has to live with the consequences."

"Great stuff, Hank. While you were out staying happy a bunch of guys like me stayed and did what had to be done. We brought the wall down and went through two wars afterward. We put our lives on the line and paid the price. But I'm sure that doesn't bother you, does it?"

"Not in the least," he said. "I didn't start those wars."

"CPT Rosenberg was relieved from command thanks to you and had his career and life ruined. Does that bother you?"

"Nope."

"That dozens of soldiers had their leaves cancelled and spent additional months pulling border duty – that bother you?"

"Nope."

"That your fellow officers were confined to the billets and not allowed to even see our families for weeks while your disappearance was investigated?"

"Not at all," Hank said, the smirk never leaving his face.

"Or that your fiancé nearly committed suicide?" I demanded.

"Oh alright, Tom. A lot of things happened after I left. But you're alright and Brenda survived. Stop trying to make me feel guilty because I don't and never will. Like I keep telling you - I accept the consequences for my own actions and my own life, and I'm happier with it than you can ever imagine." He held up his beer, wiggled the glass at me and took a long drink.

"That's enough, Hank. Now, I had better see my wife very soon."

As if on cue a soft knock interrupted us. Hank smiled at me and opened the door. Valerie entered the room. "Your wife, Mr. Miller."

Lisa entered the room and immediately hugged me. I was as greatly relieved to see her as she was to see me. "Are you alright, Tom?" she asked, worry still planted on her face.

"I'm fine, Lisa. I'm not hurt at all, don't worry."

My wife glared at Hank and he quickly launched into an extended apology. "I'm really sorry I had to do things this way, Lisa but I couldn't take the chance of some kind of scene. Tom here could have even been arrested."

Lisa looked back at me. "Fine, let's get out of here" she said.

Hank offered his hand. "I'm very sorry for my little trick, Tom. I hope the bit of chicanery does not cause any lasting hard feelings."

I put down the drink I'd been holding, smiled and reached out to return the handshake. Instead I threw a straight right and sank my fist into Houlihan's face. He careened backwards over a coffee table and sprawled out on the floor. I knocked the table out of the way and delivered a pair of rib breaking kicks. I retrieved my beer and poured it over him. Houlihan did not budge but he was breathing.

I turned to Valerie who was still standing by the door, her mouth open in shock. "When he wakes up," I said, "tell him there's no need to feel guilty, it's just another one of those minor consequences of his actions. But tell him I apologize about the little handshake trick."

I took Lisa by the hand and we quickly walked out of the building by a side exit without looking back. After finding our car in parking lot we discreetly observed it for short while in order to make sure all was safe. Once satisfied that all was clear we jumped in and headed home. As we drove I explained what had occurred after I stepped on stage. There was a piece of the puzzle missing, though.

"Just out of curiosity, Lisa," I said. "What was I "transformed" into as part of Houlihan's big magic act?"

My question provoked an unexpected gale of laughter. She finally stopped and said, "A lamb, believe it or not, a cute little lamb."

That caused me to laugh. "I guess that trick failed."

Lisa leaned over and squeezed my arm. "That's right, darling, you haven't changed one bit."

The littered, urine pungent dead end alley was neither above nor below Buggy Nichols' standards. It was a regular haunt and he'd slept here on several occasions. He pulled his collar up against the cold misty rain and grumbled, but not in real unhappiness. That fresh fifth of Southern Comfort hidden under his jacket would make up for a lot of discomfort. He'd found it on the front seat of a car, still in the brown paper bag, near a window that the owner had courteously left open.

The alley dead ended against a windowless three story tenement. A large, vacant warehouse bordered the left side. A convenient shelter but police knew the building well and routinely rousted transients, and there was no way Buggy was going to share this special treasure with his wino friends. Minus the old warehouse, Buggy's selection was confined to the side that abutted the rear entrances of four businesses. The small diner was hopelessly barricaded. The place had been broken into on several occasions and the owner had installed a reinforced door accessible only by key or dynamite. Likewise with the sports shop next to it. The proprietor of the tattoo parlor had a different solution; his back entrance was supposedly booby trapped with a rigged shot gun. True or not, Buggy declined to test the rumor. At the end of the alley sat his last and only choice, an abandoned used bookstore. To his considerable delight a twist of a rusted knob was the only effort he needed to expend.

He stepped in and closed the door. The bottom floor was long and narrow and dotted with boxes of discarded books that lie haphazardly on the floor. Dust covered, empty shelves lined the walls. "MacGregors used Books" had closed months ago, leaving another hole in the worn out downtown section of the city. Buggy laughed. Like anybody in this town can read. But the deserted book bin suited his purpose. The only drawback was a broad picture window facing the main street. Too easy for someone to look in and see him. Thankfully the building was made in the old, three story style. The second floor contained living quarters for business owners. Floor three served as an attic or room for rental. No one had been foolish enough to live in this section of the city for a long time so the upper floors stayed empty. Buggy groped his way to a stairwell that ran against the far wall.

The bare wooden steps groaned and complained at the intruder disturbing their repose. Buggy leaned against the wall. The other side had no handrail and he did not trust himself in the dark. At the top the stairwell opened to a storehouse of dusty space; long and narrowly constructed like the floor below it but divided into empty rooms. Peering into the silvery gloom Buggy considered the accommodations. Nope. Still too close to the street. Several paces from the end of the stairwell he'd just ascended another, steeper set began. This one had a railing attached to the wall on the right. Buggy grasped the rail and looked up at the dark hole yawning at him from above. Darkness. Perfect – darkness meant privacy. He reached into his pocket and hugged the reassuring hard shape of the paper wrapped bottle.

By the time he got to the top of this flight he was breathing heavily. He leaned against the wall, rested, and squinted into the dark. No partitions here; just a large, attic with slanting walls of rough lumber that made up the underside of the roof. The floor planks were the same rough cut wood and a cold, damp draft permeated the room. But the top floor had a singular advantage - it had just two tiny windows facing the street three stories below.

The floor was strewn with decayed boxes, nameless junk, and scattered, broken pieces of furniture; years of neglected trash silently crumbling in the dark. Buggy contemplated his body rotting away side by side with it. He dwelt on the idea for a while. He did not conceive of himself after death as a flesh and blood thing. No, he thought, I've been trash for so long that I'll just dry up and disintegrate like the rest of this stuff. He wondered if anyone in his family still thought about him. Sooner or later they'd have to, if only in a chance conversation. Yea, my name probably comes up; then everybody frowns and changes the subject to something more pleasant. Someday they'll conclude that I died. But at least by then he'd be a distant unpleasant memory.

Buggy walked to the one of the small windows. His perch looked out over the top of a street lamp that beamed down on a lifeless, empty street, shiny with rain. A mindless traffic light two blocks away provided the only break against the drab dark gray. His breath glittered in gray mist, clouded on the glass pane, and disappeared. The rags he wore did little against the night air. Plenty of drunks had passed out and frozen to death on nights like this. Buggy had bigger plans than that. An old rug or carpet would do yet despite all the trash he couldn't find as much as an old newspaper for cover.

I deserve a little comfort on my last night. Buggy had pondered killing himself for quite a while; the trick was how to do it. The bottle of Southern Comfort provided the answer – even the cover title was perfect. The idea was to drink until he got a good buzz going. This time when the memories came he'd totally immerse in them; no holding back. He'd ratchet it up until the emotions really flooded over and then swill down the bottle to the three quarter empty mark. At exactly that point he'd slash his wrist. After that it was just a matter of drinking slowly enough so the booze replaced the blood and the memories; until the great black whatever washed in and took him away.

Yep, tonight would be the night. Everything was set. All he had to do now was find just the right setting. Buggy continued his examination. At the other end of the attic, barely visible in the dim light, he noticed a small room, perhaps a toilet or tiny bedroom. That might be just the spot, he mused and walked purposely toward it. A white porcelain knob stuck out of a wooden door, leafy with peeling paint. The rusted iron moorings defied him for several minutes before it sprung loose. He yanked the door open and tried to discern the interior of the room but it was too dark. He lit a match. The flickering light revealed a peculiar, diminutive cubicle, approximately four feet across and four feet deep with just enough room for him to stand. A wide sturdy shelf supported by a pair of wooden posts jutted away from the wall on his right. Slanted like an architect's table it supported a monstrously oversized book. A high backed wooden stool faced the front of the book. The tiny room was otherwise barren and a bit warmer than the rest of the place. Perfect.

Buggy regarded the gigantic volume on the shelf. It looked like a monstrous version of an unabridged dictionary and had to weigh over fifty pounds. Whoever used the room obviously wanted to read the thing in absolute privacy. He wondered what kind of reading demanded such secrecy and why the guy had left it here. He pushed the chair out of the way just as the match went out. Darkness reclaimed the little room. As he fumbled for another match something tickled his ear. Buggy quickly swatted at what he thought was a spider or a fly, but his fingers snagged a knotted string. A soft click preceded a shocking burst of light that filled the room. Startled by the unexpected brightness, he yanked the string and shut off the overhead lamp, afraid that the sudden light had revealed his hiding place. But when clicked on the light and shut the door from the outside not even the smallest twinkle of illumination escaped.

He slipped back into the tiny enclosure, took a seat on the stool, drew out the liquor from his coat pocket and removed it carefully it from the wrapper. The cap made a wonderful cracking sound as he twisted it open. He brought the bottle to his lips, swallowed deeply, and raised the bottle to the light. There was nothing like a fresh bottle. Next he pulled out the knife and tested the blade on his thumb. Nothing to do now but sip whiskey and wait. My last night –

perfect! He glanced around the little room. It was almost like his own private pub. He took another pull on the bottle, capped it, and considered the object in front of him again. The curious thing measured more than two feet in length, over a foot across and easily that thick. The polished leather cover reflected a deep mahogany stain. A silver pen in a leather sheath was attached to the cover. Embossed gold letters proclaimed the title:

"THE CORRECTABLE BOOK OF LIFE"

Buggy had no idea what it meant, but it annoyed him just the same. The thing was a distraction. He pushed the book with his free arm. It didn't move a fraction. With great care he replaced the precious bottle in his pocket and tried to lift the book with both hands. The thing stubbornly sat there as though fastened to the desk. Shit! Buggy swilled some more whiskey; a big slug this time, the buzz was not coming fast enough. The dammed book. He pulled out his knife and considered slashing the thing to pieces. Nah; that would take too much effort. And for what, anyway? As big as the book was it'd take forever and all he'd have in return was a little room full of torn paper. He shrugged, cursed, and turned away from the desk. He sat for a minute contemplating the knife he held. The blade was corroded, but sharp and patches of bare metal reflected the gleam of the overhead light. He positioned the blade over the exact spot on his wrist to cut.

But his entire plan rested on achieving just the right mood. Easy, he told himself, easy does it. He downed another mouthful, took a breath, and quietly stared at the barren wall just two feet away. Finally he felt it - the buzz was getting there at last. Buggy held up the bottle and judged the remaining volume of liquid. One quarter of it was already gone! He'd have to slow down a little. Determined to do so he turned around to rest his arms on the desk. The confounded book instantly confronted him. Who could write something like that? Despite his irritation Buggy rubbed his hand across the pebbled cover and embossed letters of the title. He had to admit enjoying the feel of it on his fingers. The pages were trimmed in shiny gold, giving the book a solid, valuable appearance. He turned the cover. The first page had INTRODUCTION written across the top. The text began with no mention of an author, copyright, date, or any of the standard literary trappings. The script was heavy, black gothic written on thin, almost tissue like sheets of surprisingly tough paper. Buggy peered closer. His eyes were not what they used to be.

You have in your hands a remarkable book, perhaps the most remarkable book ever written. The Correctable Book of Life is a compilation of short biographies and events, each highlighting one or more episodes in a selected life. The biographies herein are not a random collection. The recounted incidents have been meticulously selected based on criteria known only to the authors of this book. This book is founded on two important principles:

PRINCIPLE NUMBER ONE

Every life when examined in sufficient detail reveals an incident or incidents that determined the general course of that life from that moment forward. These incidents are classified into two types:

Incidents of Choice and Critical Incidents of Choice

An Incident of Choice is a moment when a decision is made and acted upon. This may be provoked by an external event or an internal emotion. The actual provocation is not important. What is important is the act of the individual based upon that decision. The act brings forth Consequences. Consequences are irretrievable and unpredictable but inevitably provoke further Incidents of

Choice; an endless chain of cause and effect that is the Law of the Universe and the cause of the human condition.

A Critical Incident of Choice results from a number of Incidents of Choice - it is a decision and resultant action that focuses a human life in a particular direction, for good or bad. From this point onward a chain of decisions and acts unfold that drive a person to what is popularly called his or her "destiny."

Incidents of Choice and Critical Incidents of Choice register on the human consciousness in various ways. Many seem totally innocuous, trivial at the time of occurrence, and easily forgotten. Others are obviously momentous and recalled with ease. Others are shades between these extremes. Any single Choice in a person's life, however, has the potential to trigger dramatic consequences. The consciously perceived importance of the event at the time it occurs has no bearing on the impact of the consequences it brings forth. Some events lead to Fortunate Consequences, others to Unfortunate Consequences. The beneficence or detriment of these consequences is very often at odds to what is perceived at the time but that perception is critical because it strongly influences the following decision a person may make in similar circumstances. These results are sometimes disguised so artfully that they are not often recognized as beneficial or harmful until the passage of many years if at all.

The Correctable Book of Life identifies for the reader those Critical Incidents of Choice that caused the irretrievable direction in the course of his or her life. The event that provoked the Critical Incident of Choice is described in such sufficient detail that the reader will definitely recall the event no matter how trivial. Upon reading this singular event the Life Reader relives their decision and behavior of that moment. The recollection of that event then provokes a string of associated memories that manifests in a revelation.

Principle Number 2 – The Nature of Reality

Recollection of past occurrences are not remarkable, of course. But the Correctable Book of life provides the reader a further, very remarkable step - the ability to make corrections. This is accomplished because The Correctable Book of Life uses the principle of Incident of Choice leading to Inevitable Consequence to affect a new outcome: a different life than the one currently experienced.

An important distinction and explanation must be made for the reader. The book does not change the events of the past or the consequences of the past. Past events are unchangeable. The consequences spawned are irretrievable. Yet change in the present and the future life is dramatic and fully discernible.

The thoughtful reader rightly asks: How is the present transformed if neither the past action nor its consequences are altered? This is the second principle and ultimate foundation of Correctable Book of Life: The Nature of Reality. Prior to and following the Incident of Choice exists an infinitely more powerful moment - the Incident of Thought. Thought is not just the seat of all reality – for humanity it is the only reality. All else in the entire universe is an illusion of appearance colored by sense perception. Only thought – the precursor of all creation - is real for the human condition. And the human condition is EMOTION. Thought dictates emotion, emotion dictates decision. Humans make decisions to bring happiness into their life. Changing thought at any time results in change to emotion and therefore to present and future reality.

How to Use This Book

Using this work is a simple process. The table of contents lists the names of selected lives. The user, referred to as a Life Reader, locates his or her name and turns to the appropriate page. Each life history begins with an introduction briefly recounting the Life Reader's current status. A various number of chapters follow, each highlighting a Critical Incident of Choice in that particular life and the consequences of that choice. At the conclusion of each chapter the Life Reader will find a short space under the heading: I SHOULD HAVE. The Life Reader has the option of entering a different decision than the one previously chosen or leaving the space blank. A different decision – a different thought – effects change. The Life Reader, of course, has the option of not making any entry, thus choosing acceptance of the status quo. As a convenience to the reader Critical Incidents of Choice are written in red.

A final note before proceeding: Think carefully before you answer.

Buggy reflected on the passage. I don't know who wrote this thing, he thought, but the guy had one hoot of an imagination. He turned to the table of contents. Starting on the left, in small print, were rows of alphabetical lists. Thousands upon thousands of names. To the right of each name a page number was listed. Buggy found the concept fascinating. The author had compiled an astounding list; it looked like a phone directory for the whole country. Buggy didn't believe it for a minute of course. He knew a scam when he saw one but the concept was irresistible. He peeled back page after page until he finally arrived at the Ns and found the series that began with the name Nichols. Scrolling down from that point he came to an amazing entry:

NICHOLS, ROBERT PAUL.........................8,990

His flesh pimpled. The entry was undeniably him. How had they gotten his name? It ain't in the phone book. Wait a minute. A lot of people around this stinking town know my name. Okay, let's see what kind of scam this guy's running. He pulled back a handful of oversized pages and turned them over. Two more handfuls and he was almost there. He began flipping individual pages. 8,885...8,886...8,887... 8,888...8,889.... With meticulous care he slipped his fingers under the final page and silently turned it over. For a while he stopped breathing.

ROBERT PAUL NICHOLS

Robert Paul Nichols, also known by the detested nickname "Buggy." At this writing you are a fifty seven year old white male, approximately fifty pounds overweight for your 70 inches in height, down one and one half inches from your maximum at this writing. You are the first of three children and the only boy of your immediate family, born 9 January 1940 in Ricetown, New Jersey. Your hair is gray, filthy, and exceedingly thin at this point, but was at one time dark brown. Your eyes are blue. The nickname "Buggy" is in response to a tendency to laugh for no apparent reason after consuming too much alcohol.

You were a bright child born to loving parents, and you had fine dreams of accomplishment at one time. You were an intelligent, athletic, fine looking adolescent with school grades adequate enough to get you into the college where you met the woman who would become your wife and later leave you. Several years after this your promising potential degenerated into homelessness and alcoholism, dependency on handouts, and occasional stints as a laborer or dishwasher. You are not, however, above theft or other degradations to acquire alcohol.

Buggy straightened in the stool, violently startled. In just two paragraphs a bunch of merciless black letters had spelled out the sum total of his life. He wiped the water streaming from his eyes and read the awful passage again. No mistake. How?

Robert Paul Nichols. Something heavy rolled in his chest at the sight of his full name. Years had passed since he had seen it written like that. No one knew Robert Paul

205

Nichols. He was Buggy. He recalled the day he had become associated with the despised label. That moron bartender, Jimmy Rill, he's the one did it to me. Started calling me that one day - and after I spent good money in that place. He vowed to never again enter Jimmy Rill's, but he did anyway. Jimmy wasn't really a bad guy. Not that it would have made any difference; the damage had been done. He'd become Buggy Nichols. Robert Paul had vanished a long time ago anyway. He read further.

CRTICAL INCIDENT OF CHOICE NUMBER ONE:

Recall this day Robert. It is raining. You are eight years old and playing with a friend in the basement of his family home on Rosewood Street. Your friend's name is Ronnie Salzman. You are playing a board game with him called "Escape the Skeezix." The "Skeezix" is a peculiar, lizard like creature that chases pieces about the board. The object is to maneuver your piece around the board without being overcome by the monster. For some reason Ronnie is extremely good at the game; he defeats you almost every time you play it with him. This day will have the same result, but with one important exception. You spin the arrow and move your piece the appropriate number of spaces away from the Skeezix. Ronnie spins the wheel and moves his piece. You then spin the wheel and move the Skeezix. It lands midway between your piece and Ronnie's. Ronnie then spins. The monster is allowed to advance five spaces. Ronnie, however, seizes the Skeezix and moves it six paces ahead where it overtakes your piece sending it back to the start point. You protest that he has moved the monster incorrectly. He ignores you and when you attempt to prove his error, Ronnie spins the wheel again and begins to move his piece. This transgression provokes your sense of fairness and you protest more loudly than before. Ronnie tells you to shut up, get out, and go home. You accede, continue to play the game and lose. Ronnie and you remain friends but he always teases you about the Skeezix.

Think carefully before you answer.

I SHOULD HAVE:

How in the hell was that a critical moment in life? "Stupid book!" Buggy shouted. But just as quickly the short passage jolted him as the odd little incident jumped back into his mind. How did the stupid book know? He remembered the incident clearly; for some reason the memory of that game with Ronnie had popped up a few times. Each time he saw a children's board game he thought of it. Sometimes rain on a window provoked the recollection. He couldn't think of an obvious reason, yet the Skeezix remained, unexpectedly jumping up from somewhere. Thanks to the foolish thing he'd never forgotten Ronnie Salzman either. But then, so what? Why in earth is a stupid game I played fifty years ago such a critical choice? What was I supposed to do at seven years old? Yet there was the incident, written down exactly as it occurred all those years ago. It was unnerving, and now it blossomed into his mind again. Ronnie Salzman, a big, overweight guy, two years older than young Robert. He still clearly pictured Saltzman and his bushy red hair perched on his knees on the other side of the board. Then the Skeezix appeared. Angular and covered in blue scales the beast had a giant red mouth crowded with sharp, dagger teeth and long claws. The idea of the hideous thing chasing you could provoke nightmares. Ronnie flicked the arrow with his index finger. The thin strip of black metal became a blur of motion and scratching noise as it spun on the smooth laminated cardboard. It landed on the 5! Ronnie grabs the Skeezix, but moves his piece six spaces. Robert sees the action and knows he is being wronged.

"I should have won" Buggy muttered, surprised to still feel resentment. What was I supposed to do? He pondered the problem and looked at the bottle of liquor sitting on the small desk shelf, the effects of it by this time causing just enough muddle to freeze him into inaction. This was complete bullshit! Yet he was afraid to answer the question. Puzzled, irritated, and more than a little unnerved Buggy returned to the book.

CRITICAL INCIDENT OF CHOICE NUMBER TWO:

This time, Robert, you are thirteen years old and have pronounced interests in life, but one stands above all. It is a peculiar attraction, uniquely your own: Ants. No one can explain the odd preference; your parents are puzzled. But they are proud of your unusual knowledge about them. They even cater to your interest by buying books about the subject for you. Your room is home to a varied and growing collection of various sized glass containers and commercial "science kit" ant farms. You find something incredibly wondrous about the incessant activity of these little creatures. In your room you sit hour by hour, doing nothing more than staring intently at their relentless energy. Do you remember that enthralling sensation? One day something extraordinarily odd happens. You are sitting in your room alone, intently observing the activity of your favorite insect in one of the large glass jars. But you do something different that day. You put down the magnifying glass and place your ear tightly against the jar - and you hear something.

Think carefully before you answer.

I SHOULD HAVE:

For an instant, Buggy went dizzy. The carefully
crafted words mingled with the yellow light above his head.
He drifted back to his little boy room and once more fell to
the fascination of his tiny arthropod friends. A peculiar odor
tweaked his nostrils, an odor of fresh soil, grass, and traces of
whatever had been in the glass jar previously. Ah, my
wonderful ant collection! I did like doing that, he thought. It
was… peaceful.

Buggy's eyes returned to the page and ended the
reverie. What should I have done? There was nothing to be
done. He had done it, hadn't he? He'd played with ants as a
kid. He liked it a lot. The ants made him feel special, like he
held some esoteric knowledge that others did not possess; a
separate private part of himself no one else could access.

What had become of all those jars? They drifted
suddenly away, just as their strange magic inexplicably and
suddenly evaporated. The magic faded in the new
neighborhood. Buggy remembered the loneliness of the first
few weeks and how he took refuge by immersing himself
even deeper into his ant study. One sunny day in summer,
however, he went to the corner drug store to buy a comic

book. He met a boy named Eddie. Eddie had many friends and he introduced Robert to all of them. For the first time in weeks Robert had friends, boys his own age he could talk to. He invited Eddie over to his home.

Robert immediately displayed his ant collection.

"This is stupid," Eddie said. "Why do you like this stuff? This is weird, man." Suddenly the ants were not so attractive; they were a little embarrassing. But why didn't he just tell Eddie to go to hell? He liked ants. So what? Eddie liked fishing. Robert didn't make fun of that. Robert did not let go of his ants, but he learned to keep his hobby secret.

Nothing else was written after the second Critical Incident of Choice. Buggy slipped to the next page but saw the biography of someone else. Suspecting that the last user of the book had ripped out some of his pages he checked the page numbers. But no, the next page was numbered in exactly the right sequence. He was profoundly disappointed. "A couple of stupid little kid things," Buggy grumbled. "How can this crap change a person's life?" He swilled more Southern Comfort and grumbled. "I could understand if they'd written about my first drink or something. Even my first wife. Hah! There was a life changing event." Evelyn launched into his mind. How could a woman look so beautiful one day and so ugly a couple of years later?

No remarriage. Evelyn had extinguished that desire. She extinguished the idea of seeing his son, too. But the truth was that Robert really did not want custody. He wanted freedom. And the divorce granted it. Even after the alimony payments he had enough money to get by on. Never had to worry about booze, either. He was a distributor and a salesman of the stuff. Life was fun. He felt reborn. One day, several years later, he woke up wrapped around a bottle instead of a woman. Not long afterward his profession went the way of Evelyn and the rest of his family went the way of everything else. Maybe that's why there were only two things in the book. There wasn't much else worth writing about. It all happened so fast! One day I'm a kid looking at ants and the next I'm alone in an abandoned building.

In his alcohol altered mind Buggy's childhood little sister appeared; chubby, pink faced and blond. Not quite two years old Debbie used to push herself around in a little wheeled contraption visiting everyone's room. Robert's ant collection fascinated her. Every night she'd roll into his room and point her little finger at the glass containers. "Ants," she'd say. "Ants." And every night young Robert would look up from his studies and patiently answer, "Yes, Debbie those are ants." She always looked at him afterward as though Robert was supposed to do or say something else. He was never sure what but he used to go on and expound about various ant species and their peculiar behaviors. Pretty soon his sister would wheel herself out of the room and young Robert would return to his books. He thought about the last time he'd seen Debbie. Lots of guys have wives that throw them out. Lots of kids disdain their father. But you know you've really screwed up when your little sister gives up on you.

He swilled more whiskey and looked at the book. But by now the letters had melted away; he could no longer read them. A dark confusion engulfed him. On top of everything else he was now delusional. Hah! Now he'd really earned the name Buggy! A book to change your life. Right. Yet it had seemed so real. He recalled how it felt to his fingers. He remembered the words. It was exactly his life. An alcoholic's delusion? Sure was a realistic one. The biography had his life down perfectly. Buggy pictured the letters that Robert Paul Nichols spelled out on the page. A handsome name for a handsome boy. Yea, that was me.

The book – the imaginary book – said it had happened when he had given up the ants. The thought crossed his mind bitterly. I was just a kid, dammit! What the hell was I supposed to do? There was nothing to do! It was a kid's hobby; there was no I Should Have moment about it. Okay, I shoulda told Eddie to hell and kept my ants. He cursed himself for thinking about the book. He filled his mouth with liquor, swirled it with his tongue, and swallowed hard.

He felt the surge of alcohol reach deep into him. Enough of the damned fairy tale book. He groped for the knife and yanked it out of his pocket. One small slice; a straight little cut, and then just ride the rest of the bottle to an eternal rest. There's an incident they can put in the book! He fumbled to open the blade, but could not do it with one hand. Even when I go to kill myself I can't put the bottle down. He tried to place it on the table, but the surface was too slanted. With the folded jackknife in one hand and the bottle of Southern Comfort in the other he pushed himself to his feet intending to slide to the floor and finish his life there. He promptly tripped and fell. Like all drunks Buggy passed out as soon as his head hit the floor.

But sleep, the great healer and comfort of man, did not allow its balm. The book and its cryptic dark print swirled and jumped up at him, persistent as a giant dog with exasperating, unwanted affection. It nudged and pushed like a dog, too. The book even became a dog. Buggy recognized it, too. It was the giant brown and white mutt with a gold muzzle he'd had as a kid. Towser was the dog's name. He was like a cross between a Saint Bernard and a brown bear. No one even remembered why the stray had such a ridiculous name, he was just Towser, and that was that. The book had become Towser. Robert could never get rid of the dog. It was an ugly mutt that slobbered all the time and it embarrassed him. No matter how fast he ran, rode his bicycle, or hid, Towser always found him. One day he finally just gave up and let the dog have its way. He grew to love the thing.

When Towser died young Robert's grief knew no bounds. His parent tried to bribe him with a new puppy, but he would have none of that. Another dog was a betrayal. For days afterward Robert sat in his room grieving for his lost floppy eared friend. That was when he discovered the ants. He was sitting on the edge of his bed when a large black ant flew in the window and landed beside him. He'd seen these ants before, of course, but this one was different. This one had wings. Robert watched as the ant prowled around on his bedspread. He picked the insect up and dropped it in the soil of a large potted geranium his mother had put in his room. The winged ant then did an astounding thing. After probing the soil for a while it found a small depression in the dirt. It settled into the depression, calmly tore off its wings, and ate them.

Young Robert became engrossed. What was the thing doing? Later he learned that he had witnessed a female ant in the very first stage of building a colony. She mates in the air, lands, and searches for a suitable nesting place in order to begin laying eggs. Her only nourishment is the very wings upon she they flew to that spot, since up to that point she has no colony to gather food. Robert was riveted. Ants became his instant favorites. They were cold blooded and mechanical, as un-puppy like as anything could be. No betrayal to Towser at all. In a way Towser had led him to the ants.

He may have lived in a New Jersey suburb that was hardly a natural history paradise, but that made no difference to the ants. Robert easily found dozens of species and thousands of ants. His room filled with his collection. He watched them endlessly, fascinated by their relentless, never ending activity. He'd scoop up hundreds or thousands with a small shovel and dump them into a glass container. At first there was mass chaos as the little things scrambled about terrified and confused at the monstrous upheaval. Within hours, however, they miraculously organized themselves back into a perfectly coordinated working colony.

Construction of tunnels, dens, and eggs chambers was swiftly underway.

The dream took him into deeper memory, sitting in his room peering at a group of small brown ants through the side of a glass jar with a magnifying glass. He has an odd idea. He puts down the magnifying glass and places his ear tightly against the side of the glass.

It was a moment he never forgot. The ants were making noises! At first he thought he was hearing things. He reared back and looked again at the Lilliputian city. They naturally had taken no notice of the gigantic ear that had suddenly blotted out the light in their miniature world. The frenetic labor of tunnel construction and nest building continued. Robert again placed his ear on the side of the glass. And once again he heard the same amazing thing – thousands and thousands of tiny, barely audible screeching sounds, as though each individual ant in the colony was calling out to the other in some bizarre, unknown language.

He was electrified by his discovery! Nowhere in any of the literature or any of his studies had he ever read about ants having a language. Again and again he placed his ear to the side of the glass jar. The eerie sound was unmistakable – the ants were speaking to each other!

Hearing ant language and convincing others of the discovery were two different propositions, however. Robert's parents supported his obsession with ants, but this new development was worrisome. "You're not talking to them, are you son?" his father asked nervously.

Robert replied with teenaged patience. "No, Dad. But what if it was possible to learn their language? The answer did not reassure his parents. No one, in fact, was reassured about a boy who claimed ants had a language, least of all Robert's friends who howled with laughter when he explained his discovery. By the time entered high school he was known as "Ant Boy." The name was inevitably accompanied by forefingers on either side of his tormentor's head to represent antenna. Robert learned not to mention ants. By the time he was a high school senior his Formicidean friends were a memory. Like every other teenager in the world he wanted to fit in, not stand out.

Buggy jolted awake, vision of his childhood room and the gleaming jars still vivid. He tried to push the picture away. But the vision would not fade. He groped for the knife. He found it lying on the floor beside him. He grabbed at it and this time opened it quickly. The blade snapped out ready to do its work. The bottle of Southern Comfort stood upright just out of his reach. Several good swallows of booze remained in the bottle which had surprisingly stayed upright despite Buggy's fall. He leaned over, grabbed the bottle and dragged it close. "A swallow and a slice," he said aloud.

He brought the lip of the bottle to his mouth. With his right he placed the blade on his left wrist. Drink, slice, swallow. Even a drunk like me can manage this. His hand and lips burned in stinging, ragged fire. He screamed at the unexpected pain. The cut of the knife was not supposed to be so painful. He'd somehow managed to tear open his lip, too. He pulled the bottle away and saw wriggling trickles of blood oozing down his arm. The blood moved oddly and burned as it leaked along the length of his arm. He rubbed at the burning in his lips and focused his eyes on his wrist. But the blood was not blood. The blood was ants, thousands and thousands of them. While Buggy had wallowed in delirium the tireless scouts of a colony of little brown ants had found the treasure of sweet liquor and had instantly alerted the rest of the colony.

He scrambled to his feet and stumbled out of the little room. The entire top floor blossomed in sunlight that slanted in from the front windows. The beams marked a pair of bright yellow rectangles on the opposing wall and transformed dust into sparkle across the length of the attic.

He stared and blinked, and then walked to the front of the attic. Buggy Nichols had not seen a sunrise in a long time.

He stumbled back into the small room, grasped the pen and turned to his own biography. "I should have stayed with the ants,' he wrote, "in fact, I will. And I'll never back down from anybody."

Buggy carefully left the building and walked out into the sunlight knowing exactly where he wanted to go. When he at last got to the public library it was closed so he waited outside. But the time was not wasted. There was a large grassy area behind the building, and it was inhabited by thousands of ants. closely inspecting his old friends. They returned the favor by delivering instant fascination to their observer. Childlike wonder returned to his heart.

"Alright, you. What are doing?"

The authoritative voice was startling. Buggy rose to his feet as quickly as he could and came face to face with a policeman.

"Oh, I'm sorry, officer. I was observing ants."

The cop frowned and shook his head. "Observing ants. That's a new one."

"No really," Buggy said. I was waiting for the library to open so I could study the latest research on these animals."

"The library opened two hours ago," came the flat response. "Now stop this bullshit about ants and get outta here."

"Can't I go into the library, officer? I just lost track of time, is all."

"Nope get out of here. You've already scared enough people in there that's why they called me."

"Officer, my name is Robert Paul Nichols and I have a passion for observing and studying ants. I will prove it to you." Robert Paul Nichols then launched into a detailed and authoritative lecture about the species he had seen, the unique qualities of their behavior, and their effect on the library lawn.

Surprised and amused at the stubbornly dignified and knowledgeable gentlemen in front of him the policeman was impressed. "C'mon, Mr. Nichols. I'll escort you to the library and explain what you were doing out here."

Sally MacGregor grasped her cell phone and dialed her father. "I found it, Dad. Right here where you said it would be."

"Great, Sally. Bring it by when you can, alright?"

"Sure, Dad. Something's kind of odd, though. Somebody's been in here. There's broken bottle of whiskey on the floor and an old knife. They scribbled something on the bible, too."

"Oh no! That bible has been in the family for years. It's not destroyed, is it?"

"No dad. Except for the few small scribbles it looks fine."

I got off the plane in Riyadh, Saudi Arabia full of hopes for a desert sky blazing with stars. My flight ordained an evening landing and in a short sleeved shirt I was dressed for the heat. Sure, I froze in the plane, but the discomfort would be worth it. Let those fools from the states deplane while still in their sweatshirts – I was prepared. I stepped onto the gangway eagerly anticipating the embrace of warmth. I was embraced alright, by a windy fifty four degrees on the Fahrenheit scale and an over cast sky – the same weather I left in Seattle twenty hours four ago. There was to be no relief from the cool weather and no starry desert sky. Who did this to me? But the silver lining to this particular late December landing was that just about everyone in the Kingdom was in Jeddah on the annual Hajj. Had they not been over there circling and praying I'd have had a much more difficult time getting through customs. As it was I sailed through.

I walked past a fountain the size of Mount Rainier and headed to the baggage claim area for Saudi Airlines. The crowd was mostly Saudis with a good number of Westerners mixed in. Besides the wardrobe it was easy to tell the Westerners from the Saudis. We were the one getting impatient after just thirty minutes of waiting for their bags. Forty five minutes later an alarm did sound and the carrousel began to move. After ten more minutes of watching this circular farce our bags actually began to appear.

My business is military. I'm a retired soldier, twenty five years in the King of Battle – Field Artillery. Yes, I can still hear, but speak loudly. Ha Ha. I was hired as part of a contract with a Saudi-American conglomerate to advise the Saudi National Guard in my area of expertise. My job was to head up a team of former artillery guys. Good money, and most of it non-taxable, too because we actually work for the Saudis. I'd spent most of my career in Asia so the Middle East was a new experience for me.

Despite all the horror stories customs was no problem at all and I sailed through. A driver was waiting in the lobby holding a handmade sign with the company's name and in no time myself and four other hired workers were loaded into a mini-van and ready to go. Our driver, a diminutive fellow in a blue suit, pumpkin pie complexion, and effervescent personality introduced himself as Jaleel and hit the gas. As he narrowly avoided parked cars and the concrete columns of the parking garage he regaled us with warnings about how reckless most of the drivers in Saudi Arabia were. "You are not being unsafe with me," he assured us. "I am from India and we are driving the safest."

By the time we hurtled through the parking garage we had exceeded fifty miles per hour, but Jaleel had managed avoid colliding with numerous obstacles such as the large DO NOT ENTER sign hanging over the lane he drove in. I began to suspect that there was a tad more Arabian recklessness in our chauffeur than he admitted to.

With a cloud covered sky overhead and temperatures more fitting for Norway I gave up all hopes of my vision of a star crammed desert sky. I had more immediate concerns – my life. Jaleel, while continuing to insist that he was the safest driver in the in the entire Kingdom of Saudi Arabia and the greater part of the Middle East, treated us to a harrowing ride through the streets of Riyadh. My inquiries concerning the red lights that he always managed to run was inevitably answered by the explanation, "I am being very sorry, Boss. I am thinking that light was being yellow." I was thinking he was making my bladder very loose. We safely arrived at the company compound, however, where Jaleel gave us a stern warning not to backtalk the Pakistani gate guards before proceeding in. Good advice to follow. Back talking armed gate guards has never been my forte.

It must have been a great disappointment to Jaleel to decelerate at the security entrance, but I took the opportunity to massage my heart out of my throat. Five armed and uniformed security guards converged on the car like ants on a jelly doughnut and checked every square inch of it. IDs were checked and rechecked. Each of us gave our temporary badge number and carefully spelled our names. Everything was duly noted in pen on a sheet attached to a clipboard by a man who appeared to be the head guard. He waved us forward and the big red and white iron pole blocking our way was raised by another guard with help from a large counter weight.

Driver Jaleel came back to life as he slalomed through twelve alternating concrete barriers missing each by two micrometers. At the end of these barriers we were met by another, albeit smaller, contingent of guards who directed us forward into a canvas garage that hovered over an open pit. Once over the pit we stopped while one guard inspected the undercarriage of the vehicle, another inspected the outside, and a third collected our names and badge numbers again. Apparently some exceptionally clever individuals had in the past been able to change identities during the slalom between the barriers. We were not so dexterous so our identity cards were exactly the same forty feet later. Several more concrete barriers and three gates later we were in the compound. I was feeling better about this job all the time. NOT!

Jaleel dropped me off in front of my quarters where I was met by my sponsor. Mike Roberts' most notable feature was the cigarette that hung like a permanent fixture from the left side of his mouth, and his baseball cap. Affectionately nicknamed Rattlesnake Roberts for his apple pie personality, I found out later that he actually did remove the tobacco and hat during extended periods of sleep. For short naps and all other breathing moments these accouterments remained in place.

Rattlesnake lived up to his nickname immediately. "Welcome to Rydell Corporation, sir," he said. "You really got screwed on this room they gave you." He extended his hand. "Joe Doyle," I said. "Pleased to meet you." I went to shake his hand, but realized he was only handing me the villa keys. I fumbled with them while Rattlesnake looked on impatiently. From the outside, although it was dark, the place did not look bad. A one story, beige concrete building landscaped with a bedspread sized front lawn and palm tree. I didn't expect the king's quarters. When I got the door open Rattlesnake found the light switch and saved me from further fumbling in the dark. He gave me a quick tour of the living room and kitchen. Judging from the week old cookies laying on the coffee table, the moldy bread scattered about the kitchen, and an unidentifiable, objectionable odor, I was not billeted with Martha Stewart.

"Your villa mate's on vacation," Roberts explained. "Looks like he ate before he left."

"You think," I said.

Rattlesnake then beckoned me to follow him down a hallway through a layer of ankle deep dust. My room appeared cleaner than the rest of the villa, but this turned out to be an illusion of the 40 watt bulbs that brightened the room like a penlight with a worn out battery.

"If you want something to eat there's a sandwich in that bag on the dresser and there's water in the refrigerator." Rattlesnake's tone told me that he had had enough of playing the concerned sponsor.

"I've got everything I need, Mike. Thanks for the help." He left and I settled into the silence.

Out of curiosity I opened the sandwich bag. Technically, yes, it did contain a sandwich. Generally, however, most sandwiches contain more than a single slice of hot bologna laced with mayonnaise. A blue foil wrapper that contained four potato chips provided the remainder of the meal. I set down to eat. Seconds later, my stomach bursting from this hearty feast, I pulled what little I had from my suitcases and filed my goods into several dusty drawers. A minute later and I was asleep between dusty sheets. I had a lot to do in the morning.

A loud, awful caterwauling snapped me awake. I suspected some kind of territorial mating war between feral cats that populated the compound, but I was wrong. It was the Islamic evening call to prayer broadcast from one of the twenty or so mosques that surrounded the Rydell compound. Jet lag then conveniently settled in and I couldn't sleep so I trolled around the quiet villa wondering why my life had become sleepless in Saudi at the age of fifty. Most of my peers were probably sleeping peacefully within the bosom of family, or at least some kind of bosom.

But my circumstances were no mystery. Military life has an insidious side effect, you see. No matter how badly you longed to settle down in that nice neighborhood in the big house with the white picket fence; no matter how cold the nights were or how hot the days, or how terrified while diving to escape a mortar strike – no matter what - at the end of the day you loved it. Put a career military man anyplace for more than a year or two and he'll get bored. Soon he's trolling the internet for defense contractor jobs and dreaming of adventure again. Couple this with my own relentless natural curiosity about the world and there I was.

After a long night and a good twenty minutes of sleep I awoke to a phone call from Rattlesnake. I was to be picked up in a half hour. Instead of going in later to meet my crew, I'd been selected to consult with a Saudi artillery battalion for fire support training in some place called Haffoof. "Some Army officer over there saw your resume and specifically asked for you," Roberts explained. "Says he really needs you there today for some meeting he managed to set up." Wonderful. But seeing as how this was my first day on the job I figured I'd at least give it a try before I quit. Feeling like I'd been dragged through a sandy keyhole I willed myself out of bed, struggled into the shower, emerged in time to throw on some clothes and pile into a ragged SUV driven by the indefatigable Jaleel. With a neck snapping jolt we were off.

I finally got a glimpse of the Kingdom of Saudi Arabia in the unvarnished daylight, but most of what I saw here on the outskirts of Riyadh looked like dirty concrete and dirty cars. Glimpse, considering Jaleel's fondness for the accelerator, was an appropriate word, but I took in what I could. We left the compound and careened through a parking lot of sorts that served what appeared to be an apartment complex in the middle of several half finished construction projects. The cars were parked in a fashion similar to the aftermath of a demolition derby. This did not, of course, remotely faze Jaleel. He attacked the lot with the same gusto as he did a traffic light - as a challenge to his driving prowess. In no time we the haphazard parking lot was behind us.

At the edge of the lot we turned right, miraculously squeezing in between a cement truck and a racing taxi yet emerging unscathed. The scream of the taxi driver's horn let us know his opinion of Jaleel's skill with an automobile, but Jaleel was unimpressed by this rude gesture. Much to my distress it actually seemed to exhilarate him. He plunged his foot deeper into the accelerator. The cab driver took up the challenge and a ferocious race to the next traffic light was enjoined; this one thankfully just several blocks away or I feared these Middle Eastern madmen might race right off into the desert.

When we came to a brake squealing halt at the light the man behind the wheel of the taxi seemed to have triumphed as I noticed that Jaleel had clicked on the left turn signal. We were in the far right lane so I assumed that he'd let the taxi move ahead before attempting to turn. But I underestimated my resourceful driver. The instant the light changed to green Jaleel introduced me to the infamous "Saudi Sweep," a left hand turn from the far right lane. With superior reflexes, steel band nerves, and complete disregard for laws, physics, or gravity Jaleel cut off the driver attempting to follow the normal course of the middle lane and even managed to eclipse the taxi by diving back into the left lane in front of him after he made the turn. I could tell by the beaming smile on his face that he was exceptionally proud of his maneuver. Pride did not describe my emotion or the adrenaline that rocketed up my spine at nearly the same speed as Jaleel's driving.

Shrewd fellow that he is Jaleel noticed the enlarged size of my pupils. "Don't be thinking that is so bad driving, Mr. Joe," he explained. "This turning in Saudi Arabia is the correct and proper way for a skillful driver. I am understanding that they do not do this in America. Is that right?"

"Jaleel, they don't do that anywhere else in the world."

"Oh, then I am thinking that we are very fortunate to be able to do that here. It is saving much time."

I began to suspect my Indian friend enjoyed my terror. We tore down a street that I estimated as four lanes in our direction. The Saudi drivers estimated differently. The four lanes occasionally became six or seven lanes; dividing lines did not seem to impress anyone. Intersection red lights, where such innovations existed, stimulated a profound sense of challenge as each driver competed with the other in an effort to find the most innovative way to run through it. We finally cleared the traffic congested part of the city before my muscles began to tear away from my bones and tendons. We were soon on a reasonable semblance of a highway.

"How far away is Haffoof, Jaleel?" I asked.

"Not very far, boss. Maybe three hours, but it is perhaps being so that I can make it there in many less time."

"No, Jaleel!" I nearly screamed. "Three hours is just fine."

We rolled on across a monotonous landscape of sand, scrub, lightly swelling hills and rising heat. From one horizon to the other I saw nothing but sand and rock. The only thing that broke the bleak landscape was a Bedouin mounted on a camel. Like something from a movie he stood by the side of the road, a picture from the past waiting to cross the highway so he could be on his way back into the endless desert. He was an incongruously amazing sight.

Outside of that and some of the filthiest truck stops on earth the place looked a definition of the word bleak. It had warmed up considerably from the night before and I imagined what it would be like to be stranded out there under a truly blazing sun. You wouldn't last long. I almost considered asking Jaleel to speed it up a bit, but that was an action probably riskier than getting stranded in the desert. True to his word, though, Jaleel held to a steady speed and delivered me safely to Haffoof in three hours. There, at the headquarters building of the Saudi National Guard I was met by my host, one of the US active duty military advisors to the Saudi Army. Wearing the inevitable sunglasses and the new computer camouflage designed Army uniform he looked like the typical career oriented young field grade officer. But the shaved bullet head and bodybuilder physique turned out to be a front for an affable young man at home anywhere in the world.

"Major Brian Paulson," he said, "pleased to meet you, sir."

"Joe Doyle," I said. We shook hands. I told Jaleel he was free to go for the rest of the day. He smiled with mischievous delight. I could only imagine the terror he'd cause cruising the streets of Haffoof once freed of his cautious human cargo. He drove away and Major Paulsen offered to introduce me to the Saudi officers I was to train and take me on a tour of the area. We climbed into a superbly air conditioned and comfortable Ford Expedition and hit the road. After Jaleel's battered SUV the new Expedition was a dream.

First stop was the headquarters of the Saudi Army National Guard 2nd Field Artillery Battalion. The commander, Lieutenant Colonel Ali Al-Omari was a short, intense man a with heavy beard. Through LTC Ali's interpreter Brian introduced me. We immediately joined by a young Saudi sergeant holding an ornate silver coffee pot on a tray. He poured the coffee into a thimble sized cup and offered it to me with a bowl of sticky dates. Arabian coffee is not as thick even as American brew and has a slightly greenish hue; it has a unique, somewhat bitter taste, but goes very well with the sweet dates so popular in the Kingdom.

We exchanged pleasantries, sipped coffee and ate dates and maintained the pace of this ritual for about twenty minutes. Understanding the Saudi custom for proper social amenities before business I stifled my impatience, knowing that we would get down to business at the conclusion of the coffee and dates. But no sooner had I waved off the fifth cup of coffee than another young soldier appeared, this time holding a tray of tea served in small glass cups. My bladder at this point had begun to remind me that it had long ago reached full capacity and the last thing I wanted or needed was another diuretic. Diplomacy prevailed, however, and I consented to further refreshment.

The tea sipping ritual did not, thankfully, last quite as long as the coffee and dates routine, but we had now been in the office for nearly an hour. Just then LTC Ali looked at his watch and delivered a long statement to his interpreter. With relief I sensed that the time to discuss business had finally arrived. And not a minute too soon. My bladder was as the point of combustion. I mentally readied myself to deliver the training sales pitch I had prepared.

The interpreter turned to me and said, "LTC Ali wishes for me to inform you that he is very happy to make your acquaintance and looking forward to working with you. Unfortunately, he has a very important meeting that he must attend. Is it all right to meet again tomorrow when LTC Ali has more time?"

The Ugly American in me wanted ask why we in hell had spent an hour filling our bladders and neglecting the reason I had been asked to come here, but the diplomat in me again prevailed. With a smile I replied that tomorrow would be fine.

As we walked back to the car Major Paulson said, "Welcome to Saudi Arabia, sir."

"At some point we are actually going to talk about why he asked me to come to his artillery battalion, are we not?"

"Oh sure, sir. You just have to understand that they're on an entirely different concept of time than we have; that is to say they really don't have one."

"I see. Okay then, young major, where does the weary Rydell traveler stay overnight in Hafoof?"

Only one place, sir, and one place only – The Al Hasa Intercontinental. I'll take you."

"Great," I said. "Do they have a latrine?"

Paulson laughed. "They'll square you away, sir."

As we drove I mentally pictured the Al Hasa Intercontinental. I saw it crammed into a side street of a seedy neighborhood, dirty in the way that only a Middle Eastern city without adequate water, sewers, and other sanitary concerns could be. I could hear the whispers of terrorists, thieves, and murders as they conspicuously watched me enter the one and only hotel in the city while making plans about how to carve up and dispose of my body in the desert.

We stopped at the security entrance of a magnificent structure. The guard recognized "Major Brian" immediately and waved us through. I gaped at the palace in front of us.

"What is this?" I asked as we got out of the car.

"The Al Hasa Intercontinental, sir. Let's grab your bags."

"You mean I'm staying here?"

"If it's not good enough we can find something else. But this is the best around. The Al Hasa has a five star rating." He was enjoying himself. "And they have a latrine, too."

"C'mon. You mean I'm staying here?"

Mike grinned. Something about old soldiers. We just can't get used to the fact that we don't have to live in jeeps, mud, or one room hootches with bad everything. That anybody or any company would put me up in a hotel like the Al Hasa Intercontental, and foot the bill, was more than this old GI could comprehend. But there I was.

The place rose out of the desert like a magic castle; a ten story palace of beige stone and blue green glass surrounded by a stunning array of palms and gardens. Paulson swung the Expedition into a covered parking space. Still a bit in awe I jumped out but not before he'd already managed to get my bag. "Not to worry, sir," he said. "I'll take care of it." Service, too. I was about to have a mental breakdown.

But if I was a stunned mullet at the outside of the Intercontinental I was nearly incapacitated by the lobby. We walked through a metal detector and passed another security guard before entering the truly most spectacularly decorated space I'd ever seen. A luxurious, exotically designed carpet covered the floor strategically crafted to display gaps of gleaming marble. A gigantic stairwell, constructed entirely of marble the color of chocolate swirl ice cream flowed like a great river to the upper level. On either side of the stairwell hung the most monstrous chandeliers I'd ever seen. Gigantic tear drops of brass, crystal, and gold; it made you wonder how the ceiling could hold them. The whale sized gleaming orbs absorbed the sunlight and oozed out a liquid rainbow and gold shimmer that filled the lobby. Polished mahogany, teak, and rosewood furniture filled spaces unclaimed by marble, rich carpet, sculpture, and paintings. The place did not boast wealthy extravagance, it was wealthy extravagance; breathtaking and beautiful.

My host directed me to the front desk and introduced me to the man in charge, a fellow by the name of Kareem. Kareem's smile glittered like the chandeliers. "So glad to see you again, Mr. Brian! What can we do?"

The two shared jokes and laughs like old friends for a moment and Brian introduced me. "Kareem, this is my good friend, Mr. Joe Doyle," he said. "He has reservations for the next couple of days."

Kareem of the shining smile shook my hand and turned to his computer. I was certain that he wouldn't find my name in his files, but he find it he did. With a smile even wider than before he pushed several keys on his machine. Like quiet magic my reservation ticket appeared. I did not believe it possible, but Kareem handed me a room key. "Number 525, sir. Please call me for anything." The smile radiated. "I assume Mr. Brian will show to you room?"

"I've got it covered, Kareem," Brian said and turned to me. "Right this way, sir."

"I still don't believe it," I said as Kareem waved for a bellboy.

My room was a microcosm of the lobby; luxurious to an overwhelming degree. Sumptuous might be a better description. I gave the bellboy a generous 20 dollar tip, well, 20 Saudi riyals actually. At 3.75 Saudi riyals to the dollar I could afford to play high roller.

With the bags deposited in the room I walked the major back to his car. Along the way he gave me a tour of the rest of the hotel. The place had three restaurants, full sized gym, sauna, massage room, shops; imagine any measure or technique for optimal lodging experience and the Al Hasa Hotel had it, and probably more than one. The pool was unlike anything I'd seen anywhere. Mosaic tile filled the room with an artistic design of green fish, dancing blue dolphins and golden sun rays. Brian knew the guy running the shop and the guy's supervisor, and they knew him by first name. This was a soldier who did not practice being miserable. But the patch on his right shoulder was a sign he'd done at least one war tour. He deserved it.

Paulson had to get back to his unit so I walked him out through the lobby to the parking lot. As we exited the lobby I noticed a large, circular room that jutted out of one side of the hotel near an open air restaurant. It was an odd, out of place structure

"What's that place, Brian?"

"You've never seen one of those, sir?"

"Well, I don't know. What is it?"

"That's the Hubbly Bubbly Room."

"The what?" I asked.

"The Hubbly Bubbly Room," he repeated.

"The Hubbly Bubbly room," I said. I liked the way the phrase burbled about my lips. "I give up, Major. What goes on in there?"

He scrunched up his face. "Something you might want to stay away from, sir."

"You're killing me. What is the Hubbly Bubbly Room?"

"It's kind of an Arab version of a cigar lounge, only they don't have cigars, they have water pipes and flavored tobacco. You know, what we call bongs, hookahs."

I was instantly fascinated.

"That's why it's called a Hubbly Bubbly Room," he continued, "because of the sound the water pipes make."

"So why should I stay away?"

"Ahh, it's expensive for one. And it's such a traditional Arab thing that you might not be welcomed with open arms, either."

"Do they smoke dope in there?"

He laughed. "Probably not unheard of, but mainly just different types of flavored tobacco."

"Have you ever been in there?"

"Yea, once. It's sort of neat, but the fumes kind of get to me after a while. Gave me odd dreams, too."

I considered the advice. Tobacco held few charms; I'd quit years ago and even the very occasional after dinner cigar did not taste especially good. But that name. The Hubbly Bubbly Room. Intriguing.

We agreed to meet the next morning in the lobby of the hotel. I walked him to his car and headed back to my room all the while thinking about the mysterious Hubbly

Bubbly Room. What kind of nefarious activity could go on in a place like? Hashish hubbly bubbly most likely, but Paulson had said that was unlikely and the Intercontinental Hotel did not seem a likely opium den. Yet he'd been oddly vague about the dangers of the place, as though the whole thing was more than simply distasteful. Tobacco fumes and bad odor hardly constituted the most dangerous bodily harm, and if the locals did not take to Westerners in their hubbly bubbly sanctum, what of it? They could tell me to leave.

I approached the room as from the palm shrouded walkway in front of the hotel. The pavement ended abruptly in front of the Hubbly Bubbly Room onto an expanse of polished stones that surrounded the structure. Twelve, large rectangular windows curved about the front. It was impossible to see inside. Rolling waves of curtains descended beyond the darkened glass. I circled the room looking for an entrance, but by the time I had reached the point where it joined back to the hotel I could not discern a door or entrance.

I retraced my steps to the other side of the room with the same result. The entrance must therefore be someplace inside the hotel. I knew just the man to solve this mystery – Kareem, he of the gleaming smile. But when I informed my happy countenanced host of my desire to experience the

Hubbly Bubbly room, Kareem's dentures took on a noticeably duller shine. "Oh, sir," he began, the word "sir" a full octave lower than the word preceding it. I immediately sensed that I had somehow overstepped my bounds.

"There is a problem with that, Kareem?"

"Yes, Mr. Joe," he said as though it pained him. But he was obviously reluctant to reveal what the issue was.

"Kareem," I said. "I don't wish to pry, and perhaps I'm missing some Saudi cultural custom, here, but I thought the Hubbly Bubbly room was simply a place to sample various types of tobacco. Is that not right?"

Kareem hesitated, seeming to agonize over finding the correct words to explain this desert dilemma. "Did not Mr. Brian tell you, sir?"

"No, Kareem. Major Paulson said nothing about the place except that it was for smoking."

"He did not mention anything else?"

"Well, yes," I admitted. "He did say he had unpleasant dreams. But he didn't seem too upset about it."

Kareem frowned. His eyes narrowed. "Perhaps, Mr. Joe, it would help if you tell me why you wish to experience the Hubbly Bubbly room."

At this point I was feeling insulted at the interrogation. But I held my irritation in check. "It's something uniquely Saudi Arabian, Kareem, and I'm in your country for the first time" I explained as patiently as possible. "I've never been inside one and I am intensely curious."

"There are many such rooms in the country, Mr. Joe."

"Yes, yes, Kareem. I'm sure there are. But I'm not going to be in your country for a great length of time and I am here right now. Look, Kareem, just tell me why I cannot go in there. Is it because I'm a Westerner? What's the deal?"

The gleam was off the rosy smile now. "I did not say you cannot go into the room, sir."

"Then what is the deal, Kareem. Why are you being so evasive?"

Kareem appeared genuinely pained. "It is not so easy to explain, Mr. Mike." He paused. "I will see if it can be arranged, sir. Please give me some time. Inshallah, I shall arrange it." He frowned, leaned his head to the right, and raised his palms in a supplicating manner.

I was obviously being dismissed. But I hardly had much choice in the matter. "Okay, Kareem," I said. "I appreciate your help, even though I don't understand what's going on."

I retired to my room more intensely curious than ever. What could possibly be the issue here? I concluded that it had to be something to do with my Western heritage. I gave up on the idea of Kareem making the "arrangement." Let these snobby Saudis keep their hubbles and bubbles to themselves, I thought. Who needs em?

I stripped down and headed for the shower still thinking about the damned tobacco parlor in spite of my determination not to. I could say whatever I wanted to myself, but the truth was that I wanted to get in that place and see what the devil went on in there. I kept up this irritable conversation with myself as I washed. When I was done I threw the shower curtain back and stepped out of the shower. Two hotel towels, each about the size of a queen size bed comforter, hung like a pair of drapes on a gold rack in front of me. I grabbed one and rubbed myself down from head to foot.

I have this habit of giving my scalp, and what remains of my hair, an especially vigorous and rough massage after a shower. Now this tidbit of my toiletry habits is not a detail worthy recounting except for what happened when I removed the towel from around my head. Ironically it was the kind of thing I always remained leery of; a long term premonition that this might someday occur. Every time I cover my head with a towel like that I have this sneaky paranoia that someone is going to surprise me, i.e. attack me when I'm thus blind. I know it's stupid. I know it's idiotic. I know it's unfounded. Of course, my odd paranoia never came to fruition – until now. I let the towel drop from my eyes and became instantly aware of someone standing at the bathroom door.

My first reaction, and a normal one I might add, was violent fright. My next reaction was violent anger. I reached for the first weapon I could lay my hands on which happened to be the hair dryer on the sink counter. I snatched it, swung back, and abruptly checked my swing. Had the intruder been anyone else I'd have cracked their skull open like a melon colliding with a two by four.

"Jaleel!" I roared. "What the hell are you doing!?"

"Oh, Mr. Joe, sir," he said. "I am being very sorry to disturb you this way, but I am thinking this is very important, sir."

"It better be, you knucklehead! You scared the hell out of me. And you almost got yourself killed, too."

Jaleel looked at me with an odd tilt of his head and a puzzled expression. "What is this being a knucklehead, sir? What is this meaning?"

"A knucklehead is," I started to explain, and then became overwhelmed with exasperation. "Never mind that, idiot! What are you doing here and how'd you get into my room?"

"Perhaps you should be picking up your towel, sir. It is very hard to talk to you in these conditions."

"Get outta of here while I get dressed, Jaleel. Wait outside."

"Absolutely, sir. That is being exactly right and then I will explain everything." He shot the big Jaleel grin at me and wobbled his head in the peculiar Indian fashion that means yes, no, and maybe all at once.

I slammed the door behind him and thrust myself into my pants and shirt. I took a moment to compose myself before opening the door. Was my driver some kind of nut? I picked up the hair dryer again. Maybe I would have to bean him with the thing. Nah, I said to myself. If Jaleel wanted to whack me or attack me he'd have done it while I had the stupid towel around my head. I put the thing down and walked out to listen to whatever absurd explanation was forthcoming.

Jaleel sprang to his feet. He was dressed exactly as I'd seen him last. Ragged, toeless sandals covered his feet and a tattered pair of black, ill fitting pants ended in hap hazard pattern of tears and rips at his calves. His shirt was somewhat cleaner than the rest of his wardrobe, but it was hard to tell from the odd, green and purple designs. He was a fashion disaster for sure, but on Jaleel it worked.

"I am being very sorry for startling you in shower, boss." It occurred to me that Jaleel seemed to begin every sentence with an apology; I think it was his peculiar Indian version of "how ya doing?"

"You didn't startle me, Jaleel," I said. "You scared the shit out of me."

"This is bad thing, sir?"

He had to be messing with me. I waved my hand. "Never mind, Jaleel. Just tell me why you're here. And don't ask me any more questions, right? Just tell me why you are here like this. Okay?"

"I did not mean to scare you like such, sir. I was not thinking that would happen."

"Jaleel! Forget about that, will you! Just tell me why you're here. Do you have something important to tell me? Couldn't you just call me? You have my cell phone number."

"Calling is not appropriate in these conditions, sir. Besides, you were in the shower and would not have answered the phone." He said this as though it the logic was irrefutable. I deliberately calmed myself. This surely had to be some emergency; perhaps he had a death in the family and needed to return to Riyadh or something. Just then the most obvious explanation occurred to me – he had wrecked the car. Of course, that had to be it. This was not a complication I needed.

"Jaleel," I said evenly, almost growling the words. "Tell why you came here – NOW!"

"It is because you are thinking about the Hubbly Bubbly room, sir. Kareem called me. You are thinking that way, is that not right, sir?"

The statement astounded me. I was dumbfounded; almost at a loss for words.

"Yes. I'd like to see the Hubbly Bubbly room. Kareem called you about that?" I couldn't believe it.

"This room is not being a very good place for you, sir." He continued quickly.

If Jaleel's face had not displayed such a contortion of real concern I'd have considered this a bizarre hoax. I sighed and threw my head back. "Okay. Tell me why the Hubbly Bubbly room is not being a good place for me."

"It is a bad place, sir, this Hubbly Bubbly Room."

I was getting a headache. "And why is it a bad place, Shabob?"

"There is a devil in there, sir."

"What?"

"Mr. Kareem knows, sir. There is a devil living in that Hubbly Bubbly Room."

I anticipated many reasons for being denied entrance to the room: thugs, drugs, prostitutes, disreputable people of various natures, insane Bedouins - that the place was the abode of Satan, however, had honestly never occurred to me.

"Did you actually say the devil is in the Hubbly bubbly room, Jaleel?"

"Oh no, sir. I said a devil. This devil in there is not a demon of great stature, he is a lesser spirit, but he is causing many mischiefs."

I groped for an appropriate response. "And why does the hotel allow this devil to inhabit their Hubbly Bubbly room, Jaleel?" I felt ridiculous even asking the question.

"This demon was being in there before the hotel was built, sir. Could not build hotel without him."

I was too flummoxed to ask a follow up question. "Alright, Jaleel. If there is a devil in the hotel's Hubbly Bubbly and the hotel cannot rid of him, then why not just forbid anyone to enter the room? Why not just put it off limits?"

"That is not possible, boss. This bad spirit is being very clever. He has made it so that anyone who wishes to enter cannot be refused."

"So if I insist on entering, no one can stop me?"

"That is right, sir. So is it very good for you to change your mind now."

I considered this absurd advice – for about five seconds. "You're killing me."

He looked puzzled and indignant. "I am not killing you, sir!" he exclaimed. "I am trying to save you much harm!"

"Calm down, Jaleel, it's just an expression. I know you're not literally killing me. But I insist on going into the Hubbly Bubbly Room. I'm so curious about the place right now that the devil himself couldn't stop me."

"Please, don't say such things, sir." He seemed genuinely frightened but I was undeterred.

"Kindly tell Kareem that I would like to visit the Hubbly Bubbly Room."

My driver seemed resigned to fate. "I have tried to warn you, sir," he said.

"Yes, you did. And I appreciate your concern. But I have made up my mind."

Jaleel shook his head and gave me a look - the sad, soulful expression of the living for the condemned. "Kareem will call you, sir," he said. Without another word he stood up, walked resolutely to the door, and exited.

I wondered why Kareem had called Jaleel instead of Major Paulson. Kareem was obviously on good terms with the major. Wouldn't he be the obvious choice to dissuade me, a fellow Westerner, from entering the forbidden realm? The answer was obvious - Paulson did not accept this devil fantasy. Kareem must have known Jaleel as fellow true believer.

My internal commiserations did not last long. The room phone rang. It was Kareem. His tone was somber. "Someone will be up to get you shortly, sir." Mmmm. No more exhortations to reconsider?

"Thank you Kareem," I said. "Oh, Kareem, one more thing."

"Yes, sir."

"What is the appropriate dress for the Hubbly Bubbly Room? What should I wear?" I'd hate to be undressed for the Prince of Darkness.

"I suggest business attire, sir. But if you do not have such clothes a nice shirt with collar and good pants will do." Kareem had obviously responded to this question before.

I did not have a business suit; it's not the kind of thing one normally wears when working out artillery problems with foreign armies, but I did have a decent white shirt and a pair of Docker pants. At least I would not have to present myself in blue jeans. Devil or no devil, I knew the Saudis frowned on Levis.

I shaved, dressed, and considered myself in the mirror. Pretty good shape for fifty, I mused. Just then the door bell rang. Thinking that this was all a bit melodramatic approached the door prepared to deliver a wisecrack or two about the necessity of an escort to the Hubbly Bubbly Room. I knew where the thing was. But I supposed the hotel had its rules. I opened the door - and stared.

Ladies are not allowed out in Saudi Arabia unless they are accompanied by their brother, husband, or father. This much I knew. And I also knew that Saudi women did not go outside without the abaya, the long, hooded gown that modestly covers them from crown to toe. But the lady who stood smiling at me in my doorway was not covered from head to toe, and a picture of maiden modesty she was not. I did not see any male relations, either. The only male in the immediate vicinity was yours truly.

It took a minute, but I found my tongue. "You're my escort to the Hubbly Bubbly Room?"

"That is my duty and my honor, sir." She spoke perfect English but with a trace of an accent that I could not identify. Come to think of it this was the first lady in Saudi Arabia that had ever spoken to me. And what a lady. She brushed a waterfall of ebony hair back over her ear, arched

254

an eyebrow, and smiled as if amused. Her grin was irresistibly dimpled. Deep black, lilting eyes lightly accented with eyeliner gave her a bewitching beauty.

"You are not pleased, sir? Another escort can be arranged." She breathed the words instead of speaking them.

"Oh no, ma'am," I stammered. "You'll do just fine. It's just that I thought in Saudi Arabia ladies had to wear an abaya...or something."

She placed her hand over her mouth and giggled quietly. She looked down and conducted a mock inspection of herself. Her scarlet, lightly sequined dress clung to her incredible physique like a silky second skin. Nearly invisible straps held what little there was of the top of the dress and one side was cut to the thigh.

"You prefer the abaya, sir?"

"Not one bit, ma'am. I was just, you know, under the impression that you had to wear one in this country."

"Rules in the El Hasa are slightly different, sir." She held out her hand. "My name is Serena."

I took her hand and shook it lightly still feeling dumbfounded. "Pleased to meet you, Serena. My name's Joe."

"I like this name, Joe, but your full name is Joseph Michael Doyle, is it not?"

Kareem was certainly efficient. "That's right."

"Such beautiful name. Why do you hide it?"

"Americans like nick names I guess."

"Yes, but I prefer Joseph. It has a more meaning, don't you think; more depth?"

"To tell you the truth Serena, I never thought of it. I've been just plan Joe for a long time. But if you prefer Joseph, then Joseph it is." Just then I remembered my manners. "Would you like to come inside, Serena? I apologize for leaving you standing out here."

She held up a finger and waived it. "That is fine, Joseph, but we have lingered long enough. The Hubbly Bubbly Room awaits your presence."

"Oh, yea," I said. I'd forgotten about that. This lady could make a fish forget water. Suddenly a room full of men smoking tobacco had lost a lot of its intrigue.

Serena seemed to sense my reversal of opinion. She reached out and took my hand. "Come now, Joseph. You have waited long enough, and you insisted on visiting the Hubbly Bubbly Room, didn't you?" She tugged me forward gently. I shut the door to my hotel room and let her guide me into the hallway. My room looked a little better right now but turning down the wishes of this enchantress was impossible. "You're right again, Serena."

"Of course I am, Joseph. Come. You won't be disappointed."

Serena maintained her gentle grip on my hand as we walked to the elevator. I was going to the Hubbly Bubbly Room alright. A trill of warning tickled me from inside. A lot here did not make sense. Why would the hotel, after repeated attempts to stop me from entering the Hubbly Bubbly Room, suddenly make such an irresistible effort to get me into the thing? Why send this incredibly beautiful woman as my escort? It was almost as if the hotel, having finally granted me permission to enter the room, was suddenly afraid that I might change my mind. In my soldierly experience strange, beautiful girls who are suddenly very friendly were usually seeking a bit more than a dinner date with flowers.

We stopped at the elevator and Serena pushed a button. "You seem nervous, Joseph. Is something wrong?"

Yes, something was clearly wrong, but it was hard to put into words without appearing foolish. And if there is one thing that every man on earth wants to avoid (but seemingly cannot) it is appearing foolish in front of a beautiful lady.

"Well actually there is something, Serena."

Just then the elevator pinged and the door swished open. Holding both of my hands my lovely hostess swept me in. "Tell me on the way down, Joseph. You can change your mind if you'd like." The elevator door closed and Serena pushed a button. I did not notice which one. I wish I had.

The door quietly closed and filled the small space in silence. She pulled my arm slightly closer. "Are you afraid of me, Joseph?" She purred with a sweet, teasing smile.

Of course I said no. But I was. Serena and her perfume filled the elevator. Her reflection in the mirrored compartment revealed a backless dress that plunged to the base of her spine. A tattoo of a pair of vividly colorful, intricately detailed serpents twisted the length of her back bone. On her neck, just above the line of her shoulders the reptiles faced each other with drawn fangs, yet the elliptical eyes looked sleepy and full of desire instead of menace. The brilliantly colored decoration ran the entire length of her back until the twin serpent tails mysteriously disappeared in the base of her dress. It took an effort not to stare.

"Ah, I see you like my pets, Joseph. They are pretty are they not?"

"Serena," I said. "Everything about you is more than pretty. And that alarms me."

She laughed. "I will not harm you, Joseph! What gave you such an idea?"

"Just an old soldier being careful, ma'am. The hotel tried everything to dissuade me from entering the Hubbly

Bubbly Room, even tells me that it is inhabited by a devil –
but then sends up the most beautiful woman I've ever seen to
lead me to it. Don't you think that's odd?"

"You will love the room, Joseph."

Just then the elevator door opened. Serena pulled me
forward and I was suddenly standing in in a large circular
room wonderfully aglow in an explosion of color and carpet
– the Hubbly Bubbly Room. There were no chairs. Large,
exquisitely designed cushions lined the walls, each one in
front of a towering glass panel with velvet curtain and each
separated by a large glowing candle. In front of each cushion
an oversized, gleaming brass "hookah" stood at the ready
with mouthpiece pointed toward a potential smoker.

It was more than slightly confusing to be suddenly in
the middle of this room. I had not noticed any button on the
elevator leading to the Hubbly Bubbly Room and my
exquisite host had not prepared me in any way for this. She
and I were the only ones in the room.

"What do you think, Joseph? Is it not beautiful?"

"It's…it's incredible, Serena. Very beautiful. But
where are the others? Aren't there normally more smokers?"

"Sometimes, there are, Joseph. Tonight there is only
you. Please take a seat and I shall prepare your pipe."

I looked around. "Anywhere?"

"Yes, Joseph. Anywhere you like." She waved a hand around the room.

Well, at least the devil wasn't here. I looked about and considered my choice of seating. The enormous cushions were actually elaborate pillowed couches without legs. They lay like mattresses, sort of Arabian style lazy boy recliners, only there was no need to recline, the giant cushions were already on the floor. Each seated position was distinguished by a particular color that radiated out to the center of the room and created a large rainbow colored circle. Being the man I am I chose the green setting. I settled into the soft cushion between the bulging armrests. It felt wonderful.

I looked up to see Serena beaming at me. "Green, Joseph! That is a wonderful choice. It says much about you. You chose a pure color – the color of life."

"Really? It's my favorite." I hoped my modesty shown through.

Serena glided across the room toward me. She knelt in front of the hookah, tantalizing me with a glorious view of her breasts in the process, and began the elaborate process of lighting the instrument. First, she carefully opened a small compartment on the side of the instrument by inserting what appeared to be a small golden key into a slot. She gave it a slight turn and it popped open the rest of the way by itself.

She reached into the opening and retrieved a small, silken bag tied at the top with a bright blue twine.

In a single motion Serena rose to her feet while holding the bag. "I have selected an intriguing mixture for you, Joseph, a combination I created myself. I'm sure you will enjoy it."

"If you made it, Serena I am certain I'll love it." The remark pleased her. She smiled and returned to her work. The hookah was over three feet tall and gleamed in the soft golden glow of candle light. She grasped the top of the instrument and pulled. The upper half of the hookah opened to reveal a silver perforated interior that looked like the bottom of an old fashioned coffee percolator. Serena carefully untied the blue twine and poured the contents of the bag into the perforated tray. With a flick of her hand she produced a vivid blue flame which she used to light a wick that jutted up from the middle of the tray. In one fluid motion she extinguished the flame and closed the top of the hookah.

She stood erect and looked at me expectantly. "Your smoke is ready, Joseph. Have you ever experienced the pleasure of the pipe before?"

"I have to admit that I have not, Serena."

"Ah, then I must show you."

"I am your willing student," I replied, proud of my wit.

Serena took two steps in my direction and knelt on the cushions by my side. She pulled the mouthpiece close to my lips and spoke softly inches from my ear. "Breathe in the aroma slowly and evenly at first, Joseph. Inhale, but not deeply. Allow the fragrance to fill your senses softly, let the pleasure build."

She placed the tip of the mouthpiece between my lips. I did as instructed, lightly inhaling the tobacco. The scent and taste of this was like nothing I've experienced previously. I'd been a smoker for a number of years when I was in my twenties and I naturally expected something similar – harsh, bitter, and initially irritating. But not Serena's mixture. Just as she had promised the smoke was fragrant and light; a mystifying, almost sweet aroma that left a satisfying aftertaste.

I know Serena could tell by the look on my face that I approved of her selection. Her face lit up in a lovely smile. "Now, Joseph, inhale again. But just slightly more than the last time. Don't be greedy! You must allow the pleasure to develop slowly."

I sipped from the mouthpiece again exactly as she instructed. It was with an effort, however. The tobacco was like nectar. I'd never experienced anything like it.

"Serena," I said. "This is wonderful! How is it made?"

She placed her hand on my cheek. "Ah, Joseph. How American you are! Be patient."

I became aware of soft lulling music. A lullaby of flute and harp invaded my senses along with the aroma of the pipe. Had it been playing before? Serena was suddenly at my side. "Breathe deeply now, Joseph. Breathe deeply."

By now she did not have to coax me. I sought the pipe eagerly and pulled the smoke deep into my lungs. Each draught brought a new rush of pleasure as satisfying as a delicious meal. I pulled on the mouthpiece with gusto.

This was not the intoxication of marijuana or hashish. I'd experienced those vices several times in my youth and I knew the familiar gross giddiness that hemp produces. This was nothing like it at all. My senses were not dimmed in the least. My vision sharpened and my whole being became vibrant. My hearing became more sensitive; I could feel each molecule of scented tobacco as it rushed from the mouthpiece.

Still kneeling beside me Serena smiled and turned until she had her back to me. She lifted her arms above her head and swayed from side to side. The soft light cast shadows on the taught, lightly muscled flesh of her back. Her entwined serpents rippled to life, writhing in tune with her movements. Green, coppery, and iridescent the reptiles appeared three dimensional so intricately were they designed.

Serena rose slowly to her feet while she continued her sensual dance. Her scant dress melted away and her naked back rolled and swayed in perfect time to the haunting flute and harp. The reptiles rolled and swayed with a life of their own. Their tongues flickered and caressed; their long sleek bodies wrestled in slow passion. The tails of the beast curled under her buttocks and on either side and tortured my imagination as to where they terminated. I pulled on the hookah pipe harder and harder. Serena and her twin serpents filled my senses even more than the sweet herb that I could not get enough of.

Then she turned. I watched in mesmerized horror as she glided to me on her stomach, stopped, and slowly rose up like a glistening flesh colored cobra. Her breasts, in fact her entire body, was covered with a sheen of minute silvery scales. I pulled my eyes away from her body in time to see the twin stilettos arcing down to my chest.

I don't like to admit this, but I screamed, screamed in bloody terror. With an adrenaline soaked burst of fright energy I slammed into the draped covered window behind the pillow cushions. The window shattered and I sprawled out onto the graveled pathway beyond. Serena was right behind me. Her eyes had turned into elliptical slits of fury; her entire skull was grotesquely distorted, flattened on the top and wider at the jaws. She slid forward on her stomach as I scrambled frantically to my feet. It was impossible to escape. Serena was slithering toward me with alarming speed.

Suddenly she stopped. The monstrous thing that had once been the most beautiful woman I'd ever seen screeched and hissed but seemed reluctant to leave the confines of the Hubbly Bubbly Room. I bolted away from the window and ran to the hotel lobby. I raced through the cavernous room, the dazzling chandelier lights a wonderful contrast to the dull candle glow of the smoke room where I'd nearly been killed.

I looked for Kareem at the front desk, but he was not working. No one was working. The entire lobby was empty. I tried to calm myself by thinking about my options. I knew I had to get out of the damned hotel; the Serena snake thing could reappear and attack me at any time. But to get to get hold of Jaleel and to do that I had to get back to my room. I was not about to take a chance wandering around outside in the dark with that reptilian demon out there.

I agonized for a moment about whether to take the stairs or the elevator and then decided on the elevator. If the thing caught me in the darkened stairwell I'd never escape. At least I could see into the elevator before getting in. She could still surprise me at the floor of my hotel room so my strategy was to take the elevator up to the floor just below mine, exit on the lower floor, and then take the stairwell just one flight up. If the hideous thing was waiting for me outside of the elevator I could see it before it spotted me.

I approached the elevator feeling like a wild animal expecting a trap. Seeing nothing I carefully tip toed the last several steps, punched the "up" button, and sprang back into the alcove of a meeting room across from the row of elevators and waited. The blasted contraption seemed to take hours to descend. The stomach wrenching sight of half human reptile kept reappearing in my mind. At any minute I expected the deformed thing to slither around the corner and attack.

The tinkle of the bell that signaled the arrival of the elevator made me jump. I remained hidden as the door swished open, glanced up and down the hallway and peeked into the elevator. I leaped from my hiding spot into the lift just as the doors slid shut. I thought I heard a muffled sound, something like dull sandpaper rubbing against a hard surface. Serena's scales sliding against the elevator door?

The elevator ride was almost as agonizing as the wait for the car to come down. I had no idea what kind of supernatural powers the monster had. My strategy of exiting one floor below mine had to work, though. The Serena snake had crawled to get me. Apparently the thing had to move in that manner or else I'd have certainly been snared by its fangs. Small comfort but I rehearsed my next moves. As soon as the elevator doors opened I'd take a quick look outside. If all was clear I'd sprint to the nearest exit and take the stairwell up. My room was near the end of the hallway, less than twenty feet from the stairwell entrance. Once I had my keys in hand I planned to alternate from stairway and elevator until I got to the floor above the lobby. Perhaps I could smash though a window there and leap to the ground or find a fire escape. The elevator eased to a halt. After a brief pause filled with awful suspense the door slid open. Serena was waiting for me with an outstretched hand. I had somehow returned to the Hubbly Bubbly Room.

"Joseph," she said calmly. "You have not finished your pipe."

I mashed the elevator buttons frantically. Serena laughed merrily. "Joseph, please. You are where you must be."

Serena had returned to human form. She wore a full length robe of purple silk and although it clung to her tightly and outlined the same sleek body that had previously enchanted me, I shuddered to think what might lie beneath.

She stepped toward me and reached out. "My poor Joseph. Come to me; this elevator will not take you anywhere else."

I cringed to the back of the lift but Serena was right. The elevator did not budge. My fear was nearly immobilizing – nearly. Using the rear wall of the elevator like a springboard I lurched forward. She might be a demon, but she was a demon that I outweighed by at least seventy pounds. I'd escaped once before and I could do it again. I launched myself directly into her but Serena dodged my attack at the last second; she truly had the reflexes of a snake. My technique was successful but the force of my attack propelled me into the Hubbly Bubbly Room where I sprawled onto the floor. I scrambled to my feet and ran to the window I had previously smashed open directly behind the green cushions. Although she had tried to disguise the opening by drawing the drapes in front of it I knew exactly where it was and threw myself at the green drape. I collided with the solid window behind it. This time it did not break.

Although still jolted from the unexpected collision I turned and prepared to face the worst fight of my life. The golden brass hookah I had previously inhaled from sat serenely in front of me as if patiently waiting to serve my next inhalation but I was ready to use it as a weapon instead of an instrument of pleasure this time. But I seemed to be alone in the Hubbly Bubbly Room. The candles continued to burn. The room was silent. For a time I remained frozen in place waiting for the attack, listening to my breath, alert to any other sound or movement – and frankly terrified. Understand my predicament if you will. I do not frighten easily. I led a full life. I've seen more than my share of the world's ugliness and beauty; I've even been around the world on several occasions and survived an assault by four men with clubs and knives. I've been through a war, seen men shot and watched them die. I've barely escaped with my own life several times. But those events I could understand. These were soldiers or other humans trying to kill me just as I was trying to kill them. And in each instance I knew exactly what to do. I did not have to think. I just acted.

But what was I confronted with now? How do you cope with a demon? With a world gone suddenly bizarre and senseless? All the power of my body and intellect was not equipped to deal with this insane situation. I had no point of reference; no experience and nothing to grip for an anchor of reassurance. I had one thing and one thing only – the awful memory of that half human monster slithering toward me.

I had no idea why Serena had not killed me upon the second capture. She certainly could have. The fact that I was alive was a comfort, but hardly reassuring. That, too, did not make sense and its very senselessness was frightening. Where the hell was she?

"She is gone," stated a male voice. "Serena is a trifling; extremely pleasant to look at, I'm sure you agree Mr. Doyle, but exercises questionable judgment at times. I apologize for her little practical joke."

Dressed in an expensive, silvery suit the man was clean shaven from head to chin and shiny bald. He stood no more than five inches over five feet and he had an unimpressive, dumpling like physique; nearly as round as he was tall, but his tanned complexion gave him a look of health. It was impossible not to notice the brilliant red tie. It seemed to glow.

"I presume you are the devil," I said. I felt a momentary foolishness as the words left my mouth. But I was not to be embarrassed.

"Right you are, Mr. Doyle," he replied. He carefully slipped off his shoes, placed them on the small carpet in front of the elevator and then took off his jacket. He hung the garment on a hook. In his white shirt he now looked more egg like than dumpling. Short arms and legs enhanced the illusion of poultry. He looked like an egg with legs. If this was the devil he certainly was an unimpressive specimen.

"I am Jonahs Nathaniel Tamaron, Mr. Doyle," he said. "And I am very pleased to make your acquaintance."

He strode toward me with hand outstretched and I rose to meet him. We shook hands. His palms felt absolutely human.

"You look surprised, Mr. Doyle. Do I disappoint you?" His brown eyes smiled up at me.

"This has been a night of surprises that I would not exactly classify as disappointments," I said. I stumbled for a minute on the proper address. "Should I call you Mr. Devil, Mr. Tamaron, or just plain Johnas, sir? I've never met a real devil before."

"I like a man with manners, Mr. Doyle! Please call me Nate. It has a nice earthy sound, don't you think?"

"Oh, absolutely," I agreed. "And call me Joe, please. Serena liked Joseph, but I've been Joe for too long."

"I understand completely," the devil Nate said.

"And speaking of Serena," I said a trifle nervously, "where did she go?"

Nate boomed a hearty laugh. "Oh she's probably crawling around here someplace," he said and peered about the room as though looking for her. I nearly jumped.

"I am sorry, Joe. Bad joke. And you've certainly had you fill for the night. I simply could not resist."

"Funny," I said.

"I apologize, Joe," Devil Nate said, suddenly serious. "And I promise they'll be no more of that kind of foolishness. Serena has been, well, sent away for a while; a punishment of sorts for her ill treatment of you." He placed a hand over his heart as though expressing great remorse. "But I can bring her back if you prefer," he added.

A return visit from the serpentine Serena is the last thing I wanted. "That is quite alright. Where ever Serena is I have no objection to her staying there."

"Very well, Joe. The lovely Serena shall remain in banishment for now."

I was not sure what "for now" meant, but I hoped it meant forever.

"Shall we sit down and enjoy a pipe, Joe? They are prepared and waiting for us, and you never did get to fully enjoy your last sitting." He indicated the cushioned seats behind me. "The green one is still yours. I shall take the red." He grinned. A devil's pun?

I sat down warily. It's not every day that one shares a smoke with a devil or the devil. I still was not sure which one I was dealing with. Devil Nate took the seat opposite me and merrily puffed his pipe to life. He took a deep draw and pulled the smoke deep into his lungs. After what seemed a full minute he slowly released the fumes from his lungs. His face glowed with pleasure. He looked at me and nodded as if to tell me to relax and enjoy my pipe.

"Is this Serena's mixture?" I asked.

"I believe so, Joe. But don't worry. It's quite harmless without her nearby." I remained skeptical. Devil Nate waved off my concern – by replacing it with another concern. "Joe, Joe. You really must relax. I don't know when the world became so overloaded with type A personalities."

"You must forgive me, Nate. I tend to get leery after seeing a beautiful woman transform herself into a fanged snake."

"I suppose I can understand," he said.

Just to be sociable I took a quick hit from the pipe. I hardly inhaled despite the sweet aroma. But the dangerous delicious scent gave me a thought. "By the way," I said. "What was the purpose of sending Serena to be my escort if she is such a known practical joker? I would have come anyway."

"An insightful question, sir, but the answer is quite simple. Without Serena as a precursor to our meeting, would you have believed that I am who I claim to be when you entered the Hubbly Bubbly Room?"

"No," I said. "I suppose I wouldn't have. But you could have easily proven your identity, couldn't you?"

Devil Nate shook his head. "That would entail a series of stunts to convince you, Joe. All of which you would likely to assign as some magician's trickery. It would have put our association off to a bad start."

"So Serena's 'bad behavior' was not an accident?"

Devil Nate grinned. "I don't do anything by accident, Joe."

I was not quite sure how to take that statement. I thought the tone was decidedly sinister. I hesitated before asking the obvious. "My presence here in the Hubbly Bubbly Room is therefore not an accident, Nate?"

He took another long draw on his pipe. "Of course not, Joe," he said while exhaling a great stream of bluish vapors. "You did ask to come here, didn't you? Repeatedly, as I recall."

He had me there. "Yes, I admit that. And the hotel staff tried to warn me; even sent my driver up to plead the case."

"Good man that Jaleel," Devil Nate said. "Impetuous driver, but a good man."

It was time for some answers. "Okay. You're the devil, right?"

"Just a devil, Joe. Please don't overstate my status."

"I appreciate your modesty, so let me begin again. You're a devil and you live in the Hubbly Bubbly Room of the Hafoof International Hotel."

"Correct," he said. "But there is no Hubbly Bubbly Room. This is, of course, simply an illusion. Sooner or later you would have deduced that."

"Of course," I replied, not believing myself for a minute and knowing that Nate did not believe me either. Is it wrong to lie to the devil? Even a devil? I decided that even that kind of lie was wrong. "It sure looked real to me, Nate."

"That's because, and I'm sure this would have occurred to you sooner or later anyway. Only certain individuals, certain extraordinary individuals, can perceive this non-existent room."

"That explains everything, Nate. I feel much better."

"Sarcasm is distasteful, Joe; the lowest form of humor actually."

"I consider myself properly chastised. I apologize."

"No need for apologies. Under the circumstances it is quite understandable." He closed his eyes and took in an enormous draw of smoke. As he held the inhalation in what appeared to be sublime pleasure I contemplated my next question, the one I was really afraid to ask. But Devil Nate beat me to it.

He suddenly released the pent up fumes and it spewed forth like a bluish ejection from a fire hose. A perfectly tight and circular roll of smoke reached across the room. Had I not known better I might have believed it possible to walk on the vaporous stream.

"At heart, Joe I suspect you have two basic questions: First, you'd like to know exactly who I am, and second, why are you, Joseph Michael Doyle, here? Am I right, Joe?"

"I couldn't have phrased it any better." If nothing else this demon had a grasp of the obvious.

"Wonderful, Joe, wonderful. And let me complement you on your restraint as well as your intelligence. Most men are nearly intolerable in their impatience."

I had the suspicion of being set up again. If a beautiful woman is suddenly interested in me – something is up. The same principle is at work when some stranger unexpectedly praises your intelligence. Even more so if the stranger claims to be a devil. But I decided to go along with the con. What choice did I have at this point?

"Nate, great intellect is something I've never been accused of, but I am a curious man. So if you could just get back to those two basic questions you mentioned?"

The son of Beelzebub smiled, put aside his bong, and turned to face me. "Joe, you may be my favorite human."

"I am flattered, sir. But may we please get down to business?" Devil Nate was starting to remind me of the Saudi Colonel I'd met earlier. I began to wonder if he was going to tell me to come back tomorrow.

"Okay, Joe," he said, suddenly serious, "I am going to tell you everything. It is important, however, that I provide some foundation for our conversation. I am not trying to be evasive, here, only thorough. Will you permit me that digression, Joe?"

Despite my impatience I found the request amusing. Here I am seated with an actual demon, in all likelihood his prisoner, and he is asking me for permission to explain why I have thus been snared.

"Absolutely, Nate. I believe in thoroughness myself."

"Spoken like a true professional!" He clapped his hands. The room darkened to small circle of light that surrounded just the two of us.

"Impressive," I commented.

Nate waved off my complement. "I find it helps to get rid of illusions and distractions when discussing matters of great importance."

I nodded in agreement and waited for him to slide aikido like away from the substance of what he had promised, but Devil Nate seemed to at last to come to the point.

"Now then," he began. "Although it may sound very surprising, at times fantastic, these revelations are nothing more than knowledge you already possess; fundamentals that you already know. For a thoughtful man such as you these things would someday become clear, so let's just say that your visit to the Hubbly Bubbly Room is kind of a short cut to true knowledge. Does that make sense, Joe?"

"Perhaps," I answered slowly. "But I won't know until I hear all of what you have to say." It pays to be cautious with the devil, even one of a lower rank.

"True enough," he said. "It is sort of like a book of philosophy or any great work of art, actually. All the author does is phrase your existing precognitions in a logical, coherent, and articulate fashion – and because these so called original thoughts are in perfect compliance with your own conclusions they seem like genius. Does this make the issue clearer, Joe?"

After all the compliments about my intelligence it was hard to disagree, but I had to admit even to myself that Devil Nate did make a valid point. When you read something it provides great insight if it agrees with your own experience, values, or beliefs.

"Point well taken, Nate."

"That is what is about to happen to you, Joe over the course of this night. I will reveal all that you know already, but from a point of view that you have not previously considered." Devil Nate raised an eyebrow and sent a ripple of wrinkle up into and beyond his forehead. The gesture was not one that asked for my agreement, it was more of a you asked for it expression.

He continued. "The answers to those two questions, Joe, unlocks the secret of it all – everything, in fact, that you ever wanted to know, probably since the day you were born." He let the statement hang.

At this point I left the logic trail, at least the one my host seemed to be leading me on. The various unrealities of the evening were beginning to overwhelm me. I had a feeling of being slowly pulled into a dangerous current. And into waters over my head. Did I have a choice? Devil Nate controlled everything here, didn't he? Of that I was fairly certain. My last attempt at escape had ended in a tragic comedy of irony. Choice. Choice. Why did that word resonate suddenly?

Devil Nate was looking at me intently, studying my face. The eyes had lost some of the original merriment. His expression roused me from my inadvertent trance.

"Go ahead, Nate," I said bravely. "Tell me about yourself."

His eyes wrinkled back to merriment. "Certainly, Joe. I thought I had lost you there for a moment."

I looked around. "No, sir. I'm still here."

"And still with your sense of humor I see," he said. "But enough delay! It is time I introduced myself."

In a sprightly movement that belied his pudgy figure Devil Nate bounced to his feet. He picked up his hookah pipe, moved it several feet away, and placed it carefully down. "I have no more need of this," he announced.

Then he took my pipe and placed it alongside of his. "It would only be a distraction."

I nodded agreement although I did hate to give up the sweet, sweet aroma of my pipe. But if that's what it took to get through the mystery of my present circumstance I was glad to pay the price.

Devil Nate took several steps to my front. "Joe?" he asked.

"Yes?"

"Tell me what you see when you look at me."

"Is this a trick question, Nate?"

Nate pouted. "Despite what you may have read, Joe I do not deal in tricks. There really is no need. So few men understand truth that the tiniest sliver of it fools them anyway. But more of that later. For now, just answer my question with honesty. Please."

"Okay," I said and took a quick breath to consider. "I see a relatively short man some forty or fifty pounds overweight and hairless, but who seems to be in good health. I see a fellow meticulous in his clothing and with a fondness for expensive suits and loud ties. That knife blade crease in your pants is probably a permanent fixture in all of your trousers. That tan of yours has a sunlamp quality. I don't picture you sitting poolside."

"Anything else?"

"You are a fine conversationalist, polite and pleasant company."

"Does anything about me look in the least bit devilish, Joe?"

I considered the question. "Perhaps the hooded expression that rolls over your eyes from time to time, Nate. But no. If I ran into you on the street I'd have no idea that you are a devil."

"And that, Joe is a key to who I am. I was created this way. My purpose is to blend into humanity, not frighten them half to death like the fantastic creatures Hollywood makes of us."

"Us?" I immediately notice his use of the plural. "So there are more of you?"

"As the saying goes, Joe. We are legion."

I did not like the way he said that but Devil Nate took no notice. "We are many, but we are also of one, Joe. Let me explain. You have your many saints, do you not? And your trinity and Virgin Mary, etc, right, Joe?"

I loathe being drawn into theological discussions, but under the present circumstances it seemed appropriate. "Yes, that's correct."

He smiled. "And so it is on the other side of the spirit world. I am one of many, but we all are part of our one true master. I am one of many manifestations of him that I serve."

Devil Nate placed his arms behind his back, clasped his hand, and looked at the floor. He began to pace, affecting a posture of intense concentration, as though the next point required wording of excruciating care. I let him go without interruption.

He began slowly. "Joe," he said, drawing out my name with great deliberation, "What you claim you know is wrong, but what you suspect and fear is true. You know that humanity lives a life of illusion don't you?" He turned quickly and pointed his index finger at me.

"In what way?" I responded.

He rolled his eyes. "You're trying to make this difficult."

"I am not!" I protested. Devil Nate was procrastinating again.

"You know what I mean, Joe. Stop trying to assign trickery to my questions." He actually seemed offended.

"There are many kinds of illusion, Nate. Which one are you talking about?"

"To the most important one, of course, the most basic – the human illusion of reality."

I did not even hazard a guess about this one. But my demon friend was not waiting for my response anyway.

"Let's use the giant microscope analogy, Joe." I agreed as if I knew what he was talking about.

"Regard the back of your hand," he said. "Go ahead, look at it."

I did as commanded and Nate went on with his narrative. "Now if you were to focus a very powerful microscope on the back of your hand, Joe, what would you see?"

"Uh, hair follicles, maybe skin cells. That sort of thing."

The demon clucked his approval. "Now suppose I turned up the power of this extraordinarily powerful microscope. Then what would see?"

"Perhaps the organelles in the cells."

"Right again, my boy! And if I continue in this way we begin to see molecules, correct?"

"Yes."

"And then atoms?"

"Yes."

"And then neutrons and protons?"

"Yes."

"And then quarks, leptons, and all the myriad particles your scientific experts have so named, right."

"This must be some microscope."

"Oh, it is Joe, it is! Because it reveals the truth. And the truth is seen at the next level of magnification. I turn the magnification up one more notch and do you know what happens? All of those lovely particles, that great wonderful solid mass you call the back of your hand disappears into a squiggle of invisible vibrations."

Devil Nate was right about this even though I did not assign great insight to his observation. This was the basic illusion of mankind – the solidity of our existence is merely an imperfect reflection of energy waves.

"But what are those invisible squiggling vibrations, Joe?" he whispered.

"If I knew that, Nate," I answered, "I'd be one of the top nuclear physicists in the world."

He shook his head. "You'd be far more than that, Joe."

"Really?"

"Really, Joe. You'd almost be God."

A thousand separate, tiny thoughts collided at once; a thousand, separate, frightening thoughts. For a moment I went light headed again.

"What do you mean by almost?" I asked when I recovered.

The grin of a jack o lantern split Devil Nate's face. It was an unnerving expression, too, the first time since our meeting that Nate actually appeared, well, evil.

Now I know that seems a ridiculous thing to say about a devil, but you have to understand this from my situation. I'd seen a beautiful woman transform into a hideous reptile. I'd escaped through a hasty, but perfectly logical plan and ended up precisely in the same room where I began. Then, when I am thoroughly convinced of my fate at the hands of the gruesome monster a very harmless looking, well spoken, courteous stranger puts me completely at ease. He has dispatched the monster, made me comfortable, and tolerated my suspicious questions. Every preconceived notion I had about the devil crumpled under the melodious personality and cheerful demeanor of this Devil who called himself Nate.

The frightening, ear to ear grin lasted a mere fraction of a second; so quickly, in fact, that I was not sure I had actually seen it. It flashed across his face like the headlights of a swiftly moving car speeding by. And the remark about being like God? I'd read about that bargain before.

As expected, Devil Nate read me like a large print book. "Joe, you asked me a question that I promised to answer and I am endeavoring to do just that. Don't regard me with such hostility, such fear. Shall I stop?"

I felt suddenly foolish. He was right. I had asked him to explain things and he was doing exactly that. He had not harmed me in any way or even intimated that he would. There is no immediate threat, I thought. And I had to admit the guy was just plain likeable. "No, no," I said. "Please go on. It's just that, well, that talk about becoming godlike cuts a bit close to the heart; kind of Faustish, if you know what I mean."

Devil Nate clapped his hands together. "Joe, Joe. You do give me a laugh. But I can see your point and your suspicions. Remember, though, I do not truck in trickery. And we've made no deal have we? Not for your soul or anything else that I recall?"

True; he had not. "No, you're right."

"But your point is well taken. Man has a fear of becoming godlike. It is an odd thing about your species I find difficult to understand. You spend so much of your life in the attempt to garner wealth and power, yet the mere hint of occult assistance fills you with dread."

"It's not the assistance that frightens most of us, Nate. It's the final price of the goods."

"There's a price for everything, Joe. In this world and the next."

On that point I had no reply. I could only account for world of the living. "That's an argument for another day, Nate. I can only defend what I know and I surely know very little of the existence that follows this one."

"Honest and well said, Joe." He nodded slowly. "So shall we get back to immediate matter at hand?"

"Oh, yea," I said. "Please go one."

"Good," he said and rubbed his hands together. He looked like a portly college professor about to lecture on his favorite subject. "Those invisible squiggles, Joe are at the bottom of it all. Those things that you know exist, but never think of and never see, hear, or smell are the answer to it all.

"And there is one word that is the most apt description of those invisible lines of force, one highly descriptive word that explains it all." He stopped right there and smiled mischievously, knowing I was bursting to hear more. But it was not Nate's intention to make me suffer in curiosity. He went on immediately.

"That one word is this, Joe. The word is thought." He stopped speaking and paced to the far side of the room and melted into the shadows. I heard his voice call from a distance. "And on that point, Joe I must allow you some silence to ponder."

He disappeared and I immediately felt the lack of his presence. My breath returned to normal. I felt as though I'd been holding it for hours. Perhaps I had.

Thought. What the hell did he mean by that and why did he suddenly vanish? For that matter what the hell was I doing here? Suddenly I'd had enough of the mystery theater for one night. Secrets of the universe be damned, my plush hotel room and king sized bed was beginning to take priority over metaphysics. But I couldn't stop thinking about it. If the underlying reality of the universe is thought, then whose thought did it emanate from? Whose thought? God's, obviously. But a devil surely would not have gone through all this trouble to give me that message? Why not just tell me what he was really getting at and get it over with? Something more sinister lurked under all this. Was Nate insidiously communicating to me that Satan was the Alpha and Omega? The idea made me shudder.

I thought about Major Paulson. What was his part in all of this? Well, none, actually. Paulson, Kareem, and Jaleel had all tried to talk me out of a visit to the Hubbly Bubbly Room. I was the one who insisted. It was me. Serena the snake woman slithered into my thoughts. I looked around the room and ensured myself that her scaly carcass was not inching along the carpet waiting to devour me.

I wanted to smoke but the fire in my pipe had gone out. I had no matches. For some reason that thought made me feel terribly helpless. I was hungry, too. I'd not eaten for some time, but escape from the Hubbly Bubbly Room was impossible. My sense of helplessness increased to the point of paralysis. I sat on the cushion immobilized by my own fear.

"You seem to be having some difficulties, Joe. What is it?"

Devil Nate had returned. This time wrapped in a satin purple robe with oversized sleeves that hid his hands and covered the floor over his feet. He shifted from side to side in front of me, seeming to slide on a cushion of air instead of taking steps.

"Why are you telling me these things Nate? Why me?" I asked.

Nate waived his handless arms about. "I am coming to that Joe, I am coming to that! Some patience is required you know. I thought that perhaps you needed a moment or two of silent reflection. I realize it's been quite a day for you, hasn't it?"

I rubbed my face. "That is the worst understatement I've ever heard."

The remark sent Devil Nate into gales of laughter. Tears rolled from his eyes and he wiped them with his purple sleeves. His laughter turned into a strange giggling sort of short screeches. It was a frightening sound. And where had his hands gone?

At last he pulled himself together. "Joe, Joe, Joe," he said and inhaled deeply. His face went finally serious. "You have the first part of the answer you seek – the very beginning – the concept of thought. Can you imagine what happened next?"

I told him I could not. I could not, in fact think of anything at this point.

He continued without notice of my distress. "The thought had too much energy, Joe. It was impossible to maintain that status forever. So the thought took form, Joe. It was the only way. Too much energy and it would have annihilated itself; already there were clashes of energy waves that convoluted and distorted the pureness of the thought. It had to change, Joe. So the thought took form; it deliberately slowed itself and took form. Kind of gaseous at first, and then it gradually solidified itself.

"From this the universe began to form, Joe. Bit by bit the original thought coalesced into carbon, minerals, planets, animals – and finally people.

"But some traces of that original thought refused to change. Some traces of it; the traces convoluted and agitated from the original thought refused to play along and solidify into the dross matter that so eludes your human eyes. We stayed true, Joe. We remained in the purified state as the rest of the thought energy congealed into the myriad forms of gross matter.

"That is why I keep telling you, Joe - I do not deal in trickery. I deal in the truth. Because I am part of that original truth. This solid matter that you worship in the form of money or human achievement is nonsense, Joe. It's false. It's a lie created by the overlords of earth who want to keep you in your place. The truth stands before you; I am one of the original convolutions of thought. There are multitudes of us still in this pure state of truth.

"Think of it like the pure water that flows from the top of a mountain. That sweet wonderful liquid is at its highest clarity and purity at the very moment of its conception. Only at that perfect moment is it perfect. From that instance on every molecule of this beautiful substance is contaminated as it answers the pull of gravity and rolls down the mountain side; each micrometer of movement adds to its pollution.

"I and others of my kind have retained that purity. But we have gone even further. We can enter the impure state of solidity and return to the state of purity at will! Such power, Joe! You have no idea of the kind of utter bliss this kind of existence is!"

Devil Nate stopped talking. He let the silence and my thoughts fill. Actually, he had not been talking. I realized, quite ironically, that this devil had been preaching, preaching the gospel of his existence and the reason for it. But it was, after all, the answer to the question I'd asked him. Who are you? He told me. But there was still one more question to be answered.

"Are you, and your kind, all that is left of the original thought?" I asked. My voice cracked and quivered.

Devil Nate's evil grin, the great pumpkin monster I had seen before cracked wide across his face. A scarlet cavern opened from ear to ear. "Yes!" he hissed.

The robe dropped and Devil Nate's bodiless head floated in the room. "It is all so easy," he said. "Once you understand the truth." His head waved easily from side to side. The awful grin thankfully disappeared. The fleshy color of his skull faded, first to green and then to a bright white complexion mottled in gray. The gray spots took on form and contrast. I recognized a startling similarity. Devil Nate's head had become the moon.

He must have seen my recognition, indeed I am sure that is what he had intended. "Yes, yes, Joe. You are seeing me for who I am; this is the greater part of me from which I am derived."

"The moon?" I exclaimed. "You are the moon?"

"Hah!" he laughed. "I am not even a tenth part of it, Joe. I told you I am part of the original thought. But the moon is the gateway for you. Gaze deep, sweet human, and feel its power. This is the truth you know, isn't it?"

Now my head started to swim and swirl. All the while I continued to stare at the Nate moon head. It suddenly seemed far away. The Hubbly Bubbly room disappeared. I was outside staring at the moon overhead. It seemed I could not stop from staring at the thing. Then the moon began to grow. It turned gold and then yellow. It turned to flesh and a horrible gaping grin. The Hubbly Bubbly Room materialized around me again. I was back in my tobacco pipe prison.

Nate continued. "You see, Joe. You've had the power to find us all along. You've had the very thing you desire, not under your nose – but above it!" He seemed to find his little jest very amusing. "Don't you see? All this time you've been worshipping the wrong thing."

"So why me? Why am I the recipient of the esoteric knowledge? Why was I chosen?"

"Oh my persistent friend! You have not forgotten your second question, have you?"

"How could I Nate? What have I done to deserve your considerable time and consideration?"

"You saw the Hubbly Bubbly Room, Joe."

"Yea," I said with more than a touch of impatience. "I'm in the thing right now as you may notice."

"Of course you are. But to get here you had to see the room first." Devil Nate's head bounced crazily. It was hard to keep my eyes on him.

"That's the way I operate, Nate. Before I enter a building I like to see it first."

"Ah, Joe. You think your sarcasm is meaningless wit but you have hit precisely on the answer."

"Really?"

"Only those who are truly ready to receive the truth can see the Hubbly Bubbly Room. Thousands enter the hotel every year. Only a select few see the room."

"Wait a minute. Major Paulson saw it. So did Jaleel and Kareem!"

Bloody teeth now poked through the grin. "Yes they did."

"But they tried to stop me."

"And they did not succeed. Only the true believer persists. That's how we knew you were ready."

We? I did not like the direction of this conversation, I did not like it at all. The evening's events tumbled through my head. The frustration of not getting into the room was replaced by the exquisite beauty of Serena. Beauty then turned to horror which in turn transformed into amusement at my audience with Devil Nate. Now I felt fear creeping. Change was in the air again; a distasteful change.

"But why me, Nate? What have I done to earn this?"

I had thought that Nate's revolting grin could not grow any larger or more distasteful. I was wrong. It grew to even great and more misshapen proportions as he spoke and giggled. "What have you done to deserve this honor? Why you've spent a lifetime earning it, Joe!"

"Nate, I've had enough. It's time for Joe Doyle to go home."

The atmosphere did change - abruptly. Devil Nate regarded me with a sideways tilt of his head that conveyed a silent and not so subtle message of distrust. "Perhaps more groundwork is necessary, more foundation?"

I did not have time to think about the meaning of the words or to protest. Nate took a single sidestep to his right. Dressed in a dazzling, colorful silken gown that clung to her body like so much perfume Serena instantly materialized. She flashed her amazing, dimpled smile. Her face beamed.

"Oh Master Nate! Thank you so much for allowing me this small pleasure," she said, never taking her eyes away from me. "Is Joseph mine?"

Serena seemed to glide to me. She stopped inches from my face. Despite my nightmarish memories her beauty was as bewitching as before. "Come, Joseph," she breathed. "Be mine. For a sliver of time at least."

Her hand touched the side of my face. Her beauty. Her perfume. Her nearness.

"Or perhaps forever," she purred. And as she mouthed the words a slimy and glistening red tongue that terminated in a pair of slender black forks flickered between her teeth. The ebony ends of it feathered my chin. Serena's eyes bulged into the horribly familiar elliptical orbits. I fell backwards.

Sunlight. I felt it on my face and sensed it streaming pink through my close eyes. I slowly and carefully opened my eyes. To my left the light was dazzling. My right was darkness. My legs and arms felt trapped, as though wrapped in thick gauze. Fuzzy thoughts slowly gelled and bit by bit coalesced into memory and awareness. At some point in the night I must have rolled off the bed taking the sheets and covers with me. The brilliant light to my left was indeed the sun beaming through the hotel room window. The frightening darkness on my left was nothing more than the dark underside of my bed.

I shuffled out of the bed covers and sat up. An overwhelming sense of relief came over me, but I remained in the terrible emotion of my frightening dream. Never in my life had I ever experienced such a thing. Had I choked on something and gone through a near death experience? It was hard to think of any explanation. My heart began to hammer at the memory. I'd talked to a devil; I'd seen a woman turn into a snake. A dream? A dream?

Using the bed for support I stood up and looked for the clock. From the bright sunlight I assumed it was late, but it was only six o'clock. I had a full two hours before Major Paulson would arrive to pick me up.

I made sure the room door was lock then I went into the bathroom and carefully locked that door as well. Dream or not I did not intend to have any more surprises. I shucked off my underwear, stepped into the tub, and adjusted the temperature. When it was comfortably warm I turned the lever and directed the water into the shower head. Water pulsed out in rapid beats. I reached up to adjust the spray and smelled my armpits. Now I'm no lily of the valley in the morning, but something was wrong, awfully wrong.

What I smelled was not normal body odor, at least not my normal body odor. By the time a guy's my age he's pretty familiar with himself. I know exactly what I'm like after a hard day's work or after a hard work out. It ain't pretty, but it was nothing like this. I smelled rancid, disgusting; it as though I hadn't bathed in months and had slept in a sewer. And yet it was somehow an odor of disgusting familiarity. Rotten meat or death. I'd become familiar with that in other parts of the world.

I yanked my arm down, grabbed the soap, and scrubbed like a mad man for over an hour while periodically checking myself. It had to be the dream, I reasoned. Something about that bizarre nightmare caused me to perspire in some weird way; that had to be it. I got out of the shower and shaved with trembling hands. I dressed and sat down on the couch in the outer room concentrating on breathing and calming myself. My knotted muscles and clenched throat had finally begun to return to a normal state when the phone rang. I nearly sprang into the air.

"Hello?" I said, hoping the rattled fear in my voice was not exposed.

"Hey, sir, it's Major Paulson. I'm downstairs in the lobby. Everything alright?"

The young soldier's voice was incredibly reassuring. "Oh yea, Brian. I'm sorry. Jet lag catching up. I'll be right down."

"No problem, sir. I'll wait."

I hung up and slowly rubbed my eyes. Get over it, I told myself. It was a dream and nothing more. Everything is fine. Jet lag, bad food, too much coming at me at once in this damned country – it all adds up. A large mirror hung behind the small cocktail bar. I walked over to it, flipped on the overhead light, and leaned forward. I looked a bit haggard, but outside of that the reflection was the same old normal head I'd been gazing at for years. I felt better. I let out a long whoosh of pent up air.

The doorbell rang. I glanced at my watch and a quick flush of embarrassment came over me as I realized how long I'd kept Mike waiting. He'd obviously gotten concerned and came up to get me. I walked to the door thinking of some reasonable excuse for taking so long and decided that my jet lag explanation was my best bet.

"I'm sorry, Brian," I said as I turned the knob and yanked open the door. "I – ." The rest of the words snarled in my throat. Dressed in a shimmering metallic blue gown that clung to her like scales Serena stood in front of the door. Her arms were folded and her head cocked.

"My dear Joseph," she said like she was scolding an errant child. She reached out slowly and took my hand. "Come on, now. You know where you want to go."

They were all there waiting for me in the Hubbly Bubbly Room. Major Paulson, Jaleel, and the ever smiling Kareem. I'd obviously been conned; my fury nearly outweighed my fear. Devil Nate was there, too, of course. Serena led me to my green seat and gleefully adjusted my pipe.

Nate had resumed his portly and harmless human shape. But Serena resumed her serpentine persona and slithered up into his arms. She raised her snake head to a level with his and tickled him with her tongue. Nate smiled warmly.

"Now my dear," he said. "Who shall we start with?"

Serena answered with a slim lipless grin. "Our old soldier, of course."

"Excellent choice, my dear. And just what I was thinking myself."

With that the serpent woman did a half body twist and slithered in my direction. It was terrifying but not unexpected; after all I was still fresh meat in their minds.

"WAIT! WAIT, Master Nate! I am thinking you should start with me! I am the first disciple you know and you promised me many times to complete me." Jaleel was up on his feet and frantically waving his hands.

Devil Nate and Serena were annoyed at this outburst. The snake lady turned and hissed violently. Devil Nate jumped down from his hookah pedestal, his face in a snarl. "So you think to defy my decision you ignorant wog?"

At this Jaleel cowered and retreated back with palms raised. "Oh no, no, Master Nate! You are the boss, the boss of all. I am only asking for my promises, yes? I am thinking this is fair."

Devil Nate sneered. "I am thinking this is unfair," he retorted in a sarcastic imitation of Jaleel's accent. "Well, I am thinking that it is time you really understood your position in the echelons of this universe. Serena, show our rude Indian friend how your power compares to his."

Serena bowed in cobra fashion and began a slow slither toward Jaleel who was instantly horrified.

Devil Nate turned to us. "Gentlemen, I apologize for this unsightly interruption but certain things must be understood within my, shall we say, chain of command before we proceed further. Serena is about to demonstrate an echelon of power that will soon be yours, a power over humans that will bring you riches, and much amusement as you will see."

He waved his hand toward the coming drama between Serena and Jaleel. The snake woman had raised her hideous hooded face several feet above the unfortunate man who was by now backed up against the glass wall of the room. She hissed loudly and opened her gaping jaws to reveal the gleaming fangs about to sink into his flesh.

Yet at that instant my horror of the situation was overcome by the instincts of the old soldier in me. This was my driver about to be attacked; my driver, who at that moment suddenly became one of my soldiers. Nobody pulled that crap on my watch! I bolted from my seat and lurched for Serena's tail. With strength I never knew I possessed I snapped the serpent like a whip. And just as instantly her neck broke. I heard the crack. But at the same instance I heard that awful sound a huge arm curled around my neck from behind me. I was immediately choking and I could hear my own neck bones cracking.

The arm lock on my throat suddenly released, however, followed by an odd screeching. I spun about to another incredible sight. Jaleel was biting Devil Nate's leg. Kareem was pummeling his stomach and Paulson was applying a ferocious choke hold on the demon. An instant later Devil Nate was gone. As was Serena, as was the Hubbly Bubbly room. The four of us stood outside of the hotel shaded by a pair of enormous palm trees. I stood silently in shock but my three mortal companions were beaming with laughter and smiles.

Major Paulson approached me and saluted. "Thank you, sir. You have saved us."

Out of habit I returned the salute but I had no idea what Paulson was talking about. "I did what?"

The Major turned to Jaleel and Kareem with an open hand. Apparently it was their turn to speak. His smile in full beam, Kareem stepped forward. "We have been waiting for you for some time, Mr. Joe, but so was the evil one. He needed you as much as we did for his own purposes."

"Is that why you tried to talk me out of visiting the Hubbly Bubbly room?" I asked, waving at the now empty spot.

"Not at all," Kareem said. "That was merely a test of the strength of your determination. Others have seen the room and asked to enter but they were easily frightened away. Most importantly they did not have your other special quality. This we reported back to the evil one and you were accepted."

"Other special quality?" At this question of mine, Kareem turned to Jaleel. "The honor should be yours, Jaleel. You brought him to us."

Jaleel proudly stepped forward. "I am thanking you very much Mr. Kareem!" he said and turned to me. "You see boss, I discovered your other special quality during our driving."

At this I had to laugh. "Hah, you mean how I survived your driving?"

"Oh no, sir!" Jaleel said as he and the others laughed at my joke. Let me explain it this way."

"Okay," I said.

Jaleel stood upright and took up a dignified posture. "First, sir, let me introduce us formally. I am Jaleel Sidana, of the Hindu faith. Standing there is good Major Brian Paulsen. He is Jewish. And standing here by me is Mr. Kareem Nahas of the Muslim faith. And now I am thinking that you understand your special quality, yes?"

And suddenly it all made sense. Devil Nate needed a Christian to complete his triumph and rise in rank. These gentlemen needed a Christian to solidify their taskforce and win this fight against evil.

"You see, Mr. Joe. This devil and many like him have been making many mischiefs here. Now we know how to beat them!" Jaleel was jubilant and we all clapped and roared joyously.

Despite this incredible episode I upheld the end of my more mundane earthly contract and went about training Saudi soldiers in the art of fire support. As you may have surmised, however, I have a very specialized sideline that I engage in as well. I love this work; it is extraordinarily fulfilling – and a lot better than spending eternity in a Hubbly Bubbly Room.

KOGIRI ATASHI

Chapter One

Forget the legal jargon and standard military phrases. My lawyer's eyes are rolling balloons as he calls the JAG and announces he's got a lunatic for a client. *No sense going to trial; the boy is bonkers. It's padded cell and twenty four hour watch for this one. The court martial is a done deal; the kid just needs rest.* They've left me alone for a while but they'll still want a statement. I promised the truth and I'm going to deliver it no matter who believes it. So here it is.

Go ahead and call me Mike; Mike Moran. At least I was for a long time. I grew up as Mike Moran and under that personage I led a life of varied occupations. Then one day I enlisted in the Army. In due time that stalwart organization changed my name to Private Moran and later to a more compelling Second Lieutenant Michael J. Moran. But good old Mike still lived and laughed, a bit unsure of his soul and identity I admit, but ready for the new adventure. Before long I became Captain Michael J. Moran - then one night on the other side of a dirty river just south of the DMZ in Korea I saw an odd, misshapen old circus tent. I'm not sure what the hell my correct name is now but at least I know who I am.

For three weeks we had been training in the broiling Korean summer, undergoing an evaluation of our skills as an artillery battalion. It was a grueling 21 days. Summer in Korea is rough introduction to reality for those raised on televised news reels and reruns of unrealistic TV shows. Winter can be a bone chiller, but summer is the real challenge. The heat is unrelenting; mountains block every breeze and focus the sun into narrow green valleys filled with water logged rice fields and swamps periodically inundated with monsoon rains. A humid haze hangs from the sky, cicadas scream endlessly, the air shimmers, and the training area smolders. Three weeks of twenty four hour operations in these conditions test a unit.

Our evaluation was successful, though. Under the able leadership of our commander, Lieutenant Colonel Joseph Kerney we gave it all we had and shot like champions. On time and on target. Over a thousand, one hundred pound rounds into the impact area with accuracy that surprised even us. "Knockin' fleas off a cat's ass!" as my First Sergeant liked to say. Every displacement and every occupation my battery executed went like clockwork.

When the battalion rolled in after that kind of a performance everyone was feeling good. I was the firing battery commander of C Battery, 1st Battalion, 15th Field

Artillery Regiment - the best job in the Army. I had six big howitzers, a lot of other tracks, trucks, HUMMVs, and about two hundred soldiers. They could have left me as a BC for the rest of my natural life and I wouldn't have complained. With my battery safely back in the motor pool we went about the standard drill of ammo and small arms accountability, vehicle and weapon maintenance; the usual post field problem routine. For three days the troops worked around the clock. We had inspections on day four and with the okay from the old man we embarked on a three day pass.

Now when it comes to enjoying a few hard earned days off an officer is negligibly different than the men he supervises. I linked up with three of my fellow captains. Kevin Cunningham, a big, blond all American type built like a linebacker, Tommy Dolenz, referred to as the Bird Man due to the unusual size of his nasal passages, and Vincent "Vinnie" Vinzi, a short squat Italian fire plug.

Since I was the only one of us on his second tour in Korea the guys tended to follow my insightful lead in these matters. I recommended we meet at the officer's club and warm up with a few beerskis. This we did, then ate dinner and headed back to the bar too fool around a bit with some of the regular girls. Chung Oh and Su Mi could always be relied on for a good time, but you had to watch them on the pool table and the dart board, their hustling skills were superb. If they liked you then your losses amounted to no more than a round or two of drinks. If they didn't then you'd quickly feel the pinch in your wallet. Like you or not the price of their company cost money. But if you have to be hustled it always feels better when done by a beautiful girl. I bought each of them an obligatory drink. The expression in Su Mi's face held promise, but I felt the need to expand our horizons. We left the club in fine form and headed out for the adventure that awaited us across the street from the post at the "downrange" section.

Camp Casey, Korea sits at the edge of a relatively small Korean town named Tongdechong. "TDC" has two distinct sections. What we call "downrange" borders the post and is a typical GI honky tonk and souvenir sucker haven. The rest of the city, the majority of it, belongs to the Koreans and is a rightly respectable, middle class Korean town.

Needless to say, respectability was not high on our list. Our first stop was a favorite haunt, renamed countless times over the years of GI occupation. Its current incarnation, "Cheers," bears no resemblance to its TV namesake beyond the sign hanging over the entrance. Quite simply, Cheers is a dive which features two standard attractions: cheap beer and girls. Hardly a unique downrange combination, yet the place is one of those landmark launching points none of us would think of doing without. We paraded in. The girls behind the bar were familiar friends (some very familiar) and greeted us like the returning heroes we thought we were. The bar sits right in the middle of the salon. It has sort of a funny octagon shape and forms a protective barrier between the leggy beauties slinging beer and the sea of drunken soldiers beyond. The micro minnied girls and the overly loud rock music are the only entertainment. The beer is cheap, but these ladies are sly and sharp at separating Joe Willy from his money. Watch out or they'll take a beer bottle still one quarter full and ask you if you're ready for another and somehow you usually end up buying them a drink with your next one. And they're always happy to play "Speed," a card game specialty of the house that requires fast reflexes and a clear head, exceedingly rare attributes among GIs in a bar.

Having paid our respects to Cheers we wandered over to The Bucket, famous for its colorful little plastic pails of soju liquor Kool-Aid and porno video monitors. The Bucket is rumored to have a more biochemical approach to theft. They load barbiturates in the drinks to help soldiers loosen up their cash. Since I've never seen a GI downrange who needed any help whatever to get stupid with his money I don't know why they'd have to resort to that.

We bounced in and out of a few other clubs and strip joints. The summer night was alive with a thousand soldiers, "slicky boys" selling ten dollar Rolex watches, prostitutes, madams calling from street corners, and countless other tacky distractions. Garish bars on either side of the street blasted music and advertised the various delights to be found inside. There's a place for all tastes downrange, and everybody advertises outdoors. Country western, soul, hard rock, and disco boom from cheap speakers. Strip joints aren't shy at all about letting you know what they're offering, while girls sit like sleepy cats sprawled around open bars. Throw in pawn shops, fast food, karaoke, etc. Name your particular vice, muse, calling, or peccadillo (to use the polite phrase) and you can find it all on a dirty concrete strip half a mile long. And if you want something a little more durable than a hangover there's tee shirts, leather goods, blankets, sex toys, and a million other useless trinkets. Shops a little higher up the legitimacy scale hawk brass and onyx statues, leather goods, tailor made suits, TVs, stereo and exercise equipment; a blur of colorful, cheap, easily transportable items aimed directly at the lonely GI. Picture this cacophony of sin and glitter displayed under a thousand twisting miles of neon lights and you have Downrange TDC in full swing on a Friday night.

Our next tour stop was a gin mill of sinfully shady reputation called the Beak. The Beak is located toward the end of the downrange line. Maybe that's why the place is the scene of more than its share of trouble. Like us, most patrons have already paid homage to quite a few other shrines before they make it here. Loud music, smoky dance floor, a glittering bar where girls pump booze and take cash. The Beak has all the standards. Naked dancers gyrate under strobe lights while Private Snuffy buys fake smiles and phony kisses with real dollar bills. We claimed a booth, ordered a round of drinks, and settled in for the show.

I'm no sooner sitting down than I have to get up and fight the crowd blocking the path to the latrine. The room was a smelly little cubicle, entirely too small for the purpose it served. GIs are crammed into the thing and the odor competes with the worst field shitters I've dealt with. By the time I get out a cat fight has broken out between two ladies on the dance floor, probably a dispute over wiggling space. The crowd parts to give them room because everyone likes it when the girls fight, but when one of them starts to get the worst of it her boyfriend jumps in to help. Needless to say this brings in the other gal's macho ally, and most ricky tick we have a lot of GIs throwing fists. It's time for prudent young officers to leave; the MPs around here are on a hair trigger and a short leash.

My companions and I head for the door. We make it to the street in time to see the first wave of MPs hit the Beak, pardon the pun. We put a little more distance between ourselves and the epicenter of dispute. At this point the Bird Man, innovator that he is, suggests that despite this interruption we continue on and turn the evening into a full blown "Thunder Run." Vinnie and Kevin second and third the idea immediately. A Thunder Run meant catching a cab to a squalid little town on the other side of post called Toko Ri. When you wanted to raised hell you went downrange to TDC. For real, turn you into a pillar of salt debauchery, Toko Ri is the hell hole of choice.

I was all up for the run, but suddenly I had a change of heart. Maybe it was the smell of the latrine, the grinding music, or the disturbing spectacle of humanity at its grubby, alcohol and flesh seeking worst. Maybe the ritual of Friday nights and Saturday hangovers got to me. I don't know. Suddenly I was tired of it all. I decided not to make the decision unanimous.

Vinnie was perplexed. I'm normally an enthusiastic hell raiser and more than happy to meet trouble past the halfway point. "You sick?" he asked.

"Nah," I explained, "just need a change of scenery."
My friends were not really surprised by this odd behavior;
my background prior to coming into the military was a bit
unorthodox to say the least and the guys were used to my
sometimes odd preferences. My change of heart, however,
broke up the team spirit somewhat and me wandering around
outside alone was not a good thing. GIs are pretty well
indoctrinated in the buddy system for good reason. But I
convinced them not to worry; I was going to walk straight
back to my hootch and take an early retirement for the night.
My friends listened with great sympathy and understanding,
hailed a cab and said goodbye.

Now the sensible, intelligent thing to do at that point
would have been to execute my plan for an early night. I
could have woken up the next morning, reasonably clear
headed and made a pilgrimage to some cultural shrine,
something I had been meaning to do for months. One of the
main reasons I had come back to Korea was my yearning to
learn more about the country; something about the place
intrigued me. The whole time I had been back stateside I
thought about all the sights and history I'd missed while
behaving as the typical second lieutenant during my first
tour. Now I had a three day opportunity to actually do
something constructive and intelligent and I was not going to

waste it. But although I did not have the stomach for a Thunder Run, I did have a bit too much alcohol in my system for a book and bedtime. I was restless. What the hell? I thought. Why not walk around a bit, see the sights; respectable sights?

I strolled to the end of the downrange strip to the border that marked the end of the GI influence on Tongdechong. Here the GI playground ends abruptly; bars dwindle and then stop towards the end of the street; the music fades away. A wide, empty alley runs directly into a busy street crossed by railroad tracks. On the other side of that street is the respectable, truly Korean Tongdechong. I crossed over. It was like walking into another world – because it was.

I strolled about peeking into restaurant windows where patrons sat cross legged, their arms resting on low tables situated on a raised portion of the floor. Rows of shoes lined the floor waiting for their owners to finish eating. Some places had additional areas for western style dining complete with tables and chairs. Giant aquariums filled with a rainbow assortment of koi and goldfish are a standard feature of Korean restaurant windows and just walking by is an entertainment. The city lights increased, the sidewalks brightened, and I was soon in a well lit section of the city bustling with activity like the old downtown sections of America before the advent of the giant shopping malls. The street glittered with motion, light, color, and a dazzling array of sophisticated consumer goods. Pretty young girls walked hand in hand in the Korean fashion, giggling about boyfriends and pausing occasionally to stare at me. Well dressed people, Koreans rarely dress otherwise, meandered in an out of the shops inspecting and buying. Block after block of bright clean shops beaming sophisticated civilization. I had crossed into respectability, and although folks often looked at me like an alien, I felt good in this purer environment.

A couple of turns later I took a right turn and entered the alleyways of the open air market. Once again, cross a street and enter a different world. People crowded around brilliant displays of fruit, berries, nuts, vegetables, and pots of brilliantly colored beans. An intriguing array of fish, eels, clams, pig heads, hams, and hundreds of unidentifiable edibles tumble over shelves on beds of crushed ice. Mobile vendors stirred silkworm larvae in large boiling pots and the acrid smell mixed with the delicious odor of fish shaped pastries stuffed with sweet bean paste. The smell of barbequed chicken on a stick blended with sour kimchi. Barkers and proprietors touted shirts, shoes, ladies underwear, and little gadgets that would make Ronco proud. Overhead lights were strung in haphazard fashion and little portable televisions blinked in every booth. A fresh, vibrant explosion of life.

Drinking in the odor, color, and life of the market I explored every inch of it as I walked off my restlessness. After the sordid atmosphere of the GI honky tonk this celebration of light and life was a refreshing change despite the muggy heat. I wandered to the end of the market where it halts before a strip of businesses that border the Im Jim River. On the other side of the street I spied line of shops and cafes. Why not end this delightful sojourn with a coffee in one of the cafes?

I selected a nice looking place on the fourth floor of an office building. The subdued, air conditioned interior of the café after the night's journey through the market felt wonderful. I took a booth by a window and viewed the never ending activity on the street below. A smiling waitress, clearly amazed at my presence in this section of TDC at this hour, took my order and brought coffee. I sipped and stared at the city lights. From here I could see all the way down to where the street ran into a wide concrete bridge that crossed the river. On the other side row after row of high rise apartments gleamed against the sky.

An odd, out of place shape caught my eye. It looked at first like a giant, illuminated orange balloon sitting on the far river bank. Then I realized I was looking at a circus tent. A perfect addition to this night of clean fun wonders!

Excited by the prospect of seeing my first Korean circus I plunged back into the humid night. It's a good thing I wasn't looking for a Ringling class show. As I crossed the bridge it became obvious that this was small town stuff. The tent was a pretty ragged affair. It looked like a bloated discolored wart against the skyline of high rise buildings beyond. But it was fairly large and I had not seen a circus of any kind since my short stint of working in one before joining the Army.

A man sat behind a rectangular wooden crate that served as a ticket booth. He greeted me with a smile that revealed teeth as worn out as the tent and handed over a ticket. I paid the admission fee of a thousand Korean won, about fifty cents back then. The fellow took my money and pointed to the tent flap behind him. Near the entrance a forlorn group of stump tailed macaque monkeys sat tethered to a rope. "Monkey bites," he warned in English. I hadn't thought about cuddling any of them but I thanked him for the advice and walked in.

The interior of the tent was no more to brag about than the exterior, but it had the odd circus charm. There was a small raised stage above which hung supports and rigging that promised some form of trapeze act. Ropes hung from beams that crisscrossed beneath the big top. Behind the stage a gaudy red curtain hung which I surmised to be the performer's entrance.

Seating arrangements were uniquely Oriental. Most people sat cross legged on a large mat laid out in front of the stage. The wealthier clientele, of which I considered myself a member, rented a folding chair for another one thousand won.

Trying not to appear too conspicuous, I pulled my seat close to the stage and sat down. I wondered what kind of circus feats would emerge from behind the scarlet curtain. A jarring clang of metallic sounding drums preceded a sudden fanfare of taped music. What appeared to be the entire troupe poured forth from behind the curtain. The assemblage pranced onto the stage in a proper show folk promenade, made their way to the very edge of the stage, joined hands and raised them high. Several beautiful young ladies dressed in obligatory tights and circus spangles, a bald midget, and a bunch of muscular young men made up the entourage. I instantly noticed one performer. Outfitted in a powder blue, lightly sequined leotard she had the taught, lean physique of an athlete. Her hair was pulled back into a tight pony tale. She had a classically beautiful Korean face. Yep, this was going to be better than some grubby display in Toko Ri.

The performers linked hands, called out a loud "Anyang ahseo!" to the crowd, and bowed deeply. The audience, myself included, responded back with the traditional Korean greeting and polite applause. The music changed to western style rock and the first performance began in earnest. A pretty young lady I estimated to be about sixteen remained on the stage with a petite little girl no more than five years of age. The pair bowed and then retreated to center of the stage where they mounted two separate raised platforms.

Rock and roll changed to the Vienna Waltz and the artists began contorting themselves into an astounding array of pretzel like shapes that caused many gasps of appreciation from the audience. They even did a balancing act with glasses of water, standard fair for larger circuses and Las Vegas shows, but a remarkable scene under this rundown tent. The flexible young artists bowed stiffly to wide applause and were replaced by three fellows of exceptional energy who treated the onlookers to a display of tumbling, acrobatics, and juggling that even had me clapping with enthusiasm. I was in the swing of things now and thoroughly enjoying myself.

I was anxious to see the performance of the striking lady I had seen at the introduction and each time the announcer took the stage I listened carefully. My Korean is spotty, but I can pick out a few words here and there. Finally my patience was rewarded. At the conclusion of a very clumsy clown act the announcer, a little fellow with a surprisingly loud voice, introduced "The beautiful Kyung Re!" I picked out something about Tae Kwon Do, but that was the extant of my ability.

The little guy bowed off stage and the most beautiful woman I have ever seen emerged from the curtain. Right there, at the instant she walked out, my identity began to fade. I was no longer my own man. I belonged to the vision on the stage. She had a high cheek boned, perfectly proportioned Korean face, skin of polished ivory, and wide, lilting eyes made more exotic by show business make up. In a white, ankle length cape she calmly walked to the front of the stage and delivered a regally slow bow.

With a dramatic swirl she removed the cape, sent it whirling to the back of the stage, and stood solemnly in a white satin uniform with a black sash. She let out a high pitched, "Kee-yah!" and snapped into a head on, bent legged punching position. From here she executed a number of kicks, punches and blocks accented by her flying main of pony tailed raven hair.

The three young men who had previously given an outstanding performance as jugglers and acrobats now came on stage dressed in western style jeans and tee shirts. They sauntered around the lovely martial artist with obvious evil intent. The young men closed in and all three attacked at once. In a blur of strikes and spinning kicks Kyung Re left each of them sprawled on the stage. The audience applauded loudly; my big slapping hands loudest of all.

But the assault was not over. The three delinquents got to their feet and closed in again, this time carrying a variety of weapons. A man ran at her swinging a large knife. Kyung Re deftly blocked his wrist, snapped an arm lock on him, and used the force of his momentum to hurl the attacker completely off the stage. A similar fate awaited the next guy coming at her with club of some sort. The last fellow rushed in waving a board over his head. I've never seen anyone attack another person with a piece of plywood but it made great show when Kyung Re leaped high into the air and demolished the wood with a resounding crack accented by a large scream. For a comic touch the attacker stared horrified at his broken, splintered weapon, dropped the pieces and ran away. We applauded mightily. Kyung Re turned and faced the audience, snapped once more into her Tae Kwon Do punching position, then straightened up and bowed.

I was properly impressed, but the amazing lady was not quite finished yet. The little announcer joined her on stage and began speaking in rapid Korean. I couldn't understand the words, but behind him several stage hands rushed about putting together a hastily rigged hire wire act. To my immense joy Kyung Re stripped off her martial arts uniform and revealed the powder blue leotards I had seen her in before. With the grace of a leopard she scaled the rope ladder to the top platform of the high wire. In time to a selection of somber music she gave another extraordinary demonstration of martial arts, this time on the high wire. A performance I have not seen before or since.

After a tumultuous applause the show halted for an intermission which consisted of a curious sales pitch for some kind of a miracle camera. In a demonstration of audacity that would have turned Americans violent, a ticket stub lottery was held to determine the winner of the wondrous camera. Miraculously, nearly everyone in the audience held the winning numbers, to include myself. The only requirement for the winners was to come on stage and pay a "special tax" for the valuable thing. While this amusing farce took place I schemed and thought of a way to get backstage and meet the amazing woman I'd just seen.

When the unique intermission and sales presentation ended, the announcer skipped back onto the stage and introduced the next act. "Pok Dani" was the name of the next performer. I thought I heard the word, Kogiri, Korean for elephant. Now that was something I'd really like to see.

At the sound of our applause a stubby, diminutive fellow in a sleeveless, red satin jacket and oversized gold pants strutted onto the stage and proceeded to direct two dirty poodles through a straightforward, unimaginative act. He never bowed, paused for applause, or even seemed to expect any. Working his ridiculous little dogs with the air of a lion tamer went about his task with silent pride. He may not have had much going for him, but every bit of the little man projected dignity and circus blood. I'd obviously misunderstood the introduction. The canine act continued without an elephant in sight. The obedient little dogs, clad in red jackets like their master, plodded along, climbing ladders, walking a tightrope, and deftly jumping over contrived obstacles. The highlight of the act was a "shooting" of one of the dogs with a not loud enough cap pistol. The dog rolled over and played dead. Bad stuff in my opinion. But the audience, comprised mainly of parents and children, hardly cared. Sitting on the mat, enchanted by the show, it was a Friday night like few others. You don't see too many bald midgets and trained dogs around the DMZ. They howled, laughed, and gasped at every ridiculous stunt. I went along with the applause but my mind remained on the beautiful martial artist.

Then the little guy did something unexpected. He directed the dogs onto a pair of stools and turned to face the audience. In a dramatic, surprisingly loud voice he addressed the audience. Most of the Hangul-mal oratory was again too quick and accented for me to understand, but I did pick up two words: kuda (big) and koe-mul (monster). He had my attention now and judging from the excited murmurs around the tent I wasn't the only sucker hooked.

The performer executed a smart about face and took up a posture of rigid, silent attention, just long enough to build an bit of tension in the crowd. Perfect, I thought. The little son of gun actually does know his craft. At just the right moment he raised and lowered his arms in rhythm to exaggerated, deep inhalations as if to sharpen his concentration and husband strength for the challenge ahead. Sufficiently fortified he marched resolutely to the rear of the stage and disappeared into the thick scarlet folds of the performer's curtain.

Three seconds later he popped out pulling a shiny black chain of sausage size links in his short muscular arms. The chain had an immediate effect on the poodles. They barked madly, pranced around on their stools and executed flying back flips. The little showman ignored the canine protests and continued his strenuous task, leaning forward and throwing his back into the effort of pulling out the mystery hidden behind the curtain. He sweated, growled and swore. The little dogs howled.

Suddenly Pok Dani appeared to give up. The chain hit the wooden stage like a bomb and caused the audience to jump. He took an oversized purple handkerchief from his pocket, wiped his brow with great show biz flourish, drew a breath, and then bent down to resume the struggle. This time he would not fail. The audience loved it. Chain firmly in hand he let out a yell like a Norse battle cry and gave one last ferocious effort. The scarlet curtains parted and the tusked head of an elephant appeared! It was an Asian elephant, not quite full grown, but in front of the little man on this small stage it looked enormous. Its huge ears flapped back and forth as it raised its trunk and bellowed. The audience, including myself, erupted into squeals and screams.

Pok Dani continued his chain pulling farce but the real force motivating the animal was soon revealed. Once again, it was something I never expected. The curtain swayed completely open and revealed four men standing on either side of the elephant – each one holding a burning torch. The men were costumed in some sort of ancient looking, furred outfits as though portraying the image of jungle natives or something. I assumed this was just show business fanfare and some kind of a standard circus elephant act would ensure. Wrong.

Pok Dani dropped the chain again and thrust his arms out. This turned out to be a signal for the torch bearers to close in on either side of the elephant. The beast immediately sensed the threat and moved forward. Pok Dani then raised his arms over his head. The torch bearers halted and moved away from either side of the elephant which then stopped in its tracks. The audience applauded. This time I did not join in. The idea of controlling an elephant with burning torches did not sit well with me and looked dangerous besides.

Pok Dani, of course, was undeterred. He took a few steps back, let out a deep throated command and pointed with his left hand. The torch bearers immediately went into action persuading the elephant to move left. Pok Dani bellowed another command and pointed with his right hand. The torch bearers positioned themselves in such a way that the frightened beast turned to the right. This maneuver was then repeated to move the elephant again to the left and then back to the right. It was quite a spectacle for sure and even more bizarre when the performers began moving the frightened elephant in circles.

Encouraged by the increasing enthusiasm of the audience Pok Dani increased the rapidity of his commands. After several revolutions of this the confused, and likely dizzy, elephant swung wildly about and collided with the torch bearers on his right, knocking them to the floor. The flames briefly touched the rear of the animal and it let out an ear shattering bellow. It turned on the fallen men who immediately scrambled to their feet and fled, leaving the still flaming torches on the stage floor. The elephant then turned to face the other men. They backed away but held on to their torches, intimidating the animal from further attack. The elephant then faced Pok Dani who was suddenly not so courageous anymore as the animal charged toward him. The great trainer turned in panic, immediately tripped on the ridiculous chain and fell; the elephant was on him in a second. I raced to the front of the stage just as the animal delivered a powerful kick to the little man and sent him skittering toward me. The elephant intended to continue its assault and another powerful kick or deadly stomp was on the way just as I managed to grab Pok Dani by one of his golden pant legs and yank him off the stage. Hanging on to my arm for support he screamed something to the crowd as I helped him away from the stage. I did not have to understand Korean to know what he yelled because most of the audience suddenly leapt to their feet and ran for the exit as though King Kong had escaped. All was not lost, however. With burning torches still on either side of it the elephant would not move to the right or left. The drop off from the stage was only about three feet but too steep for it to go forward and the dark curtain behind the animal must have appeared like a solid wall. The elephant just stood there bellowing.

I sensed that the animal was not enraged, however. A truly angered pachyderm would have mauled Pok Dani to death and annihilated the torch bearers despite the flames. No, it was simply as frightened and confused as the humans that surrounded it. But something had to be done, and fast. A small fire was starting from the fallen torches on the other side of the stage. What to do? The answer suddenly appeared at my feet. In the frenzy of escape from the circus a family had abandoned a large bag of fruit likely purchased at a nearby open market for dinner after the show. I snatched the bundle up and approached the stage again. The elephant eyed me suspiciously but did not move. I found an orange and tossed it in front of the animal's feet. The bellowing ceased instantly as the elephant snatched up the treat with its trunk and popped it into its mouth. I repeated the action several times with the same result. Gathering all the nerve I had I mounted the stage and faced the animal. It waited for another treat.

The remaining torch bearers were obviously surprised but seemed to think that all was back to normal. They began to edge closer perhaps thinking that they could now control the animal. I vigorously waived them off and they thankfully obeyed, retreating to a position just off the stage to my right. I also moved in that direction, this time dropping apples in order to encourage the elephant to follow, which it did. This got him away from the growing flames on the other side of the stage but I was running out of fruit. Thankfully, Pok Dani proved he still had some grit. Limping from his elephantine soccer kick he began fighting the flames with buckets of water and was soon joined by a couple of other circus hands.

"Atashi!" said a feminine voice behind me.

I looked quickly around. To the front of the stage stood the beautiful trapeze artist holding up another bag of fruit. I grabbed it with relief and returned to feeding the grateful elephant. As I did she climbed up on to the stage and took up a position behind me. "Will he follow you?" she asked. I was thoroughly surprised and relieved to hear my own language, especially under the current circumstances. "I think so," I said. "Where shall I take him?"

The lady moved to my side and beckoned me to follow. I moved after her while keeping a close watch on the big animal behind me and continuing the fruity offerings. Thank God for apples and oranges. The elephant trailed along like a big dog begging for treats. It stopped just once and snapped off the chain it had been dragging; apparently the thing was nothing more than a plastic prop. Soon we had the animal outside and heading for a fenced in corral where three of the former torch bearers stood by holding open a large gate. I marched the elephant in without any further trouble and dumped the rest of the fruit on the ground. The big guy was on the bounty immediately and I exited out the gate to the cheers of circus folk.

An instant later I was the topic of an excited torrent of rapid Korean, handshaking, and hugging. The little elephant trainer Pok Dani, had tears in his eyes and would not let go of my hand. The entire troupe had me now and I did not have to understand the language that well to know I was being congratulated for heroism.

Koreans are an astoundingly gregarious people, quick to emotion and celebration. And saving a circus is apparently cause for great celebration. Ah, the twists and turns of life! In very short order I'm sitting at the head of a makeshift table outside of a circus tent on a riverbank, being toasted as a hero with generous dollops of Korean mekchu and soju liquor. The men raised a toast to my health and we drank. This of course brought forth another round. Like Koreans everywhere the circus folk drowned me with hospitality. The drinking became a feast and the feast became a raucous celebration.

I must say that I was as carried away by the spirit of the celebration as anyone else. How often in one's life do you get to be hailed as a true hero? I was a life saver, an honest to goodness brave man. Not only that I had the unique circumstance of being hailed for my deed on the center stage of a circus. It was all quite glorious. I had won the fight - and it looked like I might get the girl, too!

We were in the middle of another roaring toast to my bravery when I became pleasantly aware of the stunning beauty sitting next to me. She introduced herself as Kyung Re and her English, much to my delight was surprisingly good. She thanked me for saving Pok Dani and asked my name. I think I gave a somewhat intelligible answer but I was so overpowered by her perfumed presence and astounding beauty my throat caught.

While my eyes were filled with Kyung Re, a stream of beer in front of me turned into a river, followed by a flood of soju liquor that went to my head as well. Round after round found its way to my lips between bites of spicy shrimp, marinated beef strips roasted at the table, squid, kimchi, and a hundred tasty tid bits I could suddenly not get enough of. I indulged in the making merry as my lovely host did her best to translate the raucous exclamation of my admirers and give me some background on the elephant. The animal's name was Konto. They had recently purchased the animal and this was the first time they had used it in an act. Kyung Rye doubted they would do it again, a point upon which I heartily agreed.

My recollections from that point on are decidedly vague. They come to me now in pleasant blurred bits and flashes, like trying to recall a half remembered, delightful dream. I have a picture of Pok Dani at my side, still clad in his red jacket and gold satin drawers insisting on pouring my drink. My glass was not allowed to dry. The young acrobats and a dozen other circus workers could not seem to get enough pleasure from shaking my hand. Dazzling in spangled, thigh cut leotards that displayed supple bodies of elegant beauty several young ladies tried to speak to me, but Kyung Re held my attention.

KOGIRI ATASHI
Chapter Two

I knew my eyes were open because I could feel the insides of my lids grate against them when they moved. Other sensations made no sense. Pinholes of brilliant light pockmarked the ceiling like a planetarium. I was in something that moved, creaked, and rattled. A blanket cushioned my back. My hand rubbed against something splintered and rough. I was in a wooden box! The thought alarmed me and I jumped up. At least I attempted to. The pin holes of light were not nearly as far away as I had estimated. I smacked my head on the roof with force. The collision let loose the full range of my hangover and a floodgate of memories. I still had no idea where I was, but at least I recalled where I had been.

I rubbed my skull and attempted to more completely remember the adventures of the previous twenty four hours. I abandoned that exercise when I came to full realization of the present. I was inside of a wooden box, a moving wooden box. Now I was fully awake. I banged the side of the box with the back of my elbow and battered the end of it with my feet. In short, I went into a bit of a frenzy with an obscenity or two thrown in for good measure. My hysterics provoked immediate action. Outside I heard voices barking and yelling in Korean and the thing I was in stopped moving. I heard a rattling sound like chains being moved and the end of the box sprung open. A brilliant light shocked my eyes.

Dark outlines of faces looked at me. They seemed friendly but why had they locked me in a wooden box? Whatever the reason I was not going to give them a chance to change their minds. I scrambled out. I had trouble coming to grips with waking up inside a moving coffin but circumstances outside were just as confusing. Still trying to clear my head I was attacked by handshakes and congratulations. I recognized the circus troupe who had so warmly feted me the night before.

"Where am I? What's going on?" I asked every handshake and back slap. From the coolness in the air and the level of the sun I deduced that it was early morning. But early morning where? Mountains stretched off in every direction, jagged blue peaks with misty curtains at their base. Less than ten feet from where I stood a cliff dropped off into the mist.

My transport turned out to be a wooden cart attached to a small wagon piled high with some kind of supplies covered by a tarp and attached to a very large mule. Ahead of the mule wagon was another mule wagon contraption, and behind it another and another. Wait, wait, I told myself. I'm in a mule powered wagon train somewhere high up in the Korean mountains with a group of circus performers? My hangover raged, the thin air of the mountain filled my lungs, and the crowd of odd people surrounding me continued to pull and pat every part of my body. I reached for the side of the cart. This provoked an instant reaction of sympathy and everyone tried to help at once. Finally someone brought something that I actually needed. I gladly gulped cool water from a metal canteen, pressed my back against the cart and steadied myself.

"You are all right, Atashi?"

The stark clarity of English against the background of Korean was a pleasant surprise. Kyung Re's presence was an even better one. Even with her circus spangle replaced by jeans and an open collared shirt she was a beautiful as ever. "Kyung Re, where am I? What's going on?"

"You are with us, Atashi. You asked to come so we brought you. It was only right after rescuing the circus."

"What do you mean I asked to come here?"

She flashed a dimpled smile. "Last night during party. You kept saying how much you loved the circus. You told me it is the dream of every American boy to run away with the circus. This was the only place we had to put you. You very drunk." She laughed and translated for the group. They laughed.

"Yea, but…"

"You said many other things, some very foolish. You made everyone laugh."

"I'll bet."

Despite Kyung Re's beauty and the obvious regard her people had for me, I was getting annoyed at the situation. Why the devil didn't they bring me back to the post? Or at least just leave me in TDC? Why load me into a box and cart me away? This is crazy! Okay, okay, I told myself, trying to calm down. I can't blame them because I got drunk and stupid. "Well wherever here is, I can't stay. I have to get back."

"I am sorry but you cannot go now."

"What do you mean? Why?"

"Atashi, please speak some slower. I cannot understand when you go so fast."

Steady, I reminded myself, steady. "Kyung Re. I'm a soldier, I'm an officer. I have to get back to the Army. I cannot simply take off and go as I please. You're a very nice bunch of people, but I'm in big trouble if you don't show me how to get back to Tongdechong."

"Tongdechong is very far away."

"That's all right. I have some won and a couple of credit cards. All you have to do is get me to a town where I can catch a train."

"There is no train for many kilometers from here, Atashi."

"Will this trail take me back to a town?"

"You will walk?" The idea seemed to horrify her.

"Yes, I will walk."

She rapidly said something in Korean to the rest of the troop. This provoked an uproar. All of them raised their hands and shook their heads. Kyung Re pleaded with me. "You cannot walk alone in these mountains. It is very dangerous."

"Why? Are there bandits? Are the mountains dangerous?"

"Yes, there are thieves, and the mountains are very dangerous, easy to get lost in. We come here so often we know the way. But there are worst dangers."

"Like what?"

"Tigers."

Now I might have believed the business about dangerous mountains and roaming bandits, but in 1988 Korea I was not about to accept a population of tigers roaming around snatching lone travelers. "Kyung Re, enough of this nonsense. I don't know why you brought me here, but I've had enough. If I don't get back to the Army very soon I am going to be in more trouble than any bunch of imaginary tigers could ever do. I'm leaving."

With that I began waking back along the path in the direction from which the wagon train had come. Behind me an excited babble of voices rose. I passed the last wagon and regarded the road ahead. The trail stretched on as far as I could see, winding along the top of a ridge that zig zagged through the mountains. Where ever I was headed it was going to be a long walk. Where on earth were these crazy circus people headed to out here in the hinterlands?

Well, that was their affair, not mine. I was already in enough hot water thanks to my own stupidity. I only hoped I could get back before Tuesday morning formation. At least I wouldn't have to explain how a seasoned battery commander became a bonehead for one night and ending up running away with a circus. I might not be court martialed but I'd never hear the end of it. Kevin, Vinnie, and the Birdman now, not to mention my battalion commander would have a hell of a time with this.

I pondered the long walk ahead. Be nice if my head would stop banging. My stomach was not in top form either.

But if I've learned anything about life I know this: when things are going bad, you can count on circumstances to degenerate into something worse. And it did. Behind me the yells of the Korean circus troupe grew louder. I looked over my shoulder and saw the whole gang headed my way waving their hands, earnestly trying to make me stop. Oh please, I don't have the strength for this.

Kyung Re led the charge. "Atashi!" she exclaimed. "You cannot do this! It is too dangerous! Listen to me, you do not understand!"

"Kyung Re, you don't understand! There is no way I can stay here. I have to go back. Now either show me the way, take me to a town, or get out of my way." The hangover had the better part of my tongue and my temper was getting the better part of the rest of me.

"I cannot let you go." She turned to the three acrobats and gave quick directions in Korean. The trio positioned themselves in front of me with grim faces. Fine, I thought. At least I can understand a fight. I gauged the odds. They certainly had me outnumbered. In addition to the three in front of me at least four of the other members of the troupe were healthy enough to cause problems. The trio to my front were athletic, well muscled and obviously in great condition. I had some things in my favor, however. I was considerably

342

larger than any of these guys, considerably more desperate, and cornered.

I gave another warning and then pushed my way forward, prepared to whack the first guy hard with a double handed blast to the chest. I figured that would demonstrate my seriousness without actually having to hurt anybody. He was the largest of the group but I estimated that I still outweighed him by thirty pounds. He shifted quickly to the right trying to avoid me. That proved to be an erroneous conclusion. As he shifted he dropped down and hooked his leg in back of mine. It took just the lightest push on my shin with his other foot to send me tumbling to the ground.

I sprang up furious. The diplomatic crap was over. But that first move had put me on notice. These three could probably fight; that maneuver was classic hap ki do. My size advantage had just become negligible. I turned to advantage two and three - anger and desperation. As I got to my feet I clutched fistfuls of rocks and pebbles. I put a smile on my face. Deception is a weapon, too.

The smile did it. The troupe let down their guard just for an instant figuring I was going to be reasonable about my situation and give up. I've been accused of many things, but reasonableness is usually not one of them. I let loose with one handful after the other of my rocks. Instinctively all of them ducked and protected their faces.

I sprinted away, bolting along the path. On a flat out, long distance run there was no way these characters were going to catch me. The hangover hobbled my pace a bit but once I got my rhythm nobody was going to get me. For the first several hundred meters I ran at jackrabbit pace. My initial bolt of speed must have surprised them; I heard the yells behind me grow fainter. I did not stop to look around and I continued running for a half a mile before I realized that the yelling had stopped.

I had escaped. But escaped to where? I had no idea where I was going and no clue as to how far away the next town was. Even if I found a town, then what? Although my money was good, my Korean wasn't and some of the towns out in the back country could be pretty primitive.

I'd worry about that later. The main priority right now was to put as much distance as possible between me and that crazy circus. What the hell was their problem anyway? One minute I'm a hero for saving the little guy's life and the next thing I know I'm being kidnapped. And these jokers were serious about it. I had no idea what their motive or destination was, but the more I thought about it the more I became convinced that this was no ordinary group of wandering circus performers. Was I going to be held for ransom? Were they North Koreans?

The thought of being kidnapped by North Korean agents really got me thinking. If that was the case then I was closer to the border than I cared to be. Maybe even on the other side of it. And if they were from the north they had probably let others know that I was captured. I'll bet right now they're broadcasting my escape. I'd have to be extremely careful about who I got close to out here.

All of which brought me back to my original worry. Where was here? The path stretched ahead until it disappeared up the side of a steep ridge about a klick in front of me. The morning sun was at my back so I was heading west. There was no way to tell if that was good or bad, but at least it wasn't north. On either side of the ridge I saw nothing but jagged Korean peaks; no sign of anything civilized. That in itself was another worry. In all the time I'd spent in Korea some form of civilization was visible. The country was heavily populated. Highways and high rises sprawled out from every town. Radio towers observation posts gleamed from the highest peaks. Yet even though this was a clear day I couldn't see a thing. That was strange.

My preoccupation with my location caused me to forget about where my feet were going. One second the ground was there, the next second it disappeared and I sailed out into the cool mountain air. For a single long moment I heard air rushing past my ears. I hit the side of the mountain but my feet barely touched ground before I was hurtling headlong down the side of a giant slab of granite. Moving like an airborne ranger without a parachute I collided with a small tree and my descent became a calamity of somersaults and collisions interrupted by end over end rolls.

My fall from grace ended in a thick tangle of thorny pines and brush. Incredibly enough my abrupt reckoning with gravity delivered me into an upright position. The bad news was that I was imprisoned in this upright posture, caught by the embrace of the prickly vegetation surrounding me. For the moment that was just as well, my breath had been knocked out of me and my first concern was getting that natural function back in order. I had to admit it, Kyung Re was correct about the mountain's dangerous properties.

I took a slow mental inventory. I did not feel any great pain, but initial shock always prevented that. The full range of my injuries would reveal themselves in short order. My immediate concern was the integrity of my limbs. I twisted my head from side to side without too much discomfort. Good news there, no broken neck. I undertook a visual inspection as best I could. Nothing missing. I could feel the rest of my body and move my legs. I wasn't a paraplegic.

Relieved to have survived without excessive damage I began the excruciating process of extracting myself from the thorny maze I had rolled into like a mad bowling ball. Vines, thorns, spiny pine combs, and spiked brush gripped me like a prickly straight jacket. Every time I attempted to move I jammed myself further into the thicket and hence managed to imbed more of the stinging needles into my skin.

I could not back out of my predicament since I was still on a very steep slope so I decided to force my way further down. It meant fighting through more of the prickly brush at least my own weight would assist me. The entangling mess I was wedged into had one advantage - no one would be able to see me. I was invisible from the top of the mountain.

I sucked a deep breath and bulled through the vegetation cursing my short sleeve shirt. Every step was a stinging, flesh ripping, struggle. By the time I worked myself free I was exhausted and bleeding.

The wall of scrub forest finally thinned near the base of the mountain and I sat down on a boulder to rest. I listened cautiously. Nothing but the chirping of birds. I hoped the circus people assumed I had died in the fall. But another sound mingled with the warbling birdsong. From further down the hillside I heard a rushing stream.

I hauled myself to my feet and stumbled down the incline using rocks and boulders for support, this time taking great care of my foot placement. I came out of the woods onto a narrow plain of smooth boulders polished by what must be a regular overflow of the stream now flowing gently to my front. I staggered the last few feet to the brook, flopped down, and plunged my head into the cool mountain water. The sensation of the cold stream on my scratched, fevered face was wonderful. I sucked in the water and swallowed in gulps until I choked. My thirst slaked I slumped onto my backside and lay down facing the sun. I had to get back to the post but the urge for a ten minute break was overwhelming.

I examined the cloud raked blue sky and attempted to make sense of the past twenty four hours. Part of my misadventure took no thought at all. I had drunk too much and was now paying the consequences. I thought of all the lectures I had given to the soldiers in my battery. Don't drink too much. Use the buddy system. Don't go out alone. Provided my life and career survived this episode, I could tell them I had really known what I was talking about.

If I could just find a town, any kind of town around here and get some kind of transportation I might salvage this thing. All I had to do was get to a bus or a train station and I could make it back. Today was Saturday, at least I hoped. With luck I would be back in TDC tonight or early tomorrow, at least by Monday. I'd have to explain the cuts and bruises and the fact that I'd violated the division policy of being back on post before midnight, but at least when the sun came up Tuesday morning I wouldn't be AWOL.

I had to get moving. But no sooner had I made this decision then the head banging pain of my hangover had returned and my stomach began to churn. I became acutely aware of a hundred bruises, cuts, sprains, and tears. I rolled over to my side and vomited. The involuntary spasm cleared my head and made me realize how vulnerable I was out here. Those people might still be looking for me. I had to keep moving. Streams flow to bigger streams and bigger streams go to rivers. Find a river and you find towns and people. I had a plan and a direction. Things were looking up - and about to take a dramatic nose dive.

I leaned forward and took another cool gulp before getting up. Something crackled on the dry forest floor on the other side of the stream. I looked up quickly. The noise stopped. I took a breath, held it, and listened for the noise. Squinting into the trees I thought I saw a large animal like shape. I couldn't be sure if it was an animal, a big stump, or a fallen tree. I looked at the thing for long while. Was it moving?

The bottom of my throat knotted as my conscious mind registered what my sub conscious mind had. I pushed myself up from the stream and crawled slowly backward on all fours. This time the hidden thing on the other side of the stream moved, and I saw it clearly. I jumped to my feet and in the same moment the creature revealed itself. Once again Kyung Re had not lied.

A tiger. A gigantic, pure white monster, less than twenty feet away watched me with intense interest. I had seen the same look on house cats about to pounce on small mice and birds. I had never seen such an enormous feline! This creature easily weighed four hundred pounds; the height of its shoulders nearly matched my own. Never taking its eyes from me it silently pawed across the stream.

There are seminal moments in a person's life that he will recall with absolute clarity for the rest of his days. I am not speaking of the close call car accident or the near miss of a fall from a great height nor any mundane urban event. Such things pass too quickly. The kind of ice blood terror I felt that day is only provoked when death looks directly at you with long, calm, deliberate aim; coolly planning the end of your existence in a bloody, violent climax. The time to think about

350

the horror; time to fully contemplate it; that's what makes terror compete. I stood rooted as my destruction crept closer. The monster stopped midway across the stream and growled. A second later it leaped.

I recall seeing a long dark form outlined against the sky. For an instant a shadow fell over me and the sun disappeared. In a quick, but futile, motion I turned. I felt the one of the cat's paws swat me on the thigh, almost playfully it seemed, but the force of it threw me onto the granite creek bed. On hands and knees I scrambled away and tried to make it back up the mountain, thinking I might save myself in the thorn bushes. I'm sure the cat found my efforts amusing.

As I scratched my way up the embankment I waited for the inevitable sensation of claws and teeth sinking into the flesh of my back. Yet the cat did not immediately pursue. I actually thought I was going to make it up the rocky bank. I pulled myself up, gained a foothold on a boulder, and pushed. I gained a flat ledge of rock, only to stand up and stare at another flat wall of rock, this one rising vertically in front of me. End of the road Mike. I turned and caught the full force of the tiger's impact.

I remember a flashing glimpse of an enormous white furred head, and large cat eyes, oddly blue. I was picked up, shaken madly, thrown about like a cloth fluttering in a hurricane. I wondered when I would hear the flesh ripping away from my body. Time to die? I recalled those nature films on National Geographic, the way the hoofed animals just seemed to give up once they were caught. Now I knew why.

A cream white ceiling crossed with brown beams hovered over me. My first thought was one of irritation. This was the second time I had woken up to a bizarre sight. Those circus people have gone far enough, I thought. I threw the covers away and jolted myself out of the bed. Pain echoed throughout my body. In an instant I was again on my back. The memory of the tiger flared back. I had lived?

For a while I lie there simply breathing trying to ease the burden of my injuries. Although my head was riddled with bruised lumps I turned my neck slowly from side to side and inspected my surroundings. The place looked like the inside of an old, Oriental styled room. Several lanterns hung from the wall and burned bright yellow. I lie in a futon type bed, in front of a headboard ornately carved in brilliantly colored oak. I felt the texture of silk. From the jaws of a tiger to a silk sheeted bed. The Moran luck was holding.

Waking up alive is a wonderful feeling and I didn't complain to fate for allowing me the privilege - but the pain!

Every square inch of my flesh felt tender; skinned and raw. My right ankle was surely broken. I gingerly touched it with my left foot and found it grotesquely oversized. My elbows throbbed, my head throbbed, my knees throbbed; my hair hurt. Deep scrapes ran down both of my legs. My back was moist with what I rightly assumed to be blood; the skin had been ground off of it as had the skin on my arms. It was even difficult to move my face. The fall from the mountain had been a calamity. I was somewhat thankful for having no memory of what the tiger had done. Between a tiger and a mountain. Wasn't that some kind of proverb? It could have been worse. Dead is as worse as you can get, but I wasn't.

I fell back into a slumber, for how long I don't know, and woke to a cold compress on my forehead that covered my eyes. I tried to brush it away, but who ever held the thing firmly pushed my hand back. I heard a quick chatter of feminine voices speaking softly and rapidly.

There was no fight left in me. "I'd like to know where I am," I said. My words brought on a great volume of Korean talk.

"Wait…minute." The words were slow and heavily accented.

Then I heard a male voice, older and authoritative. He spoke and the compress withdrew from my forehead. Colors and darkness twinkled as I adjusted to the light. When my eyes cleared and I saw the same lantern filled room. At the foot of the bed stood an elderly Korean man, dressed in old style Korean hangbok. He wore white leggings that came up to his knees and a jacket top made of a course white material that billowed out over knee length trousers made of the same thread. His beard was a white, narrow waterfall; a perfect caricature of the elderly Asian wiseman. On the very top of his head a small black conical hat jutted up over a wide round rim. The thing was fastened under his chin with a black ribbon that contrasted sharply with his beard.

"You have serious injuries. Lie still."

I welcomed the English. "Atashi, how did I get here? Where am I?" My voice croaked.

"Kaja brought you.

"Who?"

"The tiger - Kaja. He brought you here."

I wondered how to take that. "I thought it would kill me."

"Sometimes he does. Kaja made you an exception."

"The tiger that attacked me by the creek brought me here?"

"Perhaps you have a friend."

I felt the scrapes along my legs. "Some friend."

The old man was either not quite right in the head or he had a bizarre sense of humor. Both possibilities worried me, but I was too tired and sore to dwell on it.

I dozed off again and it was dark when I woke. One lantern, turned down to a bare flicker, made dim shadows dance on the ceiling. The raw pain of my injuries remained, but at least not with the impact of the first time I opened my eyes. At least the hangover's gone, I told myself, proud of my optimism.

Had I actually been attacked by a tiger? Yes, I remembered the incident. No mistake about that. I could not decide about the old man and the tale about the animal bringing me here. Everything seemed dreamlike. Kyung Re's beautiful face drifted in my thoughts. Had she done this? Why?

One thing remained unpleasantly, unmistakably real: I had to get back to the Army, and most ricky tick. I couldn't lie here trying to distinguish any other reality than that. By now my friends would be looking for me. I could get away with that. If I wasn't standing in front of the battery come Monday morning, though, I'd have some real explaining to do.

With an agony of effort I forced myself upright. Difficult enough in my condition from a western style bed, from a futon it's excruciating. I managed to roll onto my stomach and push myself up. Once on my hands and knees I turned out my good ankle and got to my feet. At first the injured limb did not feel so bad. Then I tried to take a step. Pain rocketed up my leg. I immediately switched to a one legged hop, got as far as the foot of the futon, and fell down.

The crash brought the entire house into action. Korean voices echoed in alarm; footsteps approached from all directions. The room blazed with light and I was found sprawled on the floor. The old man gave two slaps of his hand and three young ladies sprang to my aid. Beautiful young girls, really. But my present condition prevented appreciation of the situation. The old man was not amused.

"Captain Moran. Do not try anything so foolish again. He pointed a severe looking fan in my direction. It looked like a weapon.

"Atashi, I have to return to the Army."

"In the morning, Captain. Go to sleep now. And do not try to get out of bed again. You cannot walk and I cannot predict Kaja's reaction the second time."

Another authoritative hand clap and I was alone in the room. The old man was correct about one thing. I couldn't walk. Another encounter with Kaja? Now there was a good reason to stay in bed. All of these worries coupled with my looming, inevitable problems with the Army rolled over and over in my thoughts. Pain is a great salve for worry, however. My battered body reminded me that I had more immediate problems and I fell back to sleep.

I woke to bright sunlight and birdsong.

The old man appeared at the doorway. "Have you had enough sleep, Captain?" I thought it a foolish question considering the night I had been through. "Not really."

"Perhaps you are hungry?"

I was ravenous. "Yes, Atashi, I am."

"Good, you must eat. You have a long way to go." Satisfied with that tid bit of Oriental wisdom he turned and left. My stomach began growling at the thought of food.

Minutes later two of the young ladies who had assisted me the night before entered the room and carefully helped me to my feet. I was still fairly banged up but I could move without the agony of the previous day. My ankle remained a serious problem, though. I didn't think a joint could swell that big.

With a silent, smiling nurse under each arm I hobbled out of the room following the delicious odor of cooked food. The girls helped me to a wooden porch outside of the cottage where the old man waited, seated at a small table. With a great deal of effort I managed to take the chair opposite him. Breakfast was typical Korean fare: spicy fish soup, rice, kimchi, mushrooms. All of which I had learned to enjoy during my time in Korea, but I was pleasantly surprised by a small plate of fried eggs on top of a bed of rice.

By now my stomach was dancing with joy, but I thought a few thanks were in order before I ripped into breakfast. "Atashi, I very much appreciate your hospitality. I want to thank you for taking me in."

He smiled and removed a long clay pipe from his mouth. "Eat."

That was all the encouragement I required. After a noisy slurp of tea I attacked the food. My host looked pleased.

I pushed myself back from the table, sipped my tea, and waited for him to speak. He had promised to explain some things to me and I did not want some western rudeness on my part to interfere with anything he had to say.

"Atashi, kamsah-hapnida. The food was delicious," I said.

"I am honored."

I thought this would be the prelude to an explanation of my whereabouts, but the old fellow serenely continued with his pipe, blowing thick blue clouds of smoke into the air. Okay. I'll play the game a little longer, I thought.

The porch on which we sat was a long, wide patio that fronted the length of the cottage. A rock garden gently interspersed with pines, ginkos, lichen crusted statues, and little clearings of emerald velvet moss lie in front of the cottage. Sunlight streamed through the tree cover, painting the garden in gold dapples and startling greens. A narrow trail of flat stones meandered away to a large, glistening pond. I could see the pond through the trees and hear the distinct splash of a waterfall in the distance.

"This place is beautiful," I offered. "Do you come here every summer, sir?"

"I am here every summer, and every winter Captain."

"Pardon me, atashi, but what is your name?"

"I am Mr. Cha. Cha, Yeung Gun."

I reached my hand out to him. "Pleased to meet you Mr. Cha. I'm Mike Moran." He took my hand shook, then held it for some time in the Korean fashion.

"Mr. Cha how is it you know my name?"

"Kyung Re and Pok Dani told me about you."

"So they brought me here?"

"No, Captain. As I told you, Kaja brought you."

Okay, fine. If the old man wants to play Oriental mystic I would have to put up with it until I got out of here. But the uneasy feeling that I was a prisoner lingered. "Mr. Cha, will I be allowed to leave here when my ankle heels?"

"You are here from your own desires."

Again with the it's my fault bit. "Look Mr. Cha, your home is beautiful and I really appreciate how you have taken care of me. But I must leave. I have to get back to the Army as soon as possible. Do you have a car? Could I trouble you to take me to a train station or a bus station?"

Mr. Cha found this very amusing. "I do not have a car. I think also that you are forgetting that Kaja brought you here. He is not likely to allow you to leave."

"Mr. Cha, with all due respect, sir, I have had about enough. I have to return to the Army. It makes no difference how I arrived here. And please stop this nonsense about being dragged here by a white tiger."

"You don't remember the tiger?" He looked perplexed, but it was a sarcastic answer.

"Mr. Cha, so many things have happened to me that I am not sure I recall anything clearly. I remember being attacked by a tiger. After that, I don't know."

"There." He pointed to the front of the porch.

"There what?"

360

"This is where Kaja left you."

"So this tiger attacks me, decides I'm too nice to eat, then carries me from I don't know how far away, and drops me your front door?" I began to get up, gingerly tested my ankle, and realized the futility of hiking to the nearest town. I could not make it back to the bedroom without assistance.

Mr. Cha shook his head and looked out over the pond. "Yes Captain, that is right. And you cannot leave."

So the old man was finally coming straight out with it now. I have been all over the world as a soldier, the Middle East, Europe, Asia and everywhere I've been the government issued warnings about terrorists and how to avoid becoming a target. I never felt remotely threatened - until this moment.

"Why am I being held prisoner here?"

"You are not a prisoner."

"Is that the script Pyonyang told you to stick to?"

At this Cha burst into laughter so hard he had difficulty catching his breath.

"Mr. Cha, I ain't laughin."

He dried his eyes with a cloth. "I am sorry, Captain. Pok Dani and Kyung Re told me that you were a young man of great humor." He raised a hand. "I am not from North Korea and you are not going there either, unless you wish to."

"Then how do you know the circus people, and Kyung Re?"

"They are my friends, all of them come here many times. They guessed that Kaja would bring you here and they were right."

"Where are they now?"

"Entertaining the emperor. They will return." He sipped his tea and looked at me over the cup. "You are fond of Kyung Re?"

If his question was designed to distract me it worked. "She is a beautiful woman. But I don't know why she tricked me into this."

"Ah - she deceived you into the circus?"

"Well, no."

"She forced you to save Pok Dani and the circus?"

"No."

"And to drink too much afterward?"

"Mr. Cha, this is beside the point."

"No Captain Moran, that is the point. Your own actions have brought you here."

"I'm not going to argue. I admit that my own actions are responsible, and I will no doubt have this same conversation with my commander, but right now my desire, and my action, is to leave."

I was still not finding the humor in this conversation. Perhaps I was mistaken about North Korean agents, although I was not yet convinced of that. My anger was tinged with a spooky knowledge that North Koreans or not, these people were deliberately keeping something from me.

"Mr. Cha, regardless of how or why I'm here, will you please tell me where 'here' is? I presume that I am still in Korea."

He stared at me evenly before he answered as though he was about to carefully weigh his words. "You are still in Korea. It is not, however, the Korea that you think you know."

"Please explain."

"Korea is not so small a country as you might think, Captain. There are ranges of rugged mountains in the interior of the country still unexplored." Mr. Cha paused.

Could be. I'd had the same thought while flying over Korea or looking at Army maps. The country is an unbelievably dense mass of peaks and mountains, all well mapped, but large areas exist without roads. The majority of the population live near coastal areas; twenty five percent of all Koreans live in Seoul.

"All Right, how far away are we from Tongdechong?"

"Many kilometers, Captain."

"Hundreds? Thousands?"

He looked at me intently. "There are distances not measured with a ruler."

More word games, more mystery. Cha's eyes were not leaving me now. He was gauging me, searching, wondering how I would react to something.

"What do you mean by that Mr. Cha?"

"Have some more tea, Captain. Some things are better off seen than told."

Whatever the old fellow had in mind I was not going to hear it today. I had the feeling I had been judged and found wanting somehow. "Great, Mr. Cha. When do I get to 'see'?"

"Better to wait until your injuries heal."

This confusing, irritating banter was going nowhere. My rising anger was mixed with apprehension. Why was he doing this? Even with my injuries I could do the old man a lot of harm. Yet Cha seemed perfectly confident I could not. The girls were not a threat. Who else lurked nearby?

"Mr. Cha, whatever game you are playing, whatever it is you think you are doing, it is going to have serious consequences. I don't know why you won't help me get back or at least tell me where I am, but I will leave here one way or another."

Mr. Cha stood up. "Captain Moran, nothing is hidden from you. You are in a very dense, secluded range of mountains in the northeast part of South Korea. There are no trains or buses. There are no telephones. You may only leave by walking. But the question of where you actually are is something you are not ready to understand. Perhaps, when your injuries heal, you will. Then, if you still wish to leave, you are free to do so."

I had an impulse to demand a map, to insist that Cha show me exactly where this no train, no bus, no telephone mountain range existed. I knew he would not do it, though. He called out in Korean and the three girls appeared. They discussed something for a while. As he spoke the girls occasionally looked at me, giggled, and quickly put their hands to their mouth. If the circumstances of my situation were different this might be remarkably enjoyable. Stranded in a beautiful valley with an old hermit and his three lovely daughters. Were they his daughters? They looked more like his grandchildren. Dressed in loose fitting white muslin hyanbangs that tucked in under the breast and expanded into billowing skirts that fell to the floor, they looked like triplet

China dolls. The girls had wide, red necktie shaped silks around their necks that fell the length of the dress. Each wore her hair in a long twisted pony tail decorated with flowing blue ribbons.

The girls approached. My host quickly disabused any naughty soldier fantasies. "They will help you to the bathroom, Captain."

I cannot relate what an exquisitely painful and uncomfortable experience it is to use an Oriental style latrine when you are minus a good portion of skin and hobbled by a sprained ankle. That sordid little episode out of the way I was eased back into my seat on the porch. Mr. Cha presented me with a drink that he claimed would ease my soreness. I was suspicious but drank it any way. He'd already had plenty of time to harm me if that was his intention. Cha excused himself and retired into the cottage. I was left on the porch by myself.

Chapter Three

I tried to calm myself. If the old guy insisted on acting like the Sphinx and refused to help me, what could I do - belt him in the mouth? Tempting, but I have my standards. And it was an unusually beautiful place. A mirror pond spangled with lillies, overhanging trees, moss covered rocks, birds, quiet. For the past two years I'd wallowed in cities, military training areas, and squalid GI haunts. Natural beauty rarely shows itself in that world. This place, the wonderful scent of it, the serenity, and its near mystical setting…

And lady who had brought me here? Where was she? Her beautiful haunting face swirled into my thoughts. Where are you Kyung Re and why have you done to me what you have? Or was Mr. Cha's reprimand correct? Had I done this to myself?

Right or wrong, Mr. Cha's accusation would mean little when I returned to the service of Uncle Sam. For now, however, I put that anxiety aside. There was nothing I could do at the moment. The grotesque condition of my ankle assured me of that, plus large portions of the rest of me started to bleed if I moved too quickly. The Soldier's Creed of using every available means to escape nagged me, of course, but Cha had one thing right - whether or not he was deliberately holding me prisoner, my injuries were.

I lolled back and gazed at the tree tops. Whatever magic Mr. Cha had blended into his concoction began to make its presence known. My head, vaguely heavy at first, felt like a bowling ball. Pain softly dissolved from my cuts and evaporated out of my ankle. I relaxed deep into the mattress of the chair. Color and birdsong melted together. I focused on the pond in the distance, but the water blurred and wavered, replaced by the misty faces of Cha's ladies. They leaned forward and placed their hands under me. I floated. They brought me back into the cottage and draped me across a long, narrow table so close to the floor that the back of my hands rested on the floor. As though it came through a long tunnel I heard them giggling and speaking to each other in tiny bell voices. Then the pond came back into focus.

For the next two days I followed a similar routine of rising, eating, lingering in my porch chair enjoying the forest and learning to use the latrine without assistance. Mr. Cha spoke to me in riddles and vague phrases, but he made no attempt to keep me in place and put no obstacle in the way of my leaving. After that he would press me to drink what he called medicine. Then would come the dream and I would awake again on the porch chair.

But I was healing fast. Whatever native cure the three maidens used on me worked wonders. Within days the scrapes and gouges disappeared and my ankle had nearly returned to normal. By the third day I could walked unassisted. I announced that I felt well enough to leave.

We had just finished lunch and Mr. Cha was hidden by a mist of smoke from his long clay pipe. He did not appear impressed. "Good, Captain. Will you leave in the morning?"

"Unless you attempt to stop me."

"I will not try to stop you."

"And Kaja?"

"But you do not believe in Kaja, so that should not pose a problem."

I had nearly forgotten about the monstrous white cat. "Okay, you got me - I believe in Kaja. His benevolence, however, I'm not so sure about. But that makes no difference - I have to go. Mr. Cha, will you help me or not? At least point me in the right direction, get me started in the morning?"

He paused before he answered and took a long puff on the ridiculous, arms length pipe. In a way he resembled the pipe he loved so much. They were both long, thing, and gray.

"I have never said I would not help you."

'Then you will direct me to the right way out of here?"

"Suppose, Captain. That you and I have different thoughts on what is the right direction?"

"It makes no difference. I have to leave no matter what you do."

"Very well. But since this is your last night with us we will have a special feast for you."

I was not sure I liked the idea of a special feast, but I agreed. I excused myself and walked down the path to the pond where a red tiled pagoda thick brown pine logs overhung the water. I lingered and gazed at the scenery. I had no idea about the sincerity of Mr. Cha's offer to help or about this final feast he'd mentioned. But when I thought about what he had said I realized that he had not offered to help at all. I had asked for a particular assistance and he had consented. Consented to precisely what I had requested - the "right" way out of here. It reminded me of an old trick soldiers play on officers they dislike. They follow orders exactly, precisely to the letter. Since no one can possibly think of all the minor tasks associated with any complex action, the inevitable result was that the intent of the order was never accomplished yet ignored so cleverly that no one could be accused of disobeying orders.

The Army. It seemed so distant in the silent peace of the pond and forest. The water lie still and clear; lily pads floated in the clarity as though hanging in air. Small silver fish darted out from under the pagoda. From far off I heard the German clock sound of what the Koreans call a "poo-koo" bird. A tiny brown gecko lizard skittered, stopped, and cocked its head at me from the brown railing. He ought to be careful, I thought. If he falls in the water those fish will have him quickly.

I could never this peaceful place. I looked deep into the pond. A large fish swam languidly, moving for the protection of the shade under the pagoda. The smaller fish scattered and the water wobbled just enough to make my reflection move slightly in sparkling sun. Kyung Re's reflection stared up at me from the water. I squinted, then jumped at the unexpected sight and turned madly around. I was alone. When I looked back into the water she had disappeared. That did it. No more of Mr. Cha's "medicine."

For the rest of the afternoon I wandered about the place trying to get my bearings and checking things out. I saw no guards or anything resembling security; apparently

Cha had not lied about me being free to go. I returned to the house and found Mr. Cha. He informed me that the dinner in my honor would begin soon. Would I please meet him on the porch when I was ready? Pushing back sleep I agreed. It was nearly dark by then. I pulled myself to my feet, went to the rear of the house, and doused myself with cold water from the well. The temperature was shocking, but I came fully awake. Mr. Cha was waiting for me on the porch with his inevitable pipe. He was not dressed in his usual white outfit. Instead he had on a formal hanbok of bright, vivid colors, a traditional garb for ceremonial or formal occasions.

"Where are we going, Mr. Cha?" I had assumed that the dinner would be here in his cottage.

"This way, Captain." He directed me down the trail toward the pagoda, but instead of continuing straight in the direction of the pond we detoured onto a small side trail. It wound through the forest and roughly skirted the pond's edge. We came to an ancient stone bridge that looked like it had been lifted from a Chinese landscape painting and crossed a gentle brook that rolled down the mountain side and emptied into the pond. I hear laughter and voices in the forest ahead. "Sounds like a lot of people Mr. Cha."

"Yes, many people have come to see you."

Odd. I had not seen anyone for the past several days except Mr. Cha and the three silent ladies who tended my wounds. "Why? Do these people know me?"

"Only by reputation."

"But why do…"

He cut me off. "Please simply walk with me Captain. This is for your honor! Why must you ask so many questions?"

Cha, I thought, you're killing me. After the last feast I in my honor I had woken up a day later in a mule train on an unknown mountain top. Okay, fine. Let the old man play his game. Come morning I'm out of here. But I wanted to find out who this Mr. Cha is before I left. Perhaps during this party, or whatever it was, I get some kind of clue about the game being played out here in the lost mountains, and more importantly where I was. And the question of Kyung Re remained. What part did she and her strange little circus play in all this?

"We are here, Captain." Mr. Cha directed me along a path of crunching white stones that glowed in the evening light. Yellow light flickered between the trees. The sound of laughter and voices grew and I could see flashes of people moving in the light. "We hold all of our large celebrations here," Mr. Cha explained.

We stepped out of the forest. A long structure, generously hung with a colorful array of glittering lanterns sat in the middle of a large clearing. The building was a long, open faced rectangle. The open side faced the cleared area. Beyond that lie the pond we had circled around. At least fifty people, all dressed in colorful hanboks like Mr. Cha milled about the open center of the hall. Magnificent, rainbow colored dresses billowed and swirled around the women. On top they wore wide sleeved, elegantly designed jackets of glistening silk and satin. Some had tiny crowns, with an array of jewels that dangled from gold couplings. The men, too, had wide sleeved, brilliantly colored jackets and pants that bowed out and tapered below the knee. Around their shins they wore wrapped leggings of various colors. All wore old Korean style shoes, odd little canoe shaped things that looked uncomfortable. Most carried long, ceremonial fans blazing in shiny metallic colors. In my tennis shoes, jeans, and a tee shirt I felt like a construction worker at a Trump party at the Waldorf.

Mr. Cha took me by hand and introduced me around. No one had a simple name. I met the Mayor, the Mayor's Advisor, the Prime Counselor, the Prime Counselor's Advisor, the Director of Harvest, the Director of Planting, the Minister, the Minister's Advisor, the Senior Flower Lady, and of course, her advisor… so many titles I could not possibly recall all of them. There were Kims, Chins, Lees, Muns, Paks, Hans, Ahns, and one or two other names that repeated with every handshake. The men graciously shook my hand and bowed, the ladies simply bowed and smiled.

A plainly dressed young lady approached and handed me a carved pewter mug filled with mekchu, Korean beer. Maybe they did know me. They inquired if my ankle had healed, how I liked Korea, thanked me for coming to visit; random, general questions and comments. No one appeared to mind that I was grossly underdressed nor seemed in any way curious that I was there at all. I supposed that Cha was right; I was expected.

But the conversation struck me as a bit too clever, too smooth. No sooner would I answer an inquiry from some distinguished gentleman about the bruises on my back than his lovely wife would press my arm and ask about my fever. Everyone seemed to have an intimate knowledge of my injuries. Not the usual inquiries that one would expect. Each person had a particular body part that he or she asked about, as if the questions had been thought out and divvied up ahead of time. Yet whenever I came close to asking my own burning question, such as exactly where this particular town could be found on a map, I was ambushed by an amusing anecdote about fishing or invited to comment on the beauties of the pond.

Mr. Cha served as my interpreter and never left my side throughout this exceedingly polite prelude to dinner. Always he guided me from one guest or small group to another, made a brief, smiling introduction, allowed the conversation to proceed just beyond the normal pleasantries, then led me on elsewhere, manipulating me as smoothly as a magician.

A large bell rang three sonorous chimes. Mr. Cha directed me to my place. The members of the party ceased all conversation and took their places behind a long, red clothed table that stretched the length of the pagoda. The atmosphere turned suddenly quiet as the entire assembly solemnly regarded Mr. Cha and me standing before them. Looking up at the seated assemble I became even more aware of my tennis shoes and jeans.

Mr. Cha cleared his throat. He addressed the crowd in a short, somber soliloquy completely in Korean. I had, of course, no idea what he was saying, but I noticed an occasional gush of "oohs" and "ahhs" from the audience plus great deal of head nodding in my direction. I cannot begin to tell you how ridiculous it feels being a center of attraction and not knowing if you are being praised or ridiculed.

Cha concluded his remarks and bowed slightly to the audience. They in turn rose and bowed deeply to him. Unsure of the proper protocol I followed Cha's lead and leaned slightly forward.

These odd amenities over Mr. Cha directed me to my seat, a place of honor in the middle of the long table. He sat at my right. "Please sit," Mr. Cha said quietly. I pulled my seat out and sat down. As soon as I initiated this action the entire group promptly took their seats and conversation resumed.

I leaned toward my host. "Mr. Cha, what did you say just now?"

"I simply explained that you are the guest of honor, that we would soon feast in your name, and that you are a man of great bravery. I explained your courageous behavior regarding Pok Dani, and said that I was certain we would hear more about you in the future."

Since I had become used to Mr. Cha's enigmatic words I gave up trying to decipher the linguistic rune about future actions and concentrated on the amazing array of chow in front of me. From left to right a dazzling variety of remarkable foods sprawled the length of the table. Fish, octopus, squid, tiny rolls of colorful vegetables, an astounding collection of oddly shaped mushrooms, giant snails split open in the middle to leave nothing to the imagination, oysters, clams, mounds of steaming rice in silver bowls, soups, - a magnificent variety of color and scent. As if this was not enough, a platoon of young serving men and women appeared and began laying strips of marinated beef and pork across small burning braziers intermittently placed along the table. My salivary glands exploded.

The gourmet delights were accompanied by generous doses of spirits. Soju came my way, as did wine, and stronger species of drink. From time to time some member of the party would rise, glass in hand and raise a salute to me. Inevitably I felt compelled to rise from my chair and return the complement. Have you ever tried to do otherwise in such a circumstance? The people at the table found this very amusing. The temptation to swill too much alcohol was overwhelming. But I wisely and warily kept my head and consumed moderate amounts. The last time an odd collection of Koreans held a banquet in honor my life had become very complicated.

During a break in the toasting and eating I turned to my host. "Okay, Mr. Cha, who are these people?"

"I would imagine that in your world they would be called VIPs."

"What are they called in your world?"

"Favored of the Emperor. You are dining with royalty." He made this remark quite seriously.

"Oh, the emperor." That was a new one. "May I ask where his majesty is?"

"The emperor lives in the Mountain Palace. Perhaps you would like to see it."

"Nice try Mr. Cha. I am leaving in the morning."

An emperor? I could almost believe it looking at the gourmet bounty on the table. And these people. These were not common folk. Beyond being well dressed and proud, the people seated to my right and left were an exceptionally beautiful physically; slender, perfectly proportioned, and glowing with health. The men were robust and healthy. The beauty of the women was striking. The serenity in their tone of voice and in the expression of their smooth faces had a physical impact. These were not laborers and farmers. I'm don't know what royalty looks like, but I was pretty sure this was as close as I'd get to it. If this was Kyung Re's home town the origin of her physical beauty was apparent. Yet she had left to travel Korea in a shabby circus?

The feasting and drinking went on for two hours or longer. When I felt I could not possibly eat another grain of rice the young men and women who had kept our plates filled promptly trooped out and began to empty the table. Wine glasses and soju cups were removed. In their place appeared silver cups filled with rich, cinnamon flavored ginseng tea brimming with sweet pine nuts.

Dinner concluded, Mr. Cha rose and the company gave him silent attention. Once again his tone was short and solemn, and once again I could not understand a word. Polite applause followed. Cha sat down and explained that the dinner had been an extraordinary success; the entertainment would begin shortly.

"I think you will find the show especially interesting. I have a caution for you, Captain Moran - please do not do anything rash, no matter how much you may find yourself inclined."

Like everything else Cha had said the past week I had no idea what he was talking about. "Nothing rash." He reiterated the command with a single raised eyebrow. What would I do during an after dinner show? Applause too loud? Whistle? And then an unexpectedly familiar figure walked to the front of the pavilion. Cha had been right to secure my promise.

Dressed in his standard red and gold satin Pok Dani greeted the audience in baritone Korean and deep, respectful bows. A rigorous applause followed. I stifled an urge to scream. Here was the little fellow whose life I had saved, the guy who got me into this mysterious calamity, greeting the crowd and soaking up applause five feet away my nose as though I did not exist.

Now that's bad enough. But what do I see next? A repeat performance of his TDC folly, complete with the little dogs jumping up to the stools for a canine hula. And talk about deja vu all over again - he walks to the tent, throws back the flap, and with the same show biz flare picks up the same fat black chain. One more time I'm treated to the grunting, heaving, brow wiping farce. He's bringing the elephant out for another act? Impossible!

"Mr. Cha, Mr. Cha!" I'm talking as low as I can, but I feel like I'm ready to burst.

Cha looked at me and put his finger to his lips. "SShhh. You promised."

"But -

"Shhh!"

Prepared to see this poor elephant tortured by torches again I took a long sip of tea and crossed my arms. I have to watch this show, not like it. This time, though, the stage is smaller and not quite so high. If the elephant gets loose in this environment all these good looking people won't be so cool. Fine. Let the little guy create another catastrophe and see if I care. Let one of the beautiful people rescue the little nut. I took a long sip of tea and crossed my arms. I felt bad for the poor elephant, though. It deserved better.

Once more into the abyss. Pok Dani repeats his taunting histrionics with the black chain. What he pulls out, however, is not motivated by flaming torches nor is it an elephant. It is an enormous snake, a python. The serpent is huge and looks even bigger in relation to the small man on stage supposedly controlling the reptile. I say supposedly because I cannot see how a snake that big can be controlled. Oh, I know the trick about keeping a tame serpent well fed and cold before bringing them out on stage. But the python is twitching and curling in an odd fashion. Its metabolism has definitely not been sated before the show. I'm determined, but the spectacle catches me by surprise just the same. Yet the crowd at the banquet table does not run screaming for the exit. This group leans forward, eyes glistening like Romans at the coliseum. Pok Dani raises his arms to the audience and proceeds to deliver some kind of speech as he points to the snake.

I figure he's giving a little prelude to the wonders he's about to accomplish with the animal. The audience nods in appreciation but the odd jittery motion of the snake has my attention. It's alert and nervous, curling back its head as though preparing to strike. And it does. In a flashing, sudden movement the reptile's jaws fly forward and clamp down on Pok Dani's arm. There is a quick whirling blur of motion as the rest of its body wraps around the little man. Pok Dani and his colorful costume disappear behind massive coils of brown scales. The snake then opens its great maw we are greeted to the grotesque sight of a pudgy, squirming little arm protruding through the coils of the monster while it begins a tongue flicking search for its victim's head. The snake rolls to its side and a bald, brown head pops out of a living barrel of reptile. With slow, deliberate motion the monster's flickering tongue guides it to the smooth pate of Pok Dani's head.

I'm on my feet and halfway over the banquet table when a hand grasps my belt from behind. "You promised!" Cha yells. At the same time two fellows run to the front of the banquet table and prepare to block my assault to the stage. But I'm in full blown hero mode now and not about to let somebody be swallowed by a snake. I smack Cha's hand away, leap over the two in front of me, and land on the stage just as the python begins to devour the little guy's head. With strength borne of adrenaline raged fear I grasp the serpent's upper and lower jaws, tear it off the human's head, and rip it apart as far as my arms can spread – and instantly know something's not right. Python heads do not feel like or come apart like balloons. And although this is my first bisection of a python head but I'm pretty sure the thing would be a lot stronger than this, and bleed, too. The damned thing is a fake!

For several moments I stand on the stage holding the fake snake parts. Pok Dani unravels himself from the phony coils and stands up. He looks at me with a tooth revealing grin. I drop the thing on the stage floor as the crowd laughs and cheers. Should I break his neck or join in the joke? Okay, I'll break his neck later; for now I just shake my head and throw up my hands. Cha eases me back into my seat as the crowd looks at me and starts chanting, "Pam Sidyunga! Pam Sidyunga!" over and over.

"What are they saying, Cha?" I demand.

I get the condescending grin in return. "They are saying, Snake Killer! Snake Killer!"

Two young ladies in sparkling leotards rush on stage, remove the fake snake, and wipe perspiration from Pok Dani's face and arms. He steps forward and raises his hand for silence. As the audience quiets he approaches the table and says something to Mr. Cha who answers with a nod. He mounts the stage again and speaks to the audience in rapid

Korean, pointing at me many times. There is much nodding and agreement.

Mr. Cha turns to me. "Pok Dani is telling everyone the measure of your worth. He knew that you would try to save him again. He says that in Tong De Chong city you risked your life to save his. Even now, after all that you have been through on his account it speaks very well that you would try to save him again, although it was, as you see, unnecessary."

Cha then rises from his seat. "You will wait here, Captain. There is other entertainment for you."

"Oh great."

With that enigmatic commend Cha and the entire banquet party rose and left. Alone with Pok Dani I sat, stunned, and trying to comprehend what had just transpired as well as everything else leading up to it. Pok Dani peeled off his encrusted satin shirt and came around to the table by my side. As he had done that very first night he poured mighty dollops of mekchu into my glass. He spoke some words I'm sure he thought were very reassuring, but I could no more understand his Korean than I could come to grips with what he had done.

"Pam Sidyunga, are you all right?"

I jerked my head up at the familiar voice. Kyung Re, as beautiful as ever, stood by my side. She ran her hand through my hair.

"Kyung Re, what is going on?" was the best I could manage.

"The council is deciding now."

"Deciding what?"

"Whether or not you should be presented to the emperor."

"Kyung Re?"

"There is nothing to be afraid of."

I stammered for words, for thought. "Fear? I am quite beyond that. Shock is more descriptive."

She was about to say something when Mr. Cha returned. "Come with me, please. It is time to face the council."

I followed them away from the banquet table. Kyung Re took my right arm and Mr. Cha gripped my left. They led me to a position in the center of the pavilion facing the members of the "council" who had begun filing back into their seats. The smiles of celebration and festivity were gone, something momentous was in the air.

Mr. Cha whispered in my ear. "Once again, Captain, do not do anything rash, nor make any move unless I tell you to." Great.

Behind me I heard a faint, rapid patter, like someone fluttering a stick on a small drum. The sound grew louder, getting closer. Mr. Cha warned me not to turn around or make any movement. I soon felt the vibrations of the drum. Whoever was beating on it was directly behind me.

The beating moved to a position just in back of my ears and became louder still. First near my right, then my left. It alternated back and forth with machine gun quickness. A large shadow moved on the ground between my legs. Disobeying Cha's admonition I turned around.

A hideous, bulging eyed thing, just several feet away peered at me. An enormous forked tongue slid from the creature's mouth, hung in the air, and waived slowly back and forth like a lazy rattlesnake. Yet this aberration was not a snake. Reptilian yes, but not any reptile I'd ever seen. A luminous, iridescent outline, vivid in the soft lantern light, glowed; ephemeral and transparent. Sharp, jagged scales, striped blue and red, arched out over goggle eyes. A long bluish snout ended in flaring black nostrils that pulsated as the thing breathed. It turned away from me and crawled, propelling itself on squat, clawed appendages.

"Continue to look up and ahead." Cha's whispered reminder rescued me from my horrified hypnotic state. I forced my eyes away from the beast and turned back around. The banquet crowd, more silent and alert than they had been during the swallowing of Pok Dani, stared intently.

In my peripheral vision I could see the monster pulling itself forward off to my right, its tail writhing back and forth. It moved slowly to my front, shook its head and arched its back. A leathery dorsal fin, punctuated with erect spines, jutted straight up along the length of its kraken back. The beast hissed. It snapped its jaws and the clack of teeth reverberated. Without warning it spun suddenly around and faced me; golden eyes narrowed and boring into my own. I steadied myself with Cha's words and concentrated on looking through the beast. On my left Kyung Re gripped my hand tightly.

The beast roared outrage. "Look at me!" it hissed. Suddenly I understood why Cha had wanted me to look away from the apparition. The beast was attempting to pull me in, trying to snare me in its power. I knew it, I felt it. I had a terrifying feeling that if I allowed myself to become locked into those golden eyes I would never be free. Its blue jowls drew back into a hideous grin of cream colored ivory. The beast approached. I wondered what kind of knife is required to open the belly of a spirit dragon.

A roar shook the air, so loud that the vibrations pummeled the skin of my face. I'd heard this guttural, frightening sound before. The dragon disappeared and for a blinding instant I saw the great white furred face of a tiger, so close that I felt its breath and the quivering air exploding from its throat. Polished dagger teeth glinted in the yellow light.

Then the tiger vanished. In its place stood an ancient, wrinkled old man in a scarlet robe that fell from his neck to his feet. A white sheet covered his head and fell over his ears, and over that a crown of spun yellow reeds twisted into the air. Jutting up from the reed crown, like a small square sail, sat a brilliant red headdress stitched with golden letters in Korean. In one hand he held a brown, hour glass shaped drum made of dyed leather. In the other he clutched a bronze tocsin that he raised over his head. A pair of wooden clappers hung from the tocsin attached by thin strips of leather. He flicked his wrist and the small wooden balls clanged sharply against the metal. He raised the leather drum above his head. The old man flipped the bronze tocsin with such deftness that he was able to play both the metal instrument and the hour glass drum in near simultaneous rhythm.

An unexpected swirl of color blossomed behind the old man. Three young ladies whom I recognized as Mr. Cha's "daughters" whirled and danced around us in a wide circle. They spun like tops in time to the old man's drums. Wide flowing dresses, layers of red, blue, green, and purple silk billowed and floated in time to their whirling dance. Each wore a hat of brilliant red from which sprouted two long feathers. The ladies whirled faster and faster matching the beating of the instruments. The ancient one's hands moved in a blur. He began a chant. The chant rose to a bellow. Then a yell, and then a scream that abruptly ceased.

The resulting silence was as startling as his outburst. Like a mist the dancers disappeared. The old man walked very close to me and stared at me, inches away from my face. His eyes were pale blue and gold, eerily familiar. He turned away, spoke to the council. The members stood and bowed. Mr. Cha and Kyung Re released my arms.

"You will meet the emperor, Captain Moran." Cha said.

I looked at Kyung Re for an explanation and realized that the old man had vanished. Kyung Re was smiling as the council sprang from their seats. I was surrounded by a swarm of handshakes and hearty congratulations. Stunned, I returned their smiles, but I had no idea as to the nature of my accomplishment.

When the last council member had voiced his opinion Mr. Cha once again took my arm. For a moment he looked at me as though searching for something he had missed. "You are free to go where you wish, Captain. Kyung Re will take you back to my home. I must stay here a while longer with the council and discuss your visit."

"Mr. Cha, I -"

"Kyung Re will take you back now."

Before I could interject another word Kyung Re deftly turned me away from the pavilion. We left the area and walked the white pebble path back to Cha's cottage.

I could say that my mental state bordered on shocked disbelief, but what I felt after my excursion into that bizarre, frightening experience, bore more resemblance to astonished numbness. In the past seven days I had been attacked by visions and events so strange that my entire reference for viewing the world shook.

"Kyung Re," I said, "it is time that you tell me what game is being played here."

"We play no games here, Pam Sidyunga."

I stopped. "You are right. Putting drugs in my drink is not a game."

"Is that what you think happened?"

"Yes, Kyung Re, I do. I do not know why, and right now I am nearly beyond caring, but for whatever reason you people are doing things to me that I find disturbing to say the least."

She looked at me steadily. "Pam Sidyunga, you cannot understand just yet. Let's go back to Mr. Cha's house." She took my hand and pulled me forward. But this time I'd had enough.

"No, Kyung Re! Tell me who you are, who these people are, and what was it that transpired back there. Tell me now, Kyung Re."

"You will not believe what I tell you."

"Stop it Kyung Re! Give me an answer or I am going back there and deal with this like the common soldier I am."

The threat worried her. "Do not go back there, please! It would be a terrible mistake."

"Then answer me."

"First you must promise to walk with me." She pulled my hand. I reluctantly gave my word and followed.

Walking ahead of me and still pulling my hand she spoke over her shoulder without facing me. "You have been initiated by the shamans. Pok Dani put on a show to display your courage. The dragon spirit was called forward to look into your heart. After that the council decided you are worthy to meet the emperor of all shamans."

"What?"

"I told you that you would not believe."

She had me there. I did not believe it. Of all the explanations I had expected to hear, shamans and spirit dragons had not entered my mind. I cocked my head and sighed. "Kyung Re."

"I warned you - and now you are angry."

"I'm angry because I want the truth, not some mythological, new age garbage. I'm done. I'm leaving tonight."

"Pam Sidyunga, are you sure can you turn your back so easily?"

"Enough with the Pam Sidyunga, Kyung Re. My named is Mike Moran. Do you understand?"

She nodded. "Yes, Pam – I'm sorry, Mike."

"I have to go Kyung Re. I don't know what kind of hallucinogen you slipped into my drink, but purple ghost dragons don't exist. Midgets and fake pythons, maybe, but I've had enough of that, too. I must go home."

"That is what we are trying to show you."

I looked at Kyung Re and stopped myself from asking what she meant. I was getting angry and frustrated at this conversation, yet at the same time the sweet pressure of her hand in mind felt wonderful. We walked without speaking to the pagoda that overhung the pond. Far away golden lantern lights of the pavilion glimmered on the quivering water.

Kyung Re raised my hand. "Sometimes you have to be shown a thing before you are ready to hear it. Can you understand that?"

"Yes."

"Tell me what you saw tonight."

"Why? Didn't you see the same thing?"

"What I saw means nothing."

"Yes that's right, they didn't put anything in your drink."

Kyung Re sighed. "Nothing was put in your drink. Tell me what you saw."

I relayed the story, not about what I saw, but about what I thought I had seen. That somebody had slipped something into my drink I had no doubt. Why they persisted in this farce I didn't know.

"Only a few people saw the spirits that appeared tonight. The mudang, the paksu, and yourself. They were invisible to all others."

394

"What are the mudang and paksu?"

"The male and female shamans, everyone on the council is a shaman."

"All right Kyung Re. Go ahead and persist in this shaman nonsense. Why am I mixed up in your little tea party?"

"Because you are chosen."

"Chosen for what?"

"You are very special. That is why you here. You are a chosen paksu. The old man who appeared is the most powerful paksu in the mountains. The females, the mudangs, who danced will only do so for one reason - they dance to show all you are chosen."

This was getting better all the time. "Kyung Re, I realize that I'm just a big dumb Irishman, and I admit to my share of superstitions. But your mustangs and pakastangs, or whatever they are, have really made a big mistake this time. Chosen or not, tomorrow I go back to the Army."

Kyung Re stood in front of me and placed her hands on either side of my head. The perfumed scent of her lovely face filled me. For an instant I wished I was a shaman. I knew precisely where I would cast my first spell.

"Mike, do you really think you can return after what you have seen?"

"I don't know what I've seen. It will bother me, I won't deny that, and maybe I'll never forget it. But I cannot stay here."

Kyung Re sighed, her hands dropped. I realized that the opportunity to kiss her had just melted away and I tried to think of a pretext to regain my amorous initiative, but Kyung Re turned her back. She leaned against the railing of the pagoda like she was contemplating the moon. If I only had more time I thought. If I could just get her away from this loony bin. She turned suddenly and face me smiling. She lifted her arms behind her neck and in a quick movement and the entire gown fell to her feet. Gold and silver light glistened on her naked body. "Are you truly sure you can turn your back on all you have seen?" She dove into the water.

For a stunned moment I watched as she splashed to the surface, diamond drops of water streaming from her face and breasts. She back stroked away from me, giggling in the sparkling pond. My clothes came off in a more awkward fashion than the beautiful lady swimming in the pond, but not much slower.

The water felt warm and wonderful, a balmy bath on a summer night. I swam after Kyung Re, but she was like a little dolphin in the water. She allowed me to get maddeningly close, near enough to feel her tantalizing warmth, then flick away as agile and slippery as an eel. I lunged again and again. Suddenly she dove under the water and was gone. I waited. She did not resurface. I called her name. I had a sudden feeling that something had gone wrong in our innocent fun but then I heard my own name being called. Kyung Re was back on the pagoda, fully dressed and grinning at me.

We made our way back to the cottage. At the door to my room I made a clumsy attempt to pull her in. Kyung Re kissed me but made it clear that an unmarried couple together under the roof of a kind host was behavior unheard of. It was a rudeness I'd have been happy to live with but it wasn't mine to make unfortunately. Kyung Re promised to see me in the morning.

I lie down spinning and reeling with emotion. Every problem I had imagined about my return to the Army disappeared. Kyung Re filled my mind to bursting. I had no doubt that she would leave with me in the morning. Escaping this bunch of crazies might prove troublesome, but that involved a fraction of my thoughts and energy. That problem I'd solve in the morning. I replayed her poolside vision over and over again, fascinated by the incredible beauty indelibly burnished into my mind. From the first time I had seen Kyung Re nothing mattered except her presence next to mine. The delicious overpowering pull she exerted; the sweet wonderful experience of her. In a week of astonishing experiences, Kyung Re topped it all.

At some time in the swirling recollections I fell asleep. The day sounds of the forest woke me and the bright sunlight signaled that I had slept later than I intended. I sprang up and dressed, my thoughts instantly on Kyung Re and how to effect our escape. Cha had better understand. If he tried to stop me in any way then his cards were on the table - and mine would be, too. I was not about to be stopped.

But first I had to find Kyung Re. I prowled from room to room. The cottage appeared deserted. My stomach felt queasy, an odd sensation. I had not had too much to drink or eat the previous night; I wondered about the residual effects of the drugs I had been given.

I walked to the outer porch and found it empty. I stifled a rising irritation. Where was Kyung Re? Another game? I stepped of the porch and went around to the side of the cottage to the herb garden. Cha was bent over tending to his plants.

"Where is she, Mr. Cha?"

He straightened from his preoccupation with hoe and faced me. "Kyung Re has gone ahead to prepare the way for you with the emperor."

"You're lying. I want to know where Kyung Re is. I'm leaving and she is coming with me."

"You will leave today?"

"Yes, today and nothing is going to stop me. Now tell me where Kyung Re is."

"I have told you, Captain. She has gone to see the emperor to prepare your way."

How I wanted to brain the old fool, to smash my knuckles into his wise old mouth! What is it with people that live in the back woods? Get away from civilization too long and they all go a little whacky. I've had soldiers from way out in the hills of Tennessee tell me some of the weirdest things ever, and I've seen some pretty strange stuff in West Virginia, even upstate New York. Now I could add Korea to the list.

Mr. Cha stepped out of the garden. He looked deep into my eyes and inspected me from head to toe like a drill instructor. "You are a slow learner. I have no idea why she has such faith in you." He put his hand on my forehead.

"Mr. Cha, please…"

"You feel feverish. Is your stomach upset?"

I was instantly suspicious. "Isn't it strange you should guess? Some more of your herbs? Like the stuff you used on me last night?"

He stepped back. "Young man, your innocence is almost as laughable as your ability to wrongly accuse. Your sickness has nothing to do with any herbs. Just as what you witnessed last night, those things that you will not admit to seeing, had nothing to do herbs, or mekchu, or soju."

"Mr. Cha there are no blue and red, see through dragons. Now I'm willing to forgive whatever you have done to me because I was in pretty bad shape when I got here and you patched me up. But I will not forgive any harm you have done to Kyung Re."

He shook his head slowly. "Captain Moran, harming Kyung Re would be a nearly impossible feat even if I chose to do so. I have told you where she is - and you will go to her."

"Oh? And how do you know this?"

"Because you will. You think that I will attempt to stop you. It is not me who works against your wishes. What you are and that what is - is. These things will stop you, not me. I will even tell you how to return to your Army, but you will not. Not yet."

"Mr. Cha, enough mumbo jumbo. Thank you for your hospitality. Now tell me how to get out of here and I'll be on my way." Either he was lying about Kyung Re or she had deliberately mislead me again. Both now seemed likely possibilities. My heart sunk and bitterness rose in its place. I chided my naivety. Me with a woman like that? Too good for you, my friend.

Mr. Cha directed me to follow him to the front of the cottage. "Take this path," he said. "Follow it just as you did last night to the pavilion. North of that you find another path, very well marked. Take it up into the mountain until it runs

401

into a high ridge. To the west is your Army. To the east is the emperor - and Kyung Re."

"How do I know you are telling the truth?"

"When you find Kyung Re you will know."

If I traded words with old Mr. Cha every day for the rest of my life I would never win the last one. I turned and left, following the path he had pointed out.

I stopped by the pagoda and stared at the glistening pond dappled in morning sunlight. The silver fish played in its depths and I thought of the agile body I had chased. One more time I replayed the most singularly beautiful event of my life. For a few moments the restlessness in my stomach eased, replaced by a hollow pain elsewhere. I had a long way to go and I had better get on with it.

I retraced my steps back up the path where it meandered through the woods and beyond the pavilion. As I looked back the solid pavilion. Its curled tiles roof tiles seemed the only pieces of reality that existed. I walked on.

The trek up the mountain, a typical Korean peak, began easily then quickly transitioned to a near vertical struggle. Using trees and boulders like misshapen ladders I dragged myself up the slope. I suffered no ill effects from my previous injuries and the last several days of rest had done wonders for my stamina. My stomach, however, was not being so cooperative. Several times I nearly vomited and the constant nausea triggered a dull headache that swelled with effort of climbing. There is no good time to get sick, but there are more convenient locales than the side of a steep mountain, miles from home. Perhaps the past two weeks had taken more of a toll than I realized; my romantic romp in the pond coupled with whatever I had consumed the night before had probably not helped. Well, that was one swim I would have never turned down. If it cost my life I'd do it again now.

By the time I reached the summit I was in pretty rough shape. I was relieved to discover that for once Cha had not played word games. The trail clearly forked and ran along a sharp, elongated ridge that stretched on as far as I could see to the east and west. To my right was the way back home. To my left, if the old man had told the truth, was Kyung Re. I sat down to catch my breath and still my fickle stomach. Far down the slope I could still make out the roof of the pavilion and beyond it, sparkling in the sun, the pond. Mr. Cha's home, and any other for that matter, were hidden by dense cover of blue green pines. I wondered if I'd be able to find the valley again.

A few more snorts of mountain air and I got to my feet. I faced the fork and thought about Yogi Berra's advice. Unfortunately, life ain't like that; it's one way or the other. I imagined Kyung Re walking out of the mist. I even carried on an imaginary conversation and convinced her to come with me, until a cool gust of wind snapped me back to lonely reality. Where ever Kyung Re had gone and whatever secrets she kept I had lost.

Yet, suppose I did try to find her? I had already been gone a week, maybe more. Another couple of days wouldn't make a difference. No one was going to buy my story about circuses, beautiful ladies, and white tigers anyway. And tell them about the events of last night? They'd have me in the psych ward at the 121st hospital in Seoul, giving urine samples every day for a month. No way.

I stared at the eastern trail that beckoned me to the sun. Strangely, it felt right; as though the true way home did lie in that direction. But I was a soldier. I gritted my teeth and headed west. I took four steps and my stomach mutinied. I might have been headed west, but my belly was going in a lot of other directions, mainly back up my throat. In an instant I was on my hands and knees fertilizing the mountain grass. Violent contractions shook my body, pain banged in my skull like a bone drum. The unexpected spasm continued long after anything of substance was left in my gut.

When it finally it passed I rolled over onto my back and gulped air, trying to ease the pounding behind my eyes and tearing at my neck. Everything ached. I thought about the stretch of kilometers that lay ahead of me and groaned. I'd had some rough road marches in my day, but this was going to top all of them.

I got up on legs that wobbled and shook. "I'm still a soldier," I said to myself - and fell down again. This time I stayed there. What the hell was happening to me? For the first time I began to get frightened.

"Captain Moran."

It was Cha. Looking like Moses with a large wooden staff in his hand, he stood over me. He had on his fustian white peasant's outfit and despite the fact that he had to have made the same journey I had just completed he was not showing a single bead of perspiration.

"Mr. Cha, what did you give me?" I could hardly speak.

He sat down beside me. "I have explained to you," he said gently. "Your sickness is nothing that I have done. It is what you are."

I had no strength to argue. Please just leave me alone, I thought. But I was so sick I was relieved to see him. At least I would not die up here.

"Let me show you." He placed his hand under my shoulder and urged me to stand. I struggled to my feet.

"Walk to the east. You will feel better." I knew what he was trying to do. Why did he insist on keeping me here? But at this point I was so sick I'd believe, or try, anything. If walking east took away the harrowing pain in my head and stopped the war in my stomach I was ready to march all the way to the sun. I took several tottering steps.

"A few more," he said. "Has this relieved your pain?"

I hated to admit it but the crazy old fool was right. I did feel noticeably better. Far from my usual self, but at least I could stand and walk without passing out.

"If you walk west, away from what you are, the sickness will plague you."

"What?"

"Shinbyong, the shaman sickness. You have been chosen, yet you resist. The result is the sickness we call shinbyong. It is inevitable. Because you resist so forcefully the shinbyong is very strong."

"Please Mr. Cha. You too with the shaman business? Kyung Re said the same thing last night."

"Because it is true." He reached into a leather pouch by his side. "Drink this. It will help." From the pouch he extracted a smaller leather bag that felt as though it contained a soggy sponge. "Squeeze it and drink."

Leery though I was of his concoctions I took the medicine. It tasted bitter, like minty, burnt charcoal. "That was awful."

"Of course, it is medicine, but it will help you for a while. The sickness will continue, though."

That alarmed me. "For how long?"

"Until you stop resisting."

"And I suppose it will help if I keep walking to the east, toward the 'emperor'?"

"Yes. And Kyung Re is there as well."

The old man had me again. "Mr. Cha, I don't know what is going on here, but how far away is this emperor's house? Is it near a town?"

"Yes, it is near a town. Several kilometers away."

I looked to the west and wondered. This east west symbolism was killing me. Then again my stomach had nearly accomplished that same trick. I did not believe that my relative position to the sun had anything whatever to do with my digestion, but the wrenching bout of puking had made me cautious about the idea of being up here alone, wherever here was. By now it was late morning. I was not internally or externally prepared for an exposed night on the mountain, and I had no idea how far I had to travel.

Cha saw my obvious hesitation. "Captain Moran, I understand your doubt. These are things you have no experience with. So prove it to yourself. Walk to the west in the direction you were headed and tell me how you feel."

Alright. Enough is enough. I shook my head, turned around, and began walking. Five steps later my stomach convulsed.

"Now turn around and walk back to me, Captain. Do this and tell me what you feel."

What choice did I have? I retraced my steps toward Mr. Cha – and felt an instant relief in my gut. I repeated the maneuver three times with the same result – Western sickness, Eastern relief. What the hell was going on here? Whether or not Cha had caused my illness no longer mattered. If he did I was going to have another episode anyway, possibly worst than before. If he had not done anything...well who knew how sick I really was. I now had a new priority – keep my stomach normal.

"Okay. Lead on Mr. Cha."

He looked at me steadily. I thought I saw a brief compassion in the impassive, craggy face. He nodded slowly and motioned me to follow. I looked at my feet and had the feeling this was going to be a long journey.

The sound of a loud growl snapped my head erect. There on the trail, less than a hundred yards away the monster stood perfectly still, its pale blue eyes intent. "Cha," I whispered. "The tiger."

"Ete-wha, Kaja." Cha exclaimed and clapped loudly.

The giant beast bounded to us, stopped in front of Mr. Cha, and rubbed its massive head against his side. Then it looked at me, sniffed several times and did the same thing.

"I believe you already know Kaja, Captain. He will accompany us to the home of the Emperor. Offer him your hand as a token of friendship."

I hesitated but obeyed. If the thing was going to kill me, it was too late now. The tiger carefully sniffed the back of my hand then licked it with a tongue like a carpenter's rasp. Again, I struggled to make sense of what I saw. The beast was frightening, but also the most majestic creature I had ever seen. Its head easily reached the level of my chest and its enormous, elongated body had to have been seven feet long. It had long, heavy fur, and except for several faint dark stripes, startlingly white.

"In the west you would call Kaja a Siberian tiger. Kaja's white color is highly unusual. The Emperor breeds them."

The monster continued rasping my hand. I hesitated to move or do anything lest I alarm the cat. I estimated it at well over five hundred pounds, perhaps six. Kaja's head was a big as my chest. If you ever want to feel completely, totally, helplessly vulnerable, stand next to a six hundred pound tiger. Feel its tongue ripping at your hand, look at its saber length teeth, and let your eyes fall to where claws the size of eight inch nails sprout from paws larger than a man's foot. You will learn true humility.

"Mr. Cha," I asked carefully. "Is it all right to move?"

He clapped again. "Kaja, GO!" The tiger abruptly ceased sanding the skin from my wrist. It jerked it head up to Cha and bounded away down the ridge. A hundred meters later it stopped and turned to see if we were following. It woofed and stamped its paws.

"Kaja is impatient, Captain. Shall we go?"

Like I could refuse.

For the next several kilometers we followed the trail along the ridge and toward the sun. All the while the great tiger kept ahead of us, constantly checking to see if we were keeping up. Cha set a pace which ensured that Kaja would not have to wait long for his human entourage. Thankfully, the going was relatively easy up here and the scenery spectacular. Cool air and a light breeze kept the heat at bay.

My stomach and the rest of me anatomy returned to normal and I actually began to enjoy the journey.

"You say this emperor breeds these animals, Mr. Cha?"

"Yes, those and several others. You will see. The tigers are quite useful. People are in general a superstitious lot. Tigers, especially large white ones, frighten them away."

I couldn't imagine why.

Ahead and around stretched mountains and mountains and mountains; an endless serrated landscape of jagged peaks rising and poking into the sky. I listened to wind, birds, and the sound of our feet on the trail. Occasionally a lizard, snake, or some other small animal scurried out of our way. Beyond that no other sound intruded. In the distance a surreal vision of a monstrous white tiger bounded easily among the boulders. By afternoon we had reached the end of the ridge line and Mr. Cha halted for a break. Three hours of steady marching and the old fellow was as fresh as when I had first seen him.

He pointed to the way ahead. The trail plunged down and disappeared into a tangle of pines. Beyond that rose another obstacle of rock and pines. I knew another and another rose beyond that. Mr. Cha informed me that from here on the march would be considerably more difficult.

From his back pack he gave me a small water pouch which I quickly drained, then instructed me to squeeze some more of the herb mixture into my mouth. I obeyed without argument. We shared a quick meal of rice cakes and honey which my stomach accepted without argument. After resting for what seemed like no more than two minutes we resumed the march.

Cha's statement about increasing difficulty was a shameless understatement. Korean mountains can be an anguishing trial for legs and knees. There is no gradual rise, every peak explodes like a rocket trying to reach the sky then plummets just as violently down the other side. On the way up legs and calves burn to the point of collapse. When you think you can go no further the summit is gratefully reached, but the descent is reverse struggle against gravity. The intervening boulders, trees, and roots that aided the ascent become life threatening obstacles determined to send the traveler face first into the rocks. In no time you begin to wish fondly for the ascent.

This trial of rising and falling kept on until evening. I marveled at the stamina of old man Cha. I was still in my twenties and having a tough time keeping up with him. How was he? Sixty? Seventy? If he'd spent his life making journeys like this he must have legs like steel bands. My swiftly deteriorating pride was the only thing preventing me from asking him for another break. Kaja, of course, appeared hindered only by the humans struggling to keep pace behind him.

At the bottom of another excruciating descent we faced a barrier of rushing water that careened over weathered globs of brown granite. Against a darkening sky the black green outline of one more mountain soared upward on the other side of the stream. I felt like a long distance runner who thinks he is just around the corner from finishing an unbearably long race only to find a sign announcing that he has another thirty kilometers to go. I found it hard to believe that Kyung Re had already come this way.

Cha must have been amused at the way I gaped at the mountain. "We are not going up there," he said. "From here we follow the water."

I said a silent thank you.

The path along the water was a mercifully lighter march than the cross mountain travail. Hidden by twisted pines a narrow trail curled along the rushing water. The path had its fair share of twists, dips, and turns, but compared to the mountain trail it felt like heaven.

The valley had become completely dark when Mr. Cha finally halted the march. "We will stay here tonight," he announced. From his back pack he produced two thin blankets, gave me one, and fished out two more helpings of honey and rice cakes. I gulped mine down and slumped onto my blanket.

The next day a wondrous scene greeted me. We rested on a flat stone shelf that jutted out some twenty feet above the river offering a tremendous view of the valley. All along the waterway waterfalls spilled haphazardly among overlapping boulders, falling through a mottled checkerboard of sun and shade. Directly below a clear pool of mountain water sparkled in the sun and magnified a reddish brown bottom of crushed granite.

"Swim," said Mr. Cha. I noticed he had already been. He sat on a rock drying himself in the sun. He was shirtless and had pulled his white baggy pants above his knees. Except for the paleness of his legs and the sparse, scrawny hair on his shins there was much to admire about Mr. Cha's physique. The man was a taught, muscular picture of aging grace.

I clambered to the pool and stripped off my clothes. Remembering my wonderful night with Kyung Re I jumped into the water and discovered that this was not the warm lily pond of the valley. The mountain water gripped and shocked. In seconds all traces of sleep disappeared, but the pool was such a beautiful gem I could not bring myself to jump back out. Suddenly an enormous splash exploded in the water. It was followed by a shattering roar.

"Kaja likes you, Captain," Mr. Cha called.

Indeed the great cat had plunged into the water beside me and was thoroughly enjoying his morning swim. To my immense discomfort Kaja sprang to full height and pounced on me, his gigantic paws falling over my shoulders. I was knocked backward and floundered under the chilled water expecting the cat to hold me there until I drowned. But as I popped to the surface Kaja was waiting for me in a posture of playful expectation. Sorry, big fella, I thought. If you are waiting for me to jump on your back and play you'll have to wait until we get to know each other a lot better. The big cat gave up on me and began wildly pursuing imaginary fish.

I climbed back onto the ledge. Cha offered more rice cake and honey.

Cha pointed up the valley. "We have just a short way to go. How is your stomach? Are you feeling better?"

"I feel fine. But I still don't believe in shamans."

"We will see."

"How much farther do we have to go, Mr. Cha?"

"Oh, we are very close now, less than two kilometers."

"Why did we stop?"

"The path is dangerous in the night and there is much to learn." He looked at me quietly for a moment. "Sit down, Captain." He indicated a place next to him. I sat on the sun warmed rock.

"So far you have not accepted what myself or Kyung Re has told you."

"Mr. Cha, I only know that I fell under the spell of a lovely young lady. This is not a mystery. It has led to some wildly unforeseen circumstances; that I admit. But shamans and demons? Yea, I've got a hard time with that."

"Then you may have a harder time ahead."

"I will be especially careful about what I eat and drink."

"You must be careful about many things."

"You bet. Especially if I don't get back to the Army. I don't imagine the emperor's palace has a telephone?"

"The emperor is not to be the subject of your sarcasm. Now be still and listen."

Cha was upset. This was the first time I had seen him display any emotion stronger than a raised eyebrow. I apologized. Whatever fairies danced in his old Korean mind I supposed I had no right to mock them.

Cha spoke as a patient father to a petulant child. "In the home of the emperor you must show respect. Although you have witnessed many things, you do not believe what you see. And that is fine, Captain. A healthy skepticism is good. But soon you will see and be a part of events that you will find increasingly hard to dismiss.

"Even so, you have the right to dismiss. You may choose to disregard all you will see. That is your right. But that choice will not be easy nor will it be pleasant. You are here because you are mudang, you are chosen. You may disbelieve that with all of your heart, but what is, is."

I tried not to be flippant or condescending. "Mr. Cha, the only is I know right now is what is going to happen to me when I get back to the Army."

Leaning on his staff Mr. Cha stood up. He placed the rolled blankets into his knapsack, put on his shirt, and motioned me to follow. I quickly dressed and fell in behind him. He then gave a command to the big tiger which exploded out of the water and shook itself dry; an action that prompted a small rainstorm. From this point on the animal stayed some distance to our rear.

Cha took several steps, turned, and looked back at me. "One more thing, Captain."

"I know," I said. "Don't do anything rash."

I thought I saw him smile.

The path we followed along the mountain stream widened and eventually curved away from the water. It entered a forest valley of thick trees and began a steady incline. The path could no longer be called a forest trail. It had become a narrow road of granite cobblestone, rather pleasant to walk on. At intervals along the road stone statues of bizarre animals and odd figures of human warriors cropped up. The figures were old, encrusted with moss and lichens. I recognized a number of ancient Taoist and Buddhist symbols.

We emerged from the forest to an open area of watered fields bordered by sharp cliffs. A wooden bridge bisected the fields. On one side of the bridge a verdant rice field glimmered in the sun; on the other side emerald green elephant ear plants bobbed and waived in a large pond. Tiny waterfalls sprouted from the shear rock face of the cliff on the side of the elephant ear plants. Silver trickles of water shimmered down the rock. A slow current drifted across the pond, under the bridge and into the rice field, then disappeared into dark forest on the other side. The little valley was a jewel.

We crossed the wooden bridge. It terminated in a wide trellis of thick, knotted vines that looked as though they had been growing here for a hundred years. Cha's white tunic turned a pure, glossy green as we passed through the leafy tunnel.

On the other side of the trellis a solid pavement of worn, uneven granite began to rise. Small structures, tiled in familiar Oriental red and thatched with brown grass in the old style bordered the road on either side. The places were small, single room structures with brilliant, flower filled terraces in front of each. Hummingbirds, dragonflies, and clumsy bees buzzed and streaked in the bright sun.

At the end of the row of houses the road curved to the left, crossed an ornately carved stone bridge that spanned yet another mountain stream, then widened into a lovely lane overhung with large, well tended trees. Other structures sprouted up, larger than the ones farther down, with intricately carved roof tiles and eaves of brilliant colors. Some were open pavilions with spectacular Oriental roofs supported by enormous red columns and no walls. Stone statues of enormous turtles, pillars in the shape of writhing dragons, and tigers with wildly exaggerated features decorated the area. Carved wooden dragons and tiger heads jutted from the eaves under the roofs. It was a place full of life without a living person to be seen.

The lane came to an abrupt halt at the mouth of a cave. Above the cave a mountain ran up to the sky. A waterfall cascaded along the right side of the cave and fell into a circular pond some thirty feet below. A polished wooden railing lined the lane here; I leaned over it and enjoyed the cool, moist air that swirled from the depths.

Mr. Cha led directed me to the cave and we paused at a small fountain near a colorful statue of a ferocious warrior. "He guards the entrance to Buddha," he explained. "Say a prayer and drink water from the cup. Then we will go inside."

Why not? I recited a short request for an end to my journey, filled the metal cup near the fountain and drank. The water was sweet and cold. We entered the cave and I savored the cool air. At first I could see nothing except the white outline of Cha's jacket. We turned a corner and a glow of golden light poured out ahead of us. Tucked far back in a rocky alcove sat an enormous statue of Buddha. I doubted if it had been carved from pure gold, the statue was more than fifteen feet high, but it was brilliant gold in color. Surrounded by hundreds of softly flickering candles in the dark recesses of a cavern the affect was overwhelming. I mimicked Mr. Cha's bowing and praying, but at the same time I wondered why a shaman would pray to Buddha.

This ritual concluded we left the cave and walked back into the now uncomfortably hot sun. Cicadas screamed an endless whining rhythm and I wished for another mountain stream. But Mr. Cha led me toward the steepest obstacle I had seen so far.

This time the climb was made as much by arm as by leg. Thankfully, the thoughtful monks or whoever inhabited this place had implanted a wooden hand rail for the purpose. It was a rickety and temperamental support, however, and I took great care to ensure secure myself to rocks and wiry little pines as well. Once more I marveled at Cha's ability. This road march he was leading could test the fiber of an Army ranger, yet the old guy was right there in front of me all the way without a sign of slowing down.

After forty minutes or so of steady climbing we reached the summit, a barren jumble of brown granite boulders. I stopped and peered back into the valley we had come through. From here every structure was a tiny speck peeking from little spaces wedged between clumps of green pines. The valley trailed off and curved, following the water and who knew where beyond that. I would have liked to enjoy more of the scenery but Mr. Cha was impatiently calling to resume momentum for the march. I was glad I did not know him when he was younger.

We crossed the rocky summit and descended for a short distance until the slope leveled into a tree covered ridge. A well trodden path cut through the forested ridge and the shade was a welcome relief. We traveled along the ridge for about another kilometer all the while gaining altitude while the trees became thinner. The slow rise abruptly turned upward to another peak of jumbled boulders. Mr. Cha nimbly worked his way up the rise and waited for me outlined against the sky. I scrambled along the rocks, gained the summit, and stood up fully expecting to see one more mountain and one more ridge and beyond that a million more. I expected anything except what I saw.

A knife edged ridge ran from where we stood to a single peak that rose like a monolith from a clear valley floor. The ridge looked as though it had been formed from a colossal earthquake had caused both sides of a larger formation to collapse, leaving a surreal ribbon of rock hundreds of feet high and no more than several feet wide.

The valley spanned north and south of the natural bridge. To the south it terminated in maze of mountains that stretched into the distance. Bisected by a winding, gleaming river the northern expanse spread further. A lone peak jutted beyond the river, and on either side of it the plain rolled like a carpet of emeralds. Endless sharp pinnacles of rock hemmed in the valley to the west and east, as though God himself had pushed back the spiny mountains to give this magic place a chance to soak up the sun and sky.

"It's the most incredible thing I've ever seen," I remarked.

Mr. Cha was not wasting time gawking at the scenery. He waved impatiently so I followed him onto the ridge where a narrow foot path was worn deeply into the rock. I said a silent thanks to the generations before me who had beaten the trail. The only break from a fall would be a jumble of cracked granite boulders hundreds of feet below. At the far of the ridge I noticed a jagged cavern gaping in the side of the mountain. I estimated the wide crooked hole at about fifty feet high, but it loomed larger with every step.

As we approached the mountain a wide stone terrace, seemingly built into the side of the rock, spanned out from the cave. We stepped onto the terrace and approached the entrance. From the shadows a figure emerged, the only other soul beside Mr. Cha I had encountered on the entire journey. Dressed in a gray robe characteristic of Buddhist monks he moved to the entrance of the cave, crossed a long silver spear in front of his chest, and silently stared at us. I hoped Mr. Cha had the right password. The guy was enormous. He towered over me and his weight easily would have been greater than the two of us combined.

Mr. Cha spoke to the giant in a dialect of Korean I did not recognize. At the end of his soliloquy he pointed to me and said "Pam Sidyunga." The giant stepped aside and let us go by.

We entered the cavern. But cavern does not convey the dimensions of the enormous rip that sliced into the heart of the mountain. A large truck could have easily made in through the passageway. Although torches burned brightly, the roof of the cut remained invisible. The floor was flat, dark rock, worn and polished. The walls, though rough hewn by nature had obviously been domesticated over many years by the caress of untold human hands. I knew that lava flows were capable of creating such oversized corridors, but I had never known one that led into a mountain. This was like a train tunnel, and like a train tunnel it emerged on the other side of the mountain. From here another splinter of a ridge extended, this one descending to the south away from the wide valley. For a while it looked as though we were heading back into the wild expanse of pointy cliffs and peaks I had seen beyond the solitary tunnel mountain. Yet the ridge curved downward and to the left falling between two smaller prominences.

We passed the peak on our left and the ground fell away to a sight so extraordinary that I cannot adequately describe my feelings. There are times when a man sees something so astounding, so beautiful, that his eyes water in awe; an image so wondrous that it sears and burns itself deep into the mind and remains forever.

Cha motioned me to move, but I ignored him. I stood rooted, stunned. A series of carved stone bridges dotted a verdant valley and decorated a gem like brook that curled and glittered amidst the green. Shimmering waterfalls, turquoise lagoons, jagged cliffs and arching rock formations enclosed the place. Throughout the length of the valley colorful pagodas laced with marble statues that gushed silver streams of water into blue pools sprouted between the trees. My God, I thought. Shangri La exists!

Mr. Cha shook me from my trance and we descended into the magnificent gorge. There were people here. Quite a few in fact. All dressed in the old Korean style. Most milled about, some in the costumes of monks, but most in the colorful dress type formal uniforms I had seen at the celebration near Cha's place. They took notice and smiled as Mr. Cha and I walked though the amazing town, but none acted in the least surprised at my presence. Oddly languid and peaceful everyone appeared completely as ease. They smiled, nodded, and bowed, then went on their way strolling about in quiet conversation. I saw no modern utilities, wires, or anything that resembled the modern world.

Mr. Cha was obviously a well known personage in this extraordinary neighborhood. At every turn people rushed to greet him, bowed deeply, and shook his hand. He replied with warmth and a courtesy I had never seen in the remote old man. More confused than ever I stumbled along, dazed at what I was seeing, unable to comprehend the splendor of it. Was this a lost civilization? A movie set? A dream? My head spun.

Cha led me along a slender road of white marble that curled through the amazing place. We made numerous twists and turns, climbed several sets of steps. I lost track of how many fountains, waterfalls, and koi filled ponds we passed. Finally we ascended an exceptionally long span of steps that led to a tall pavilion set with a gleaming, scarlet red marble floor that contrasted against four enormous columns of pale blue. Above the columns the roof extended over eaves crowded with a dazzling array of carved figures, emblazoned in color. In the middle of this building stood the most dazzling sight of all.

Kyung Re turned as we approached. In an astonishing hangbok of ivory white she was more than the exotic, stunning beauty I had first seen. Framed against the red marble and blue columns she became a queen. I had an urge to run to her, dive into her beauty. But her regal appearance stopped me. How could I even think about embracing this woman? Kung Re answered my dilemma by approaching me with open arms and a knowing smile.

"I have been waiting for you, Pam Sidynga!"

I expected her to jump into my arms but Mr. Cha cleared his throat and stomped his staff letting us know that this public display was unseemly. "Kyung Re, this fellow has an audience with the emperor tonight. He must be cleaned. Look at him."

Cha's words made me once again at my less than regal appearance. Simply by approaching Kyung Re I probably soiled her dress. But that hardly seemed to matter to Kyung Re who continued to hold my arm closely. "I will ensure he is wondrously clean for the emperor."

"Ha!" the old man snorted. "I'm sure you would. Let the ladies clean him. At least then we will know he has had a proper bath and not another water frolic."

No sooner had the words left his mouth than I was assaulted by two stout woman who separated me from Kyung Re began hauling me up the remaining steps away from the pavilion. I looked desperately back at Kyung Re, but she simply stood smiling next to Mr. Cha. "Don't worry, Pam Sidyunga," she called. "They will take excellent care of you and I will meet you later."

The two matrons who had captured me were as sturdy as Korean Ssirum wrestlers. At this point, however, my curiosity at this incredible place was so great I no longer cared. Shamans and emperors and purple dragons might all be an illusion but the incredible sights all around me were not. Now I was determined to go through with this entire mystery right to the end. My hosts led me away through a leafy pass and then to a wide columned passageway. The passageway terminated at a dark opening cut into the granite of a mountain. We stopped at the entrance and I was instructed to remove my shoes.

When I stepped inside I realized that the cut was actually a hall that opened into a spacious, marble floored clearing extending into the base of the mountain. Overhead the pink granite of the cave glistened from moisture. In fact, the entire area was misty with moisture caused by a series of steaming baths inlaid into the marble floor. A large shallow pool in the center pulsed with hot, blue water that rose from a vent in the bottom of the pool. The water of this large pool overflowed into narrow troughs that connected to a perimeter of smaller baths. The floor, pillars, and squat benches of the bathing hall were comprised of red and white marble. Very Roman like, I thought.

I was directed into a smaller bath near the edge of the hall overlooking a forested slope that fell away down the side of the mountain. Whoever had constructed this place not only had to be a master engineer, but damned good geologist as well. Since I had not seen any form of electrical or gas power I assumed the heated water came from vents deep inside the mountain.

I was not allowed to admire the construction of the place for very long. At the side of the bath my guardians immediately began to remove my shirt and attacked the buckle on my pants. Now I have been in Asia long enough to suspect what was coming next, but I still clung to the naïve hope that I would be allowed the privilege of cleaning myself in some kind of privacy. That particular wish was naïve indeed. Neither lady showed the slightest hesitation about stripping the remainder of my clothes and unceremoniously pushing me into the bath.

The water was frighteningly hot. My immediate instinct for survival caused me to spring out of the bath. At least I attempted to. The guards had apparently been through this ritual with unclean males before, however. They splashed into the water with me, locking my arms and shoulders once again, and ensuring that escape was impossible.

Resigned to my fate I began the awful process of lowering myself into the scalding water. In this at least my captors were tolerant. They allowed me all of two minutes to adjust to the bath before assaulting me with soap. And a thorough assault it was. Not a single inch of flesh on my body, no matter what the protrusion or cavity, missed their unabashed fingers. When I was at last fully encapsulated by foam and somewhat enjoying the sensation, the ladies attacked me with a rough stone and proceeded to grind the skin from every square millimeter of me.

The rinsing, perhaps better referred to as drowning, followed. For this procedure I was commanded to rise from the bath I was in and enter another receptacle. Flanked by my tormentors I stepped naked onto the cool marble floor and walked to the nearest clear bath. The rinsing barely allowed me time to breath. Finally, satisfied that not a single speck of soap remained, I was commanded to rise from the bath. Both ladies eyed me suspiciously, as though I were deliberately hiding some unseen cache of microbes. Somehow I managed to pass inspection. Trial completed I was given permission to soak in the large pool.

With very business like air of having finished a job well done, the demons of the bath left me to enjoy myself in solitude. I leaned back and soaked in the soothing water. My wounds had long since healed by then and the soreness of the long road march had been rubbed out of me by the scrubbing. I leaned back, rested my head on the marble floor and allowed my body to float listlessly. Despite all that I had been through and all of the preposterous things I had seen I was incredibly tired. I gave in to the lull of the water and exhaustion and relaxed. I was soon awake, though, and determined to find out more of this strange place. I stood up and discovered a new and very real problem. My clothes were gone. The bath ladies had taken them, at this moment they were probably being burned in flames to rid the world once and for all of their contaminating germs.

"Pam Sidyunga?"

I squatted immediately at the sound of Kyung Re's voice echoing in the bath. "Over here," I called.

She approached to the side of the pool and smiled. "Would you like some clothes?"

"Very funny."

She held out a set of distinctively un-western style clothes. "I'm afraid you will have to wear something a little more Korean," she said. "I've brought you a towel, too."

431

With more than a little embarrassment, and to Kyung Re's great amusement, I climbed out of the bath. I toweled off slipped on the clothes. Garbed in the latest style of 19th century Korea I felt like Gulliver. Kyung Re appeared pleased at the transformation. "Now," she said. "I will show you to your room."

"Kyung Re, I don't want to go to a room. I want to go to a telephone. You don't under-"

She put her finger to my lips. "Shhh. Trust me for a few moments longer."

For a long moment she kept her finger over my mouth and stared into my eyes. "Can you stop speaking for a little while and listen?"

I pulled her hand away and tried to stifle my frustration. "Kyung Re. When do you propose to tell me what is going on? I have been away from my post for a week. I am AWOL, and about to be considered a deserter. I will go to prison for this. And if you are mixed up in this so will you."

My speech did not impress Kyung Re in the least. She picked up my hand and pulled me away from the bath. "No one knows where you are, and no one will find you. Let me take you to your room and I will explain all that I can."

KOGIRI ATASHI

Chapter Four

As we entered the passageway that led back to where I had first seen Kyung Re she pulled her hand from mine. "Public displays of affection are inappropriate," she announced. You must learn to control yourself with more patience, Pam Sidyunga."

"I was not raised in Korea, Kyung Re."

"Obviously."

Obviously I was not going to get the last word either. We walked back toward the pavilion, but instead of continuing along the same route, we detoured away from the public part of the "village" and headed for the outskirts of the valley. Here, on rocky land that sloped up to meet the mountains were a number of small, thatched roof bungalows fronted by tiny gardens. Kyung Re directed me to one of the structures crouched behind boulders and bent pines. "This is where you will stay," she announced.

She pushed open the door, a rough board pine affair, it looked barely able to keep out the slightest breeze. Small, open windows on either side provided enough light for me to see a futon style bed next to a knee high table in the corner. Some kind of writing utensil lay on the table, but I could see that in order to use them I would have to sit cross legged. The pillow on the bed looked just like what is was, a block of wood with a wide arc carved into the middle.

"My room?"

Kyung Re simply shut the door and walked to a lantern that hung from the wall. She lit the flame and a surprisingly bright light illuminated my new quarters. "Well," I said. "The Army has put me in worse."

Kyung Re seemed to be in no mood for jokes. "Pam Sidyunga, please sit down and let me explain what I can to you."

I was certainly in favor of that. I squatted next to her on the bed.

She thought for a moment before speaking. "In some ways you are right, Pam Sidyunga - you are not entirely here of your own choice."

"That hardly surprises me, Kyung Re."

"But you must understand that what you are is the main reason you have come here."

But by now I'd had enough esoteric explanations. "Look, Kyung Re, I'm done arguing as to why I am here or who brought me here. I admit it. If I'd been behaving myself that night I saw you in the circus I wouldn't be here, okay? That part I'll take on the chin. But right now I need to know one thing, no, make that two - exactly where am I and what is this place."

Kyung Re closed her eyes and nodded. I interrupted her meditations. "And no more misty explanations, dammit. I have to have a straight answer this time."

She pulled her head up and regarded me as though attempting to gauge something in my words. Finally, she twisted her torso and she face me squarely. "Pam Sidyunga. What would you say is the heart and soul of your country?"

"What on earth do you mean by that question?"

"I mean, what central thing defines you as Americans? What one thing, if taken away, would make America cease to be what it is?"

I thought about it for a minute, but the answer was obvious. "I suppose it would be individual freedom and the adherence to that value. Take that away and America is no different than any other place."

"Yes," she said. "That is a good answer. I know you realize that in Asia we adhere to a different set of values. Individual freedom is not the soul of our nation. Our traditions, religion, and piety to those who have come before us is much more in our hearts. But the freedom of the people is also important."

"All right, Kyung Re. What's the point?"

435

"You wanted to know where you are, what this place is. This place, and those of us who live here are the living embodiment of Korea's soul."

I tried to understand what Kyung Re was talking about. "You mean like monks; this is some kind of a monastery?"

"We are much more than chanting priests."

"Okay. What do you do?" I was more skeptical than ever.

"We guide the new Korea with old wisdom."

I remained clueless. "And how do you guide your country hidden in a valley from the past? Why not go into politics or something, try to change it like everyone else does?"

Kyung Re sighed. "I told you this would not be an easy thing to understand. Our way is not like that. We do not go out and force people to do anything. We guide, we persuade, we push indirectly. The traveling circus you saw is just one of our many ways."

"Which brings me to the point, Kyung Re. Why me?"

At this point she broke into a wide smile. "Ah," she said. "Now we are back to why you have brought yourself here!"

"And exactly why did I decide to bring myself here?"

She closed her eyes and smiled. "It's all so simple, really. Any life is nothing more than the sum of the choices that person makes. You have made many which have brought you here, from the time you were born until the day you volunteered for the army of your country and saved Pok Dani. But you made those choices based on who you are. We provided the path for you to make the choice and you did."

"Great, great. I got it. I take responsibility for my life. I'm fine with that, Kyung Re. But now my free will and power of choice tells me it is time to return to the Army."

"That is right, Pam Sidyunga. But that is something which is now very hard for you to do."

"So tell me why that is, especially in light of your lecture about my own actions leading me here."

She took my hand and looked directly into my eyes. "How can I explain?"

I waited in silence for her to go on. She seemed genuinely tortured about how to tell me more.

The wooden door swung wide and Mr. Cha entered. He thumped his gnarled staff. "Kyung Re, you have said enough. I will take responsibility now."

Kyung Re rose quickly to her feet and bowed. "Yes, Ajossi."

Ajossi? I recognized the word. Kyung Re had just referred to Mr. Cha as uncle. But in what sense?

I thought to ask, but Cha squatted in front of me. "Captain Moran, or more appropriately, Pam Sidyunga, let me explain it to you by telling you a story. It may not satisfy you completely, but it is necessary for your meeting with the emperor."

"I'm listening, Mr. Cha."

"Good." He turned to Kyung Re and bade her to sit. "There was once a young man. Much like yourself, he had a restless, curious nature. He lived in a small village, a peaceful place, surrounded by green rice fields. His parents, although possessed of an average income, gave him all that he needed. They had even managed to secure him to a great university where he could become a scholar and thus live a life much better than their own. In short this young man had all he could ask for - loving family and a fine future.

"But as I said he had a restless, curious nature. The little village and the future of a scholar was not to his liking. He wanted to see the world; to experience it for himself, not through books.

"So one day he bade his parents good bye. With a small bundle of belongings over his shoulder he set off. By the end of the first day he had passed well beyond the rice fields of his village. By the second day he was treading upon winding roads he had never seen before. And by the third day he stood on top of a tall mountain contemplating the next day's travel in new and wondrous places.

"He looked back in the direction from which he had come and relished his freedom. Although his supplies were low and he thought fondly of his parents and the village he had left behind, he had no desire to return. The young man surveyed the world from the height of the mountain. He went to sleep very contented, knowing that all paths lie open to his whim.

"The following day he rose and saw a beautiful sunrise brimming over the mountains to the east. He chose that direction and set off.

"He traveled for many days. He traversed wonderful landscapes and met many fascinating people, staying in each place no longer than he wished. Each morning when he awoke, he would decide a direction and go. For many months this life made him exceedingly happy.

"One day, however, he came to the edge of a wide river. The water appeared shallow so he stepped in and began to walk across. But when he reached the middle, he stepped into a pocket of deeper water and fell. The rushing current carried him away. No matter what the young man did he could not stop himself, even though it seemed as though the water was so shallow he should have been able to. He tried many times to stop but was finally swept over the side of a waterfall."

I waited for Cha to go on and realized that is tale was complete.

"Wonderful. Did he live?" I asked.

"That does not matter."

"Then what does?"

"That the young man was no longer the same person on the other side of the waterfall."

"So you're telling me I'm about to be swept over a waterfall - and there is nothing I can do about it?"

"The current is very powerful."

I looked at Kyung Re. "Yes, Mr. Cha. It is."

"You have felt the sickness," he reminded me.

I could not lie about sickness. I had felt it all right. Just the same I was not entirely convinced that Cha himself was not behind this turmoil in my stomach.

Kyung Re spoke. "Pam Sidyunga, your soul will lead you home."

I'm not sure what it was about Kyung Re's announcement, but it hit me with deep, striking power.

Perhaps it was a sudden, powerful realization that she was right; a hidden raw nerve of truth that I had always known, but tried to ignore; some thing I did not want to face. I started to speak - and couldn't. Kyung Re placed her hands on either side of my face and turned me around that I faced her. "Give in to what you feel. It will be so much easier."

Her eyes widened and in an instant I knew I had to leave or I'd certainly end up going over the waterfall. I jumped to my feet. "I'm leaving, now. East or west, one way or the other I'll find my way back." I got up, reached for the door, and grabbed the handle. Before I had opened it halfway the pain ripped through my stomach like a chain saw.

Cha's face loomed. "He is stubborn, isn't he?"

I heard Kyung Re answer softly. "Ne."

Kyung Re stroked my head. "You will learn soon, Pam Sidyunga. Very soon."

With that Cha announced that the time for my audience with the emperor had arrived. Kyung Re and Cha took turns coaching me on the proper protocol for my debut, with Cha never tiring of dire warnings about the consequences of acting rash. He need not have wasted his energy. The last wrenching attack of stomach pain had taken a lot of the fight out of me. I had no alternative but to wait, at least for a while longer. I still wasn't sold on the "shaman sickness" diagnosis but whatever the cause, I could not afford an attack like the last one while wandering the back roads of Korea. I almost wished the business about witch doctors was true. At least it would not be as serious as the other dire alternatives crossing my mind. What the hell was wrong with me anyway? I resigned myself for a visit to the "emperor" and attempted to relax.

The palace sat at the far end of the valley from where I had entered it with Cha. With the old man and Kyung Re as my escorts we walked back to what I called the "public square," that place where I had first seen Kyung Re. From here we followed a winding footpath that took us along the brook that flowed through the town. The land kept up a slow, steady upward slope so that before long I could turn and see the rest of the valley. Kyung Re pointed further up the slope. "There is the palace," she said.

I had to blink to be sure of what I saw. In the fading light a distinct outline of a very high stone wall rose over the tops of the pine trees. Although I could only make out one part of it, and that looked several hundred feet long, Kyung Re assured me that I was only seeing a fraction of what was a very large palace. If I was only able to see a part of the place then the emperor must live very large indeed. Until then I had not actually thought much about where the man would live. I had, in fact, assumed that his existence was a fantasy. Another of my cherished assumptions was about to be proven wrong.

Along the road to the palace we were joined by a number of other folks, all intent on the same destination. I felt slightly foolish in my Korean garb but I was not the only one dressed like he had stepped out of a cultural history book. Just like the dinner Cha had taken me to before, the gentry were out in full regalia, decked out in the color and flair of ancient royalty. This ought to be some party, I thought. Ladies and men wore colorful hanboks that swished and glittered in the amber sunset. As before, I noted that they were an exceptionally attractive people; no warts or blemishes here, and surprisingly tall for Koreans. Some of the men were nearly my height.

One thing in particular differed about this gathering compared to the night of my dinner feast. The laughter and easy conversation were gone. Everyone walked in silence, nodding briefly to each other and then continuing on in somber dignity. The atmosphere affected me as well as Cha and Kyung Re. My mood changed from flippant irritation to slight apprehension. Perhaps this emperor actually existed.

We closed ranks from all sides as the road narrowed to a single wide lane that crossed a green meadow. Statues of tall, menacing warriors in ancient battle regalia lined the road and glared down at us. If the idea was to intimidate, then it worked. Even these proud, beautiful people seemed reluctant to raise their heads, as if the stone gods would deem it a challenge and strike them down.

Drenched in a rose gold sunset we approached the palace gates. The giant wooden doors were open, parted outward in ominous welcome. Beyond the gates and dominating the interior stood a large circular, ancient looking structure constructed of polished lumber. Burnished by age and stained red brown the edifice had been built from hefty trees of a size no longer seen in Korea. A patio, or walkway of sorts, supported by wooden columns twice the width around as telephone poles surrounded the building. At the tops of the columns where they met the curled eves of the roof, colorful dragons and contorted, fanciful creatures snarled at us. I marveled at the creations, thinking not only of the artist's imagination and skill, but his considerable acrobatic flexibility it must have taken for such a task.

Cha pulled at my sleeve and motioned me to stop. He whispered. "The Dragon Temple. It is here the emperor receives audiences."

The rest of the gentry who had made the pilgrimage came to a halt and gathered. We waited without speaking, facing another pair of monstrous wooden doors. No one spoke, and I knew better than to ask what was about to occur. By now the sun had secreted itself behind the mountain cover. Faces were covered by the dark. In the distance thousands of "pookoo" birds began their familiar, spooky nighttime chant. Occasionally a screech owl or some creature I could not identify barked or screamed an epithet into the night. In the way unique to steep mountains the darkness thickened rapidly. The crowd surrounding me, some fifty people strong, suddenly disappeared. Cha and Kyung Re disappeared. My hands and body became invisible. All sound ceased. The suspense became overwhelming. What was the purpose of the silent gathering? What was I doing out here? All this talk about shamans. Perhaps they were all simply mad devil worshipers - with a convenient sacrifice at hand. I was suspicious and alert all over again and very near to doing something very rash when three bellowing gongs shattered the thick night silence.

Unless you have actually heard the sound of these monstrous Korean bells you cannot imagine the jarring, vibration rich impact they have. Some are over fifteen feet high and eight feet across. A stout wooden log hangs from a pair of heavy chains and serves as the striking mechanism. Two acolytes take positions on either side of the log and drive it into the bell like a battering ram, producing a sound of such overwhelming richness that it can be felt throughout your entire body. The ancient instruments vibrate and rattle the surrounding atmosphere long after a single strike. If I had not spent years listening to artillery fire the unexpected boom would have caused me to back flip out of my skin.

But the bell jarred me out of my self absorbed, erratic thoughts and it proved to be the signal for the opening of the twin giant doors. A narrow crack of yellow light glittered for an instant between the seams and hovered with startling brightness on the faces of those in its path. A second later both doors swung wide and a warm yellow glow filled the night. The full color of the costumed assemblage came back to life. And as the color blossomed so did the joviality of the crowd. Voices and laughter sprang up; a complete contrast to the dark somber mood moments ago. Everyone began to walk forward toward a heavy planked exceptionally wide stairway.

"We go to the Dragon Temple," Cha said as he and Kyung Re motioned me to move along.

The top of the stairwell was like emerging into a surreal, circular cavern. Blazing in torch light a riot of color mad, bulging eyed dragons decorated the walls. A pair of enormous round pillars extended from the floor to the ceiling which seemed over one hundred feet high. Red and green dragons clawed their way up the columns and disappeared into shadows at the very top. The floor itself was a mosaic of dragons spitting, clawing, yawning. The satin, iridescent kaleidoscope of the hanboks blended perfectly with the dragon figurines.

We came to a halt at the front of the circular, flat interior that made up the center of the temple. Except for the space in front of us the circle was tiered into three levels. The first rose several feet above the floor and was empty. The next level was only a foot higher than the first but was filled with ore painted dragon statues, leafed in gold and contorted into every conceivable position. The third tier, higher and wider that the other two, supported rows of huge drums, ceremonial instruments still played in modern Korea. Each instrument was actually made of three separate drums, all held aloft by carved wooden dragons of polished red mahogany at a height to that they could be played by a standing person. On the far right stood a single monstrous drum. I could have stood inside of it.

The people buzzed and talked softly as they fell orderly to their places like western Christians prior to Sunday service. The men and woman fell into five rows which seemed to be arranged according to some unknown rank.

They did not sit in cross legged fashion, choosing instead a kneeling posture, a traditional Oriental position of submission and respect to one vastly superior to oneself. I had seen children kneel in similar fashion when addressing their parents and grandparents on ceremonial holidays, but this was the first time I had witnessed adults behaving this way. The way that the hanbok of the ladies puffed up about them made them appear as though they were sitting on an unseen stool amidst a gigantic flower display.

Cha and Kyung Re led me to the middle and front of the kneeling audience. I had the feeling I was about to put on display yet again. I looked at Kyung Re and she nodded, indicating that I was to kneel. I hesitated. Kneeling in front of anyone is a difficult thing for an American to do under any circumstances. But if I was ever to find out what was going on here and somehow make my way back to the world of reality I had to play this game by the rules of the owners. I recalled Cha's constant scolding about rash behavior, and knelt.

My knees had no sooner touched the floor when a flurry of figures rushed from the shadows at the fare end of the stage. A line of beautiful young ladies in swirling hanboks of red and purple satin burst into the light. Clutching oversized drum sticks they separated into two lines and sprinted to the ceremonial drums on the third tier. Each lady faced an instrument. One drum in front of her, and one perpendicular to either shoulder. They raised one drumstick to the giant timpani in front and raised the other into the air. A lady in a solid purple handbok the appeared from the shadows pushing a gigantic drum of some kind supported on a wheeled platform. She solemnly marched to the center of the stage, raised both arms and stopped. The silence of the room throbbed in anticipation of the thunderous cascade to come.

And it did! The lady struck her instrument a single arcing blow. The sound thundered in the enclosed temple. I felt air molecules dance on my skin. She struck again and the ladies surrounding the room joined her tempo briefly and stopped. The woman at the front began a solo performance beating the instrument with slow tragic blows that exploded in bass vibrations. The tempo of her rhythm slowly increased. The ladies on the accompanying drums joined her again and filled the room with renewed thunder.

They spun about on cue, drumsticks a blur of motion and attacked the drum to the right, them turned quickly and assaulted the one on the left, then back to the center. With movements that seemed of magic they played each of the three drums in near simultaneous motion, at times even bending over backwards and playing the opposing drum upside down.

The drums thundered and exploded in the temple; my insides rumbled to the throb of them. I'd seen similar performances before, but that was from an auditorium looking at a few musicians that were part of a paid performance. This was something different. Here I was surrounded by the crushing sound; lifted by it from all sides in an ancient temple from an ancient time. I was hearing the music as it had been played in centuries past for powerful monarchs. This was music for an emperor.

Now I understood why prehistoric men were so enamored of the power of the drum. Its force was undeniable. Rumbling like small volcanoes each stroke seemed to penetrate deep inside the body. It was almost like becoming weightless, as though the body ceased to exist and became part of the air instead.

Suddenly the ladies drubbing the instruments along the walls stopped. The single woman on the monster drum continued to boom out a slower and slower rhythm. Then, she too, ceased. The air stopped without a sound. Like a flurry of whispers the girls scurried away from their drums and fled once more into the shadows.

The sudden silence after the prolonged thunder of the drums was oddly peaceful. Drenched in the powerful quiet I seemed to forget where I was; for the first time in days I no longer cared about where I had to be. I simply accepted that I was alive. I felt at peace.

Another lady, her hair pulled back into a gleaming ebony swirl held in place by a long golden pin, them emerged from the shadows and walked to the edge of the raised platform. She held an instrument that resembled a large lute with a flattened bottom to make it stable on the floor. She sat down, placed the instrument in front of her, and began to pluck it with precise, deliberate tweaks. Each note sprang up sharply and wobbled in the air for long moments until it was joined by another.

In the midst of this soothing play the mood of the audience changed again. I could feel them stiffen and lean forward. They were obviously expecting something, or someone. The long awaited emperor? I hoped so.

A familiar, frightening snarl rattled the air and Cha quickly reached for my arm. And there was Kaja in all his gleaming white furred glory, prowling to the center of the stage. The entire audience rose as one; Cha's firm grip on my arm provoking me to do the same. Kaja, the tiger was the emperor? As soon as the thought entered my mind it was displaced by another presence on the stage, this one very human. Every member of the audience stood and bowed deeply; the lengthy, very low bow reserved for a child greeting his father. Of course, I followed suit.

Standing posture regained I beheld the man on the stage. He was an ancient fellow for sure. I judged him to be well into his eighth decade, perhaps beyond. The smiling, portly face beaming down upon us certainly did not fit my preconception of a fierce Asian emperor. No, this man looked more like a kindly grandfather, or great grandfather. Shaggy white eyebrows arched down to his cheeks and below that bloomed a robust white beard. In his red flowery red robe I was reminded more of Santa Claus than Genghis Khan. But what he did next really got my attention.

The man turned his gaze to the enormous tiger at his side and made a circular waving motion with one hand. The huge beast immediately sprang to its feet, positioned itself behind the old fellow, and laid down. To my utter amazement the man then sat down on the back of the tiger which remained motionless with its head resting between its front paws. Impressive, I thought, but then again these were circus people.

"Tangun, Tangun, Tangun." The audience began a soft, vibrant chant that filled the large room. There was obvious reverence in the mantra and it continued for some time. Yet something about the sound of their odd chant sounded vaguely familiar. Something to do with martial arts? Ah! That was it. "Tangun" was an upper level form taught in the original style of Tae Kwon Do. The memory came back to me. It was named in honor of the Mountain Spirit, Tangun, the legendary founder of Korea and the Korean people. My flesh pimpled at the realization.

Tangun raised his hands the chanting ceased. Cha gripped my arm directed me up onto the dais into a position directly in front of Tangun. The ancient man rose as well and beamed his warming smile upon me. Without prodding from Cha I bowed deeply. It felt completely natural. The visage before us returned the bow in paternal fashion. I had obviously done the right thing.

Tangun stared directly at me and held my gaze for several long moments, the look of benevolence never leaving his face. Tangun then addressed the crowd in a warm sonorous voice of which I could not understand a word. The audience, however, was rapt. Although I could not understand Tangun's speech the effect of it on his listeners was plainly apparent. I watched and listened intently as the audience transitioned from wide eyed smiles to frowns, head nodding to head bowing, and at last to reverent silence as the speech ended.

But there was more. Tangun looked at me and pointed. "Pam Sidyunga," he said and then slashed his hand like a knife in front of his chest. He then pointed at me and bellowed, "Kogiri Atashi!" The entire audience jumped to their feet and repeated the odd phrase over and over as I turned to look at them. This strange chant continued for about five minutes and suddenly stopped.

I looked back at the stage. Tangun and the Kaja the tiger were gone.

No one spoke; the room remained silent. Once again, I obeyed the quiet prodding of Mr. Cha, this time to the rear of the temple where I was directed to stand. The assemblage turned and faced me. Cha raised a hand. One by one each person approached me, shook my hand, bowed, and departed the room. Each wore an expression of grim acceptance. Kyung Re was the last. There was obvious sorrow on her face. I felt like I was being prepared for execution.

"Kyung Re!" I demanded. "What is going on?"

She responded with a slow shake of her head. "Ajossi will explain," she said, indicating Mr. Cha. She then departed as the others had. I was alone with my host.

"Alright, Mr. Cha," I said, "no more games, no more suspense. What is going on?"

"Perhaps it is very good, perhaps it is very sad, Captain. It is for you to decide," Cha said and then stopped for another of his maddening pauses.

"Then tell me, dammit!" I shouted.

Cha smiled at my outburst and nodded. "The great Tangun is so very wise. He has looked into your spirit," he said. "And although I am sad to say this to you, Captain, you are not to be made shaman."

I did not know whether to be relieved or angered at this pronouncement but I certainly was confused. "So I went through all of this for nothing? All this to find out I'm not good enough? So what happens now, now that you people have destroyed my career and probably my life?"

"Captain, please. Only nothing is for nothing. Everything in this world and the next has meaning and purpose. That is what you have endured. You have a brash and very strong spirit; that is what Tangun saw and what he explained. He has determined that this inner spirit of yours is better served in ways other than the way of the shaman. You are a soldier, Captain, a warrior, but something much more important. It is in this way you will best serve the Korean people, and all people."

"Mr Cha, my days as a soldier and warrior, and much more, are in shambles and getting worse every day unless I get back to my unit."

"That is arranged for you," he said.

KOGIRI ATASHI

Chapter Five

My journey back to Camp Casey and the Army began as it started – in the wagon of a donkey powered train. Kyung Re was not even there to say goodbye. Oh well. I guess the news of my not being shaman material took me down a few notches in here opinion. The trip took a full day before arriving at a small city where I was able to board a train that took me all the way into Seoul and from there back to Tongdechon. I walked back to Camp Casey from the train station fully expecting my court martial. I checked in at the front gate still outfitted in my ridiculous Korean outfit. The gate guards stared and snickered as I approached but by some miracle I'd manage to hold on to my ID card so they let me enter. Probably figured I was some officer knucklehead trying to go native. I turned away and prepared to make The Walk of Shame up the road to my hootch. Casey is built on a steep hill and shaped like a long rectangle with a main road running up the center of it. Most of the billets are at the top of the hill. The Walk of Shame was the standard joke for drunken soldiers who had to make this journey after missing curfew. That was me alright. But I hadn't taken two steps when one of the guards started yelling.

"Wait, sir! Wait! Hold on!"

"Okay, sergeant," I said. "What is it?"

"Well, sir, a lot of people been looking for you. We were ordered to inform LTC Kerney as soon as you showed up. We just called him and he's on his way. He said not to let you go anywhere until he gets here."

I groaned and shook my head but what could I do? When something's inevitable it's inevitable. Kerney would drive to the gate in his HUMMV accompanied by the XO and a couple of other officers, take me to his office, and listen to what I had to say. Then he'd read the charges I'm probably going to face and send me to JAG for advice. The commander was a good man and I truly admired the guy but he had no choice in this matter. And that is exactly what happened. Fifteen minutes later I'm sitting in my hootch spilling out the details to the JAG, Lieutenant Colonel Neal, while he sits there taking notes and trying to keep a straight face. This goes on for about an hour and then I'm left to myself to write up a statement and get some rest. There's an MP outside of my door, of course.

The next morning my phone rings. It's LTC Kearny.

"How you doing, Moran?"

"As well as can be expected, sir."

"Alright, listen. I want you in my office at 0900. Class A uniform. Got it?"

"I'll be there, sir. Anything else?"

"Not right now, Mike. See you at nine," he says and hangs up.

Once again I know what's coming. The formal charges are going to be read, a date set for my trial, and the conditions of my confinement until then specified. I check the clock. It's only 0500 so I go back to sleep for a while, at least I try to. This whole Army thing started with such promise. How in the hell am I supposed to tell my old man that his son is being court martialed? How am I going to ever live with a dishonorable discharge? I'll never get a decent job anywhere. Shit! Shit! Shit! This kind of crap ransacks my mind over and over until I look at the clock again. It's 0730. Shit!

I'm half asleep, pissed off, and disgusted at the whole situation but I gotta do what needs to be done. After a half hour of groping around to find all the parts and pieces of my dress green uniform I lay the thing out on the bed and put it all together. We hardly ever wore Class As in this assignment

458

and it felt strange to put it on, especially after all I'd been through. Once I check myself out in the mirror, though, I feel a lot worse. This'll be the next to the last time I'll be seen in this outfit. Never figured it would end this way.

There's a banging knock on my door. "Captain Moran, are you ready?" It's LTC Neal, the Jag.

"Yeah, I'm ready, sir. Let's get this over with." I open the door and Neal stares at me a while as though conducting an inspection of my uniform.

"Well, do I look alright?" I ask.

The JAG nods. "You'll do," he says and we begin a silent walk down to the commander's office. The Executive Officer, Major Riggins meets us at the door. He salutes LTC Neal and directs us to the battalion conference room where we hold our briefings, update to the commander, etc. As soon as I enter the room I notice that something is seriously serious. My commander, LTC Kearney is standing at attention. Right next to him stands our Division Artillery Commander, COL Harrison. And as if that were not enough a three star general is standing there, too. To his left are two Korean civilians I don't recognize at all. Great. What are they going to do, take me out and shoot me? I turn and look at the JAG for an explanation but he looks just as confused as I am.

I can't help but remember Cha's admonition. "Don't do anything rash!"

LTC Kearney speaks. "Stand at ease, Captain Moran." I hardly feel at ease but I affect the posture and slump away from my position of attention.

My commander nods to COL Harrison, a gruff, no nonsense Viet Nam veteran. If there is one man in the world I rather not deal with right now it's COL Harrison. He steps forward and shakes my hand. "How you doing, Moran?"

To say the least, the question is a surprise. "Not very well, sir," I manage to say.

"Alright," he says. "Captain Moran let me introduce you to the Eighth Army Commander, Lieutenant General Rollins."

The general now steps forward and shakes my hand. "Pleased to meet you, Captain Moran. And now let me introduce you to the Mayor of Seoul, Mr. Kun Goh."

The mayor takes my hand and bows to me; I return the gesture. In a very serious manner he begins speaking in Korean. As soon as he stops the other Korean civilian translates.

"Mr. Goh wanted to come here and meet you personally, Captain Moran, and thank you for saving his grandson and the lives of so many people. What you did took great courage." Before I can say a word he opens a blue folder and prepares to read from it. LTG Rollins calls the room to attention. The Seoul Mayor speaks and the interpreter translates.

"On behalf of Seoul citizens I have the privilege of awarding this to Captain Michael Moran of the United States Army. Thanks to your bravery and courage many people were saved from injury or death, including my own grandson. Please accept this award as a token of my appreciation."

"Kogiri Atashi!" says a familiar voice behind me. I turn around and can't believe what I'm seeing. There stands Pok Dani looking up at me with a beaming smile. In his hands he holds a glass ball on a golden jade stand. Inside the ball is a small statue of a beautiful elephant with an upraised trunk. He hands it to me with a low bow.

There's another swirl of handshakes and bows, and five minutes later I'm alone in the room with my commander.

"Well, Mike, you screwed up but at least you screwed up the right way."

"Check, sir. But what happens now?"

"It's this way, Mike. All the charges against you, AWOL, curfew, etc. are dropped in accordance with the

461

recommendation from LTG Rollins. And here's the reason why. What you did was truly heroic. You risked your life and saved people. That's the main reason. But as you know there has been a deterioration in relations between the Army and the Korean public. When word got out about you stopping that elephant attack it was a public relations dream come true down there at HQs. You even saved that elephant, by the way; it's at the Seoul Zoo now."

"I can't believe this, sir. I swear I won't be any more trouble EVER! And I really apologize for causing all these problems."

"Apology accepted, Captain. But don't worry about causing me any further trouble, you've got a new assignment."

Oh boy, here it comes, I thought. I'm sure Kearney could tell by the look on my face I knew this meant bad news.

"You're being reassigned to Eight Army Headquarters in Seoul as one of General Rollin's aides. Don't worry. We'll make it look like a promotion instead of relief of command at your change of command ceremony. You're a good man, Mike but I can't let you go back to battery command after being AWOL for five days no matter what the reason, especially after that story you told the JAG."

"Sir!" I protested. "It's absolutely true! All that weird shit actually happened! I don't have an explanation for it but it happened I'm telling you."

Kearney gave a condescending nod. "Okay, Mike, I'll take your word. But I do not recommend repeating this to General Rollins or to the Stars and Stripes reporter waiting to interview you. Tell the reporter all about the incident at the circus and leave it at that. As for the General tell him exactly what the Koreans told us, that you were injured while helping to round up the elephant and it took you a long time to get back; after all that pretty much the truth, right? But only if he asks. Otherwise you might find yourself with another new assignment. Understand what I'm saying?"

"Check, sir."

So now I spend my days running a million little errands for LTG Rollins. But I now have considerably more free time off and I spend every minute of it at the Seoul Zoo helping out with their elephants. Over there I'm not Captain Moran or Michael or Mike. I'm **Kogori Atashi** – the Elephant Man. I thought I could never be happier until one day Pok Dani comes to visit and I'll bet you know who was with him. I have a feeling that Kyung Re and I will be together for a long time.

463

96711396R00254

Made in the USA
Columbia, SC
31 May 2018